How to
Teach Students
Who *Don't*
Look Like You

2 EDITION

Dedicated to Dan Alpert
You cause positive change in the world
and
To all the teachers who take risks to improve their classroom instruction
and passionately believe that ALL children can learn at high levels

How to
Teach Students
Who *Don't*
Look Like You

2 EDITION

CULTURALLY RESPONSIVE TEACHING STRATEGIES

Bonnie M. DAVIS
FOREWORD BY CURTIS LINTON

CORWIN
A SAGE Company

CORWIN
A SAGE Company

FOR INFORMATION:

Corwin

A SAGE Company

2455 Teller Road

Thousand Oaks, California 91320

(800) 233-9936

www.corwin.com

SAGE Publications Ltd.

1 Oliver's Yard

55 City Road

London EC1Y 1SP

United Kingdom

SAGE Publications India Pvt. Ltd.

B 1/I 1 Mohan Cooperative Industrial Area

Mathura Road, New Delhi 110 044

India

SAGE Publications Asia-Pacific Pte. Ltd.

3 Church Street

#10-04 Samsung Hub

Singapore 049483

Acquisitions Editor: Dan Alpert
Associate Editor: Megan Bedell
Editorial Assistant: Heidi Arndt
Permissions Editor: Karen Ehrmann
Project Editor: Veronica Stapleton
Copy Editor: Trey Thoelcke
Typesetter: C&M Digitals (P) Ltd.
Proofreader: Scott Oney
Indexer: Gloria Tierney
Cover Designer: Rose Storey
Graphic Designer: Christina Kubota

Copyright © 2012 by Bonnie M. Davis

Printed in the United States of America.

A catalog record of this book is available from the Library of Congress.

ISBN: 978-1-4522-5791-4

This book is printed on acid-free paper.

SUSTAINABLE FORESTRY INITIATIVE

Certified Chain of Custody
Promoting Sustainable Forestry
www.sfiprogram.org
SFI-01268

SFI label applies to text stock

14 15 16 17 18 10 9 8 7 6 5 4 3 2

Contents

Foreword   vii
    Curtis Linton

Preface   ix

Acknowledgments   xvii

About the Author   xxi

How to Read the Book   xxiii

PART I. LOOKING INSIDE OURSELVES   1

  1. Our Culture: The Way We View the World   3

  2. Reflection Questions for Examining Our Inner Selves   19

  3. Exploring Our Racial Identity Through Our Racial History   25

  4. What Is Race?   37

  5. A Day in the Life . . .   47

PART II. LISTENING TO AND LEARNING FROM OTHERS   57

  6. What Do We Need to Know About Culturally
      Diverse Learners?   59

  7. Latino/a/Hispanic Learners: A Personal Story   75

  8. New Immigrant Learners of the Twenty-First Century   89

  9. What the Research Says About Learning Gaps   95

10. How to Build Relationships With Culturally Diverse
     Students and Families   111

11. Creating a School Culture That Welcomes Students,
     Staff, and Families   123

PART III. INTEGRATING NEW KNOWLEDGE 135

12. **Strategies to Teach and Engage Culturally Diverse Learners and ELs** 137

13. **Moving Students From Apathy to Passion: Learning to Love Reading and Writing** 155

14. **Standards-Based, Culturally Responsive Lessons That Engage Learners** 169

15. **Readers and Writers Workshop: A Model for Standards-Based, Culturally Responsive Instruction** 183

16. **Teachers in Today's Classrooms Share Their Lessons** 195

PART IV. A CALL TO ACTION 239

17. **A Call to Action: Sponsoring Academic Student Support Groups** 241

18. **A Call to Action: Taking Care of Yourself** 259

References and Resources 267

Index 279

Foreword

I distinctly remember the first time I filmed an interview with Bonnie Davis shortly after the first edition of *How to Teach Students Who Don't Look Like You* was published. Sitting in her Southern California apartment, Bonnie emphatically stated, "Teachers don't brag enough!" When I asked her to explain, Bonnie recounted her experience as a high school English and writing teacher when she learned how to connect with students from a wide variety of backgrounds. She shared how she discovered that she was a *very good* writing teacher, but not a great math teacher. She not only knew internally for herself, but would tell students directly, "If you need to write a great college acceptance essay, come to me! If you need help on math, go somewhere else." Through her years of teaching, researching, and studying, Bonnie discovered explicitly what it took for a teacher to successfully connect with each and every student, no matter where that student came from, nor how different the student might be from Bonnie.

This forthrightness of a teacher's skills and abilities is profound in the life of a student—students enter school not to collect seat time or even grades, but to prepare themselves for the intimidating world that lies beyond the school walls. This is made even more intense for students who do not fit the majority norm in terms of race, economics, language, and background. Today's youth rely on teachers who will stretch themselves to meet the needs of the student. It begins with the teachers changing their practices, beliefs, assumptions, and biases, and ends with the student succeeding because a caring adult has provided equitable access and support to the necessary learning. In order for students to succeed, the paid professional—the teacher—must change what she or he does to support the learning and engagement of each and every child in the classroom.

The very title of this book, *How to Teach Students Who Don't Look Like You*, speaks truth to the fundamental reality of achievement gaps within schools—the overwhelming majority of teachers are white, middle class, and female, whereas the students on the negative side of the achievement gap are overwhelmingly of color, from poor backgrounds, and increasingly male. Now that Bonnie has spoken truth to an issue that tends to be untouchable—race and racial privilege—the conversation can finally move to what to do about this educational reality. Bonnie wrote this second edition in order to incorporate important new learnings, insights, concerns, and experiences she has gained over the past six years since the first edition was released. Not content to just raise the issue, Bonnie addresses it directly: what does a teacher need to do daily in the classroom to transcend the differences between her- or himself and the student?

Bonnie is fundamentally a practical teacher, and that is the reason why she has so successfully helped thousands of teachers modify their day-to-day practice in the classroom. I have always deeply appreciated Bonnie's ability to bring me down to earth in my work, writing, and ideas. This is what she brings to teachers: direct and applicable strategies that address the skills, beliefs, dispositions, and strategies a teacher needs to apply on a day-by-day basis in the classroom. After having filmed thousands of highly effective teachers across the United States, I can attest that what Bonnie proposes herein is substantiated by the observed practices of the very best teachers. These strategies are key to academically succeeding with today's diverse students.

Within this practical framework, Bonnie has identified clear classroom examples on video that you can access to see these strategies in practice. My company, the School Improvement Network, has partnered with Bonnie to feature these video segments on our on-demand professional demand platform, PD 360. To access these videos, go to http://www.schoolimprovement.com/experts/bonnie-davis.

As a reader of this book, you will have ongoing complimentary access to these resources. Follow the instructions on this page to access these classroom examples and engage in an online dialogue with other educators who are applying these strategies in classrooms in every state and province. This online community, moderated by Bonnie, will be your gateway to model classroom examples, new strategies, lesson ideas, and reflection on who you are as a teacher—and what you have done to connect with students who differ from yourself.

Education has entered a promising new age of rapid progress and accelerating expectations. The goal of college and career readiness has been established for every student, which means that a school's duty now is to assure that students gain the necessary knowledge and skills to engage successfully in college-level study and advanced career training. Students can only gain this type of proficiency by engaging in a personalized learning environment wherein they learn at an optimized level determined by their individual readiness and self-driven pace.

The only way this high and lofty educational goal of college and career readiness can be achieved is by each and every teacher knowing how to individually support and facilitate the learning of each and every student. If difference between teacher and student presents any type of a learning barrier—whether overt or hidden—the student will not rise to his or her potential in the classroom. When a teacher knows how to effectively teach students who differ from her- or himself, that is a teacher who can succeed with every student.

This is the power of an equitable education—a learning environment that guarantees each and every student will receive the individualized support they need to succeed. And this is the power of Bonnie's work—explicitly laying out what a teacher has to do day by day to help every student successfully prepare for his or her exciting life that lies ahead. After engaging in this learning, my hope is that you will go forth and apply these strategies step-by-step every day—your students will be the lucky beneficiaries!

Curtis Linton
Vice-President of Content Development
The School Improvement Network

Preface

Six years after the publication of *How to Teach Students Who Don't Look Like You: Culturally Relevant Teaching Strategies* (2006), I am at it again, writing my teaching life. I have had the good fortune to continue to work with educators across the country during these years and have learned and grown through the work. These educators work in urban schools, suburban schools, and rural areas, and I support them through ongoing workshops, observations, coaching, e-mails, and phone conversations. After working three to five years in several districts with scores of different teachers, I can document their progress from isolation to collaboration, including their use of culturally responsive strategies, peer observation, and professional learning groups. As a result, I realized I needed to write a new edition of this book to update the research in the field and give you access to the latest and best I have learned.

WHAT IS NEW?

This new edition contains the following new material:

- Updated research on culturally diverse learners
- Updated research on classroom instruction
- Common Core State Standards
- How to teach English language learners
- How to teach Latino/a/Hispanic learners
- How to teach new immigrant learners
- A chapter examining what race is and is not
- Suggestions for using technology and PD 360 alignment
- New engagement strategies for culturally diverse learners
- New lessons created by teachers using them in their classrooms today
- Additional student support models
- A wellness chapter for you, the teacher!

The book contains a wealth of new material, research, strategies, narratives, and lesson plans to be both a resource for you and a companion on a journey as we travel together in our quest to become more culturally responsive in our instruction.

WHAT IS STILL THE SAME?

I am *still* an older White female who can only share with you what "I know I know" at this time in my journey to understand culture, race, class, gender, and students who don't look like me. I can't write this book with the understanding or life experiences of a Person of Color or a young student in today's world. I will never know or understand their experiences. I consider myself an antiracist, yet I must remember, "even antiracist educators reproduce a racialized social system" (M. Pollock, 2008, p. 348). I have no other choice; I am part of the system. To continue this work, I pledge to do my best and work within this unequal system to try and change it. This book is my attempt to do that, but it is only what *I know I know* at this time in my journey.

Another thing that is still the same is the focus on African American students. African American children were the students I taught who did not look like me and the students I wrote about in my first book, *African American Academic Achievement: Building a Classroom of Excellence,* which I self-published in 2001. When I wrote *How to Teach Students Who Don't Look Like You,* I incorporated most of the self-published book within the body of the new book. As a result, even though this book contains no chapter dedicated solely to African American students, they are still a majority focus, and examples of African American student experiences are woven throughout the book. In addition, much of the earlier book is retained, based on the feedback from thousands of educators who have used it as a learning journey.

THE JOURNEY FRAMEWORK

Feeling the need to conceptualize this learning journey within a framework, I was fortunate to work with Kim Anderson, a licensed clinical social worker and expressive arts psychotherapist, to create a model for us to use as we tackle the challenge of becoming culturally responsive to the diverse learners in our schools. This model, cultural consideration and equity skill building, has evolved over time in three additional books: *The Biracial and Multiracial Student Experience: A Journey to Racial Literacy* (Davis, 2009); *Culturally Considerate School Counseling: Helping Without Bias* (Anderson, 2010); and *Creating Culturally Considerate Schools: Educating Without Bias* (Anderson & Davis, 2012). In this book, however, we return to the most direct model to begin our journey.

This framework is a simple flowchart of four steps:

- Looking inside ourselves
- Listening to and learning from others
- Integrating new knowledge
- A call to action

We name this journey a journey of *cultural consideration* because we believe that cultural consideration supports the inclusion of all aspects of culture while stemming from the basic principle of respect. This term also differentiates our work from others in the field. At the same time, we respect, acknowledge,

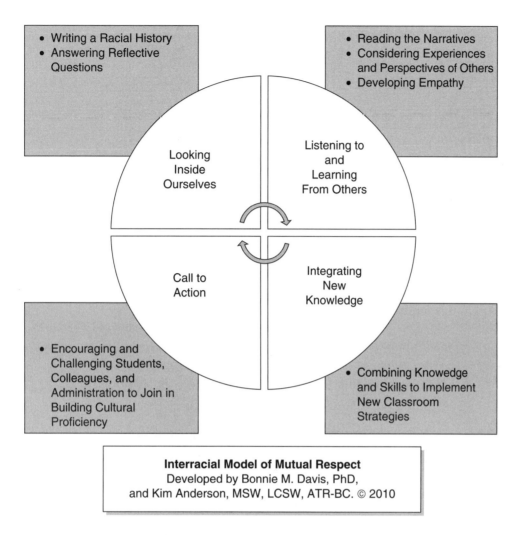

- Writing a Racial History
- Answering Reflective Questions

- Reading the Narratives
- Considering Experiences and Perspectives of Others
- Developing Empathy

Looking Inside Ourselves

Listening to and Learning From Others

Call to Action

Integrating New Knowedge

- Encouraging and Challenging Students, Colleagues, and Administration to Join in Building Cultural Proficiency

- Combining Knowedge and Skills to Implement New Classroom Strategies

Interracial Model of Mutual Respect
Developed by Bonnie M. Davis, PhD,
and Kim Anderson, MSW, LCSW, ATR-BC. © 2010

and cite in this book those pioneers and current thinkers in the fields of social justice, diversity, and cultural responsiveness.

EQUITY 101

In addition to the work with cultural consideration, I worked with Curtis Linton, coauthor of *Courageous Conversations About Race* (Singleton & Linton, 2006), on a series of books titled *Equity 101*. In these books, we explore the issue of equity through the lens of expectations, rigor, relevancy, and relationships. Curtis and I coauthored *Culture* and *Practice* (Linton & Davis, 2012), two of the books in the series. These books offer an in-depth look at both the culture of your school and the instruction in your classrooms. Aligned with this series, the School Improvement Network offers online videos of teachers through their PD 360 professional development tool. This online tool allows teachers to observe other teachers using culturally responsive strategies in their classrooms. I am one of the teachers in the videos, along with hundreds of others.

This book contains references to these videos, so you may check them out as you read about the strategies in the book (see http://www.schoolimprovement.com/experts/bonnie-davis).

CULTURAL CONSIDERATION AND EQUITY SKILL BUILDING

Passionate about the issue of equity, I see this book as one tool for investigating what equity looks like in our classrooms and what strategies we can use to support it daily. For me, these strategies include instructional strategies, cultural strategies, and relationship strategies; therefore, this book focuses on these strategies. With an emphasis on strategies and equity skill building, we use the model of cultural consideration and equity skill building to support our journey in this new edition of *How to Teach Students Who Don't Look Like You*. As you begin this journey, what do you want? Do you

- Search for strategies to engage students and close the achievement and learning gaps?
- Seek to understand the cultural differences of your students?
- Look for ways to build relationships across cultures?

If you are like many teachers, you continue to look for ways to improve your classroom instruction. As a classroom teacher with more than four decades of experience, I, too, was always searching for new strategies, understandings, and lessons to support the changing population of students who yearly entered my classroom.

This book is a result of that search. It is an organic document, one that can continue to grow as you interact with the book and your colleagues.

The chapters take you through the following stages:

- A general recognition of culture and how it shapes the lens through which you and others view the world
- The personal narratives and racial histories of educators
- A discussion of race and its impact on learners
- An examination of research on culturally diverse student cultures
- A discussion of achievement and learning gaps
- How-to strategies for teaching within a Common Core State Standards–based learning environment
- Research-based instructional strategies (K–12) to implement across the disciplines with a focus on literacy
- Several academic and leadership support group models
- Suggestions for owning your own wellness
- A references and resources section
- Alignment with PD 360 online professional development videos and support

You can read the chapters in the above sequence, or you can open the book anywhere and read an individual chapter, much like a book of short stories tied together by a common theme. You can read and respond in the book, using it as a private book study and a professional development tool. Or you can use it with your professional learning groups and collaborative staff meetings. The chapters are educator friendly and meant to be discussed and responded to informally and honestly. The research, strategies, and culturally considerate classroom lessons found in the book are designed to support and improve the academic achievement of all learners, especially culturally diverse learners.

HOW DID YOU LEARN WHAT YOU KNOW ABOUT TEACHING?

How did you learn what you know about teaching? I learned what I know about teaching from men in a prison, women in a homeless shelter, and affluent middle schoolers, as well as high school and college students in suburban, urban, and rural areas. The men taught me that even though the common denominator in our prisons is poverty, it does not equate to a lack of intelligence. Some of the most intelligent and best writers I taught were these men. The women in the homeless shelter taught me that our students must find and share their voices in the classroom, for when we allow students to find their voices, their writing glows. All too often students in our society lack this opportunity, and they sometimes find less productive means of "screaming" who they are. Also, they taught me that our lessons must connect to the lives of our students in order to engage learners and support them in attaining skills for career readiness and college. And scores of middle schoolers from an affluent school district taught me that it was not enough to walk into their classroom with a doctorate in English and more than twenty years of teaching experience at the high school and college levels—these children demanded instruction that challenged and engaged them. No longer could lectures grab and keep their attention. I had to learn what "I didn't know I didn't know" about good instruction. I learned from all of my students during the thirty years I spent in the classroom and the fifteen years since I worked with adult educators, and that learning is found in this book. This book focuses on students who may not look like you, may not come from similar backgrounds, and may not approach learning like you. Just as the student populations I have taught have informed my instruction, your students speak to you with their needs (or perhaps they scream at you with their needs). In addition, your life experiences add to your teaching repertoire.

WHO ARE CULTURALLY DIVERSE LEARNERS?

Who are culturally diverse learners? They are the homeless children, the migrant children, and the immigrant children learning English. They are children dealing with gender issues and those with learning disabilities. They are special needs children, as well as children from diverse cultures—students perhaps not previously included or successful in our classrooms. To provide these learners with culturally responsive instruction, we must build relationships and hold high expectations, provide rigorous content knowledge while making explicit the hidden rules of learning, and teach students how to learn as well as what to learn.

WHO IS THE AUDIENCE FOR THIS BOOK?

You are! This book goes beyond instruction and offers you a special opportunity to dig deep inside yourself. Unlike many excellent books that provide research-based instructional strategies, this one includes a section that focuses on race and privilege and its impact on educators: one Black American female and one White American female, the mother of mixed identity children, and one White American male, the father of Asian children. Reading their stories and discussion of the topic of race gives you a glimpse into the racial complexities of our educational landscape and examines a topic seldom found in educational literature. These chapters are designed not for the timid but for educators ready and willing to examine privilege in our society and continue this personal and professional journey into understanding the impact of race.

Who is the audience for this book?

- First and foremost, this book is for teachers from a teacher. The information and strategies are for preservice teachers, beginning teachers, veteran teachers—all of us.
- Administrators at every level who wish to enhance the knowledge base of their staff and provide opportunities for collegial dialogue and learning.
- Professional development chairs, supervisors, mentors, and coaches whose job it is to encourage teachers and provide culturally responsive materials for them.
- Professional learning communities, whether they be a group of two or 200.
- College and university instructors and their students in preservice and graduate courses in which students need or require information on culturally diverse learners.
- Central office administrators engaged in a districtwide effort to become more culturally responsive and close learning gaps.

SET GOALS FOR YOURSELF

As you read, consider setting goals. For example, you may wish to read this book in order to improve instruction or make your instruction more culturally responsive: your end result may be improved student achievement. Your goal or action plan may include one chapter per week of study with your professional learning group, followed by trying one new strategy and reporting back the following week on its effectiveness. You may even want to include peer observations. Whatever you decide, setting goals tunes our brain to focus on our needs and to filter out the rest.

Alan Blankstein, in *The Answer Is in the Room: How Effective Schools Scale Up Student Success* (2011), reminds us that, yes, the answer is in the room, and the most valuable resource you have is "focused commitment over time" (p. 42). Therefore, you may find repetition in the book; some strategies are repeated in more than one place. This continues to focus and, hopefully, commit you to trying the strategies. Join your professional learning group (or start a new one) and discuss together as you read, study, and reflect your way through the book. I welcome your professional conversation, comments, and suggestions. You may e-mail me at a4achievement@earthlink.net.

Enjoy!

Acknowledgments

First and foremost, I want to thank and acknowledge Dan Alpert, my editor at Corwin. He is an advocate of social justice and an agent for social change. He is my mentor and friend. Next, I would like to thank a group of close women friends who supported me through the writing of this book: Kim L. Anderson, coauthor on *Creating Culturally Considerate Schools: Educating Without Bias*, shares her wisdom, vision, practical knowledge, and friendship, and she midwifed me through the first edition of this book and remained by my side for the past decade. Mary Kim Schreck, author of *Transformers: Creative Teachers for the 21st Century* (2009), provokes and critiques my thinking about classroom instruction, pushing me to learn more and think differently. Dorothy J. Kelly, my close friend since the 1980s, daily challenges me to consider the world from a different perspective and generously shares her soul in this book. Dr. Elizabeth Krekeler, a woman with a brilliant mind, pushes me to think "out of the box." Susan Heggarty is my friend and partner in the educational work across the state, and Nan Starling is a consummate educator who finds the best in all learners, including my son.

Thanks to Curtis Linton, who offers me a young male's perspective and provides me with limitless opportunities. Thanks and love to my dad, and my sisters, Susan, Ruth (who gave me special help), and Mary, and their families. Special love and thanks to my children, Leah and Reeve, and their families. And to Fred, aka Hudson, you continue to reinvent our worlds.

I wish to thank the administrators and teachers of the school districts where I have provided ongoing professional development during the past six years: Omaha Public Schools, Omaha, NE; West Contra Costa Unified School District, Richmond, CA; Rockwood Public Schools, Eureka, MO; Kyrene Unified School District, Chandler, AZ; Chapel Hill–Carrboro City Schools, Chapel Hill, NC; Kirkwood School District, Kirkwood, MO; and Independent School District 196, Rosemount–Apple Valley–Egan Public Schools, Rosemount, MN. In addition, thanks to the organizations and districts who support my work.

Thanks to the many educators who gave permission to be included in the book: Brenda Alvarez, Kim Anderson, Todd Benben, Tracey Black, Maricris Cruzat, Cecilia Distefano, Tiffany Holliday, Jessica Jones, Kimberly Jones, Dorothy Kelly, Michele Lamon, Keith Leonard, Nancy McCormac, Roberta McWoods, Graig Meyer, Betty Porter Walls, Deb Preuss, Damian Pritchard, Heather Ross, Laura Sammon, and Barb Swalina. Thank you for the work you do!

I wish to acknowledge the reviewers of the first draft who gave me excellent feedback.

Finally, were it not for the folks at Corwin, you would not be reading this book. A special thanks to the Corwin team in charge of editorial and production processes: to Dan Alpert, acquisitions editor, Megan Bedell, associate editor, Heidi Arndt, editorial assistant, and Veronica Stapleton, project editor. With Diane DiMura, copy editor, added to the mix, I felt completely supported throughout this process.

This would not have happened without you.

PUBLISHER'S ACKNOWLEDGMENTS

Corwin gratefully acknowledges the contributions of the following reviewers:

Christi Boortz
Grant Writer/Coordinator
Florida School for the Deaf and the Blind
St. Augustine, FL

Peggy Dickerson
University Field Supervisor
University of Texas at Dallas
Richardson, TX

Jessica Smith Kennan
Assistant Principal
De Anza High School
Richmond, CA

Amanda Mayeaux
Master Teacher
Glen Oaks Middle School
Baton Rouge, LA

Graig Meyer
Coordinator, Blue Ribbon Mentor-Advocate Program
Chapel Hill–Carrboro City Schools
Chapel Hill, NC

Barbara Rose
Professor
Miami University
Oxford, OH

Scott Thomas
Educational Equity Coordinator
Eagan School District 196
Rosemount, MN

Rosalinda Velazquez
Teacher
Alessandro Volta Elementary School
Chicago, IL

Derrick Wallace
District Level Administrator–Public Education
Ladue School District
St. Louis, MO

Betty Porter Walls
Assistant Professor, College of Education
Harris Stowe State University
St. Louis, MO

Ava Maria Whittemore
Minority Achievement Coordinator
Frederick County Public Schools
Frederick, MD

Deborah D. Wragge
Professional Services Coordinator, Staff Development
Educational Service Unit 7
Columbus, NE

About the Author

 **Bonnie M. Davis**, PhD, is a veteran teacher of more than forty years who is passionate about education. She has taught in middle schools, high schools, universities, homeless shelters, and a men's prison. She received her bachelor's degree in education, her master's in English, her MAI in communications, and her doctorate in English. Dr. Davis is the recipient of numerous awards, including Teacher of the Year in two public school districts, the Governor's Award for Excellence in Teaching, and the Anti-Defamation League's World of Difference Community Service Award. She has presented at numerous national conferences, such as Learning Forward, Association for Supervision and Curriculum Development, National Council of Teachers of English, National Association of Multicultural Education, and others.

Dr. Davis's publications include the first edition of this book, *How to Teach Students Who Don't Look Like You: Culturally Relevant Teaching Strategies;* as well as *How to Coach Teachers Who Don't Think Like You: Using Literacy Strategies to Coach Across Content Areas; The Biracial and Multiracial Student Experience: A Journey to Racial Literacy;* and *Creating Culturally Considerate Schools: Educating Without Bias* with coauthor Kim L. Anderson. Other publications include the *Equity 101* series with coauthor Curtis Linton and numerous articles on diversity and literacy instruction.

Dr. Davis provides professional development services to districts across the country, giving keynotes, workshops, and ongoing support through her consulting firm, Educating for Change. She may be reached at www.educatingforchange.com or by e-mail at a4achievement@earthlink.net.

How to Read the Book

As stated in the preface, you can read this book, much like a book of short stories, by beginning with what interests you most—but *please* read the preface first. Each chapter can stand alone. Or you can read this book from beginning to end, hopefully discussing the book with your colleagues in a professional learning group. You will find repetition in the book since many of the strategies fit in more than one place, but this offers you the opportunity to acquaint yourself again with multiple ways to use the strategies.

DISCLAIMERS

Throughout the book, terms referring to student groups are used interchangeably since they are interchanged in many of the articles and books written about these students. Also, in some cases, the labels for identities and races are capitalized and in other cases they are not, based on the context and the sources of the information. Finally, the educators who wrote for this book occasionally use capitalization and grammatical constructions that may differ from the preferred Corwin style. These constructions remain in order to retain the integrity, individuality, and voice of the narrator.

LOOKING INSIDE

The first five chapters offer you the opportunity to look inside, reflecting on your cultural lens, racial identity, the construct of race, and the daily lives of educators who both look like and don't look like you. We begin with what may be considered the hardest part of the journey, and it builds a foundation as we move outward, examining the lives of students who don't look like us.

LISTENING TO AND LEARNING FROM OTHERS

In Chapters 6 through 11, the journey focuses on listening to others and learning from them. What is it you *don't know you don't know* about students who do not look like you? How can the research inform your practice?

INTEGRATING NEW KNOWLEDGE

The third part of the journey, Chapters 12 through 16, focuses on instruction. This section may feel like a different book, but it really is the same book actualized in the classroom. You learn lots of instructional strategies, and you find many lessons created by teachers in today's classrooms. Create your own lessons using the models and enjoy!

A CALL TO ACTION

Chapters 17 and 18 are the final part of the journey and focus on a call to action. What can you do to support the academic achievement of students who don't look like you? What can you do to take care of yourself? What can you do to encourage your colleagues to continue the journey with you?

PART I

Looking Inside Ourselves

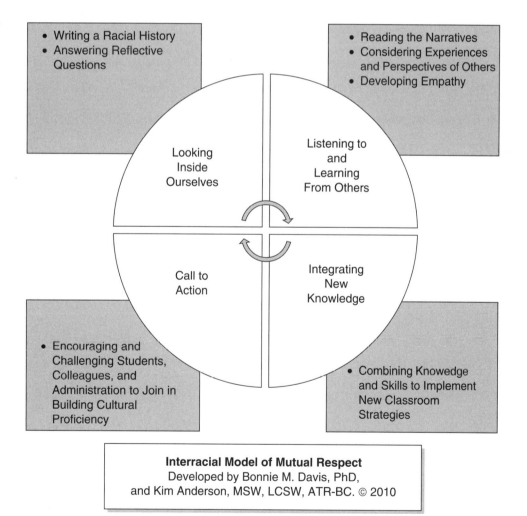

- Writing a Racial History
- Answering Reflective Questions

- Reading the Narratives
- Considering Experiences and Perspectives of Others
- Developing Empathy

Looking Inside Ourselves

Listening to and Learning From Others

Call to Action

Integrating New Knowledge

- Encouraging and Challenging Students, Colleagues, and Administration to Join in Building Cultural Proficiency

- Combining Knowedge and Skills to Implement New Classroom Strategies

Interracial Model of Mutual Respect
Developed by Bonnie M. Davis, PhD,
and Kim Anderson, MSW, LCSW, ATR-BC. © 2010

1

Our Culture

The Way We View the World

How do you view the world? My granddaughter, age four, already categorizes people by how they look based on their skin color. When a White person comes into her preschool, she speaks English, and when a Person of Color arrives, she speaks Spanish. My granddaughter is Mexican, Black, White, and Puerto Rican. How does she see the world? She sees the world through the lens of a young child who already understands that skin color places us in different groups. At four, she just thinks it has to do with language rather than power. She is brown and does not look like me. Her father, my son, has an African American father. He is Black and does not look like me. My experience as the biological White mother of a Black male and grandmother of a child of mixed ethnicity and racial identity is one of the reasons I wrote this book, a how-to book for you, educators who fill today's classrooms and search for better ways to connect with and teach students who don't look like them. Having taught English for thirty years in public schools, I want to share, in my experience, what works and what doesn't.

This book is a new edition. The first edition was read by thousands of educators, and for this, I am honored and grateful. This new edition evolved because of the following: new research and developments in education since 2006; the adoption of the Common Core State Standards (CCSS) and the challenges they present; advances in technology; new research and practices for culturally diverse learners, including English language learners (ELs) and new immigrant learners; and issues of color and race that continue to affect learners. In addition, I have learned, and want to share strategies, as a result of working with thousands of educators across the country. Also, the earlier edition barely touched on the Latino/a experience and ELs. Yet with the arrival of my granddaughter and my personal introduction to Latino culture, I knew I needed to include research about and strategies for the fastest growing group of children entering our schools today—Latino/a learners. As a result, in this book, there are new and expanded sections on Latino/a learners, as well as twenty-first century immigrant learners. These additional sections, along with more personal narratives and many more how-to strategies, build on the first edition and offer a more comprehensive resource for your instructional practice.

WHAT ABOUT YOU?

What do you see when you enter your school? If you are like many teachers, you see a sea of smiling faces, some that look like yours and others that don't. This book offers you an opportunity to read and think about those children who may not look or even think like you. The first five chapters in the book build background knowledge about your cultural lens and how you view culturally diverse learners in your classroom and school. In Part II, we examine our inner worlds as we navigate the outer world and sometimes experience it differently based on our race, gender, ethnicity, age, class, sexual orientation, and other factors. The remainder of the book offers an examination of the learning environment and classroom instruction. This book combines the affective and the cognitive, the *what* and the *who* of teaching, the external and the internal worlds in which we live and work. Let's begin with the children you see when you walk into your school.

Describe the children in your school.

_____

_____

_____

Describe the faculty and staff in your school.

_____

_____

_____

Describe yourself.

_____

_____

_____

HIDDEN RULES: BEHAVIOR EXPECTATIONS

Hopefully, you are reading this book with others, either in a book study with your staff or within your professional learning group. If you are, you are working and discussing with others. When we work in a group, we must understand what is expected of us. Similarly, when we work with students, we must state explicitly what we expect of the learners in our classrooms. Many students just seem to "know" what to do and expect in our classrooms. However, others, often our diverse learners, may not be privy to the hidden rules or unspoken codes of our classrooms. These hidden rules or unspoken codes offer immense power to those who wield them. We who possess the knowledge of our hidden rules are the gatekeepers to success or failure for those who do not possess the knowledge (Delpit, 1997). Because of this, we must be sensitive to the cultural lenses of our diverse learners and create an equitable field of opportunity for all.

In order to have an equitable playing field of opportunity, we must state clearly our behavior expectations for the task at hand. In discussions, many adults and students hesitate to give input when the discussion focuses on such scary subjects as race, class, gender, sexual orientation, or culture. Many remain silent rather than risk offending another human being. In order to support open discussion, we offer a set of expectations stated below. During your work with this book, the facilitator can present group expectations, model them, and set the tone for the discussion. This is good teaching. It also gives the facilitator the authority to intervene if a participant interrupts another speaker or speaks out of turn. In other words, the facilitator states explicitly the expected hidden rules or unspoken code of an educational setting. The teacher must do the same in the classroom.

Consider using the following expectations for your group's work with this book: *Today, we examine issues that challenge us to think deeply and respond honestly. We need to agree to follow behavioral expectations.*

- Take care of yourself. If you need to leave the room, do so. (Obviously, this one is for participants in a presentation or workshop, not your classroom.)
- Safeguard your reflective time by remaining quiet; then share during sharing time.
- Listen deeply. Do not interrupt anyone who is speaking. Wait until the person has completed his or her statements.
- Do not hog airtime. Share airtime equally with your colleagues. Each person has unique and valuable comments to contribute.
- Leave your outside concerns outside the room. Focus deeply on the stated topic.
- Save a few minutes during your break just for yourself—take a short walk, stand alone and think, be alone. Reflection encourages new learning.
- Do not stereotype people or their actions when you discuss the issues. Instead, use qualifying words. For example, use these words when appropriate: *few, some, sometimes, I've observed.* Do not use *most, all of the time,* or make stereotypical, generalized statements. When we describe the actions of others who differ from us, we will refrain from language that stereotypes others.
- Remember that each of us has lived a unique life. No one can ever know exactly what your experiences have felt like for you, and you can never know exactly what another person has experienced. Therefore, use only *I* messages and *do not* tell any other person what his or her experience has been. Don't even tell another person that you know what he or she

is feeling. This can be especially offensive to a Person of Color if you are a White person who says, "I know exactly what you're feeling." I, as a member of the dominant group in the United States, can never really know what it is like to be a member of a nondominant group.

- Give this experience your best. Our society seldom provides a forum for us to speak frankly about the effects of race, class, culture, and gender upon one's life experiences. Don't be surprised if you feel uncomfortable during some of the discussion. Glenn Singleton and Curtis Linton (2006) remind us that when discussing issues of race, we will feel uncomfortable and experience no closure. For many of us who want to "do" or "fix" things, this is unsettling; however, such discussions are about learning more of what we don't know we don't know, rather than fixing the situation.
- Respect each other's privacy. Please do not share the personal comments made during your discussions outside the workshop or classroom.

By following these expectations, you will leave this experience with a new respect for the other participants and, hopefully, closer relationships with them.

Generate additional behavior expectations for your interactions with your colleagues or your students.

_____

_____

_____

OUR CULTURAL LENS

If you picked up this book, you probably teach a culturally diverse group of children. This chapter offers you an opportunity to examine your cultural lens and reflect on how culture impacts our daily lives. Our culture is the lens through which we view the world. By better understanding our own cultural lens, we may better realize the importance of honoring the cultures of each student in our classrooms. In the following chapters, you will find numerous strategies that honor the culturally diverse cultures found in our schools.

We can't deny that our children are changing in complexion and complexity, and you may find yearly more children in your classroom who don't look like you or each other. As educators, we have more opportunities than ever to learn about each other and to share our cultural knowledge with our students.

In 2007, 44 percent of students were children from linguistic and culturally diverse backgrounds, with 10.8 million children coming from homes where a language other than English is spoken, with the majority of that being Spanish. In addition, 46 percent of all fourth-graders were eligible for free or reduced-price lunch (Planty et al., 2009a, 2009b, quoted in Saifer, Edwards, Ellis, Ko, & Stuczynski, 2011). In 2008 the approximate number of long-term English learners (LT-ELs) was about 6 million, and in 2009 about 8 million (Calderón & Minaya-Rowe, 2011).

What does this mean for you? Are you equipped to teach children whose culture differs from your own? Professionals today must examine their own culture and its inherent values, consider the different cultures and values of their students and the students' families, and explore how to meet the needs of each student by acknowledging, respecting, and accommodating the culture and value system of the family (Artiles & Ortiz, 2002). Examining *our* culture is one place to begin.

Each of us views the world through a unique lens. Each lens is composed of a diverse spectrum that includes many facets of our lives. Think of it as a pair of glasses that allows you to see the world differently from every other person who inhabits it. Every person wears a lens that colors his or her own view. This individual way of looking at the world is our individual perspective through which we judge events and people around us. Our heredity, environment, and previous experiences comprise our worldview. In using this book to better understand our worldview, we have an opportunity to take an "inside-out" journey (Terrell & Lindsey, 2009, p. 3) that begins with the self and then travels outward through research, anecdotes, and personal stories of educators, culminating with chapters filled with how-to instructional strategies and lessons to reach and teach learners who may not look like you.

WHAT IS CULTURE?

Culture is the totality of ideas, beliefs, values, activities, and knowledge of a group or individuals who share historical, geographical, religious, racial, linguistic, ethnic, or social traditions, and who transmit, reinforce, and modify those traditions. A culture is the total of everything an individual learns by growing up in a particular context and results in a set of expectations for appropriate behavior in seemingly similar contexts.

In their book *Cultural Proficiency: A Manual for School Leaders*, Lindsey, Nuri Robins, and Terrell (2003) define culture as "everything you do that enables you to identify with people who are like you and that distinguishes you from people who differ from you" (p. 41). They state that culture is about groupness because a culture is a "group of people identified by their shared history, values, and patterns of behavior" (p. 41). Culture provides us with a blueprint of the hidden rules of our group, a map for living that offers consistency and   · predictability in our everyday actions (Lindsey et al., 2003). These hidden rules are known as *cultural expectations*. Cultural expectations help us keep outsiders outside and insiders controlled (Lindsey et al., 2003), thereby sustaining our group culture.

As a White female, I belong to the majority of public school teachers in the United States, and I operate, often unaware, from an unofficial handbook of White Women's Hidden Rules that guide my behavior. Operating unconsciously by these hidden rules, or unspoken codes of conduct, I may assume my culturally diverse learners will know and understand them. In fact, I may expect them to adapt to my White female culture because it is the "air I breathe" in the public school classrooms where I teach. My culture is so familiar I do not recognize it as specific to my culture and assume others can adapt easily. This adaptation is called *acculturation,* which is the process whereby the culture, values, and patterns of the majority are adopted by a person or an ethnic, social, religious affiliation, language, or national group. Acculturation is something I expect my students to do effortlessly and willingly when the process may be neither easy nor acceptable to them or to their peer culture. In effect, when I expect students to acculturate to my culture, I ask them to "leave their cultures at the door."

CULTURALLY RESPONSIVE TEACHING

Rather than expecting acculturation, Geneva Gay, in her book *Culturally Responsive Teaching: Theory, Research, & Practice* (2000), suggests developing culturally *responsive* teaching practices. In doing this, we incorporate teaching practices that respond to the cultures of the students in front of us. Gay states that the key anchors of culturally responsive teaching are its "simultaneous cultivation of the academic success and cultural identity of ethnically diverse students" (p. xiv). These features "serve as benchmarks for organization and assessing the quality of specific teaching ideas, programs, and actions" (p. xiv). When we cultivate academic success through high expectations, rigor, relevance, and relationships (Linton, 2011) while honoring the cultural identity of ethnically diverse students, we practice culturally responsive instruction.

What do you know about culturally responsive teaching?

_____

_____

_____

Consider the following anecdote and reflect below.

> In a workshop on culture, an educator explained her practice of dealing with a diverse group of English language learners by saying that she tells her students to leave their cultures at the door when they walk into her classroom. Do you agree or disagree with this strategy?

_____

_____

_____

This educator fails to understand that she may be asking her students to leave their cultures at the door, but daily she walks in with hers and teaches them by and through White female cultural norms. In a class comprised of multiple ethnicities and cultures, she is missing out by not capitalizing on students' *cultural capital*—that is, the strengths and experiences of her diverse students—and by not honoring their home cultures.

We cannot leave our cultures at the door, for our culture is the lens through which we see the world. It is not a veil or a family crest—these are manifestations of a culture. Our culture is the totality of our ideas, beliefs, values, knowledge, and behaviors. It is not something we can take on and off, even though some from culturally diverse groups have learned to be bicultural and "code-switch" as the situation requires. To code-switch means to assume the cultural norms or practice the hidden rules of a different culture in order to be more accepted by that culture. As a White female, I don't think I can ever know what it means to code-switch daily; I don't think I can ever understand the tremendous energy it must involve and how tiring it must be to live that way.

HOW WERE YOU ACCULTURATED?

I was born and acculturated into a nuclear two-parent family that was White, middle class, small town, midwestern, Catholic, and conservative. These parameters formed the young adult lens I used to view the world.

What was your young adult lens?

_____

_____

_____

Describe your culture today. Which parts of your young adult lens still describe you (several of mine have changed)?

_____

_____

_____

CULTURAL PROFICIENCY

We weave in and out of several kinds of cultures during our day. To become culturally proficient in each of these, we may need to widen our understanding of culture. Cultural proficiency is the "policies and practices of a school or the values and behaviors of an individual that enable the person or school to interact effectively in a culturally diverse environment" (Lindsey et al., 2003, pp. xix–xx). It is an approach, not a theory, program, or silver bullet. This does not mean you must know everything there is to know about others. That is impossible. Rather, it means that "you have the self-awareness to recognize how you—because of your ethnicity, your culture, and your life experiences—may offend or otherwise affect others," as well as what you offer to others (Nuri

Robins, Lindsey, Lindsey, & Terrell, 2002, p. xii). Being culturally proficient allows you to use "teachable moments" to share yourself and learn from others (Nuri Robins et al., 2002, p. xii). We have learned much from the work of Nuri Robins, Lindsey, Lindsey, and Terrell about cultural proficiency and are grateful to them for their groundbreaking work. Building on their work, we add the skill of becoming *culturally considerate* when relating to culturally diverse students, planning and delivering instruction, and creating culturally responsive environments for learning. Cultural consideration supports the inclusion of all aspects of culture while stemming from the basic principle of respect for each living human, celebrating and norming the differences among us.

ORGANIZATIONAL CULTURE

Your school consists of several cultures. You work in an occupational culture and an organizational culture. Your occupational culture, if you are an educator, is education, and educators often share beliefs, dress, and language (jargon sometimes referred to as "educationalese"), in addition to other factors.

Your organizational culture is your district and your school site. Even within your district, you will find school cultures that differ. Elementary, middle, and high school cultures differ. Each school differs from other schools in a district, yet they share some commonalities because they are in the same district. For example, the neighborhoods that surround the schools may be similar, influencing the schools' culture, or they may vary economically, influencing the schools' culture. If you teach in an elementary school, you may find more in common culturally with teachers who work in elementary schools in other districts than the teachers who teach at the high school in your district. In one district, teachers may work hours in their buildings at the end of the school day; in another district, teachers may be out the doors as soon as the buses leave (and sometimes before). There is a difference in the work culture between the two.

Think about a "hot beverage" culture. Does your faculty lounge offer coffee or tea to teachers? If so, do you pay for it? Who makes it daily? Which teachers drink it? Who cleans up the drink station? In visiting schools, a substitute may find a wide range of hot beverage cultures. In some schools, there is free coffee and tea, the staff drinks it, and someone is assigned to make the coffee and tea and clean up the area. In other schools, there is none. Between these two, there are schools where coffee and tea duties are rotated through the staff, the staff chips in to pay for the services, gourmet coffees and teas are available, staff is allowed to take the drinks into their classrooms, and so on. However, substitutes coming into the building need to know the hidden rules of the hot beverage culture at the school if they want to participate in the hot beverage culture. They may need their own cup or correct change to participate in the school ritual, and if they find themselves without a cup or cash, they may find no one willing to assist their acculturation into the school's hot beverage culture. Cultural expectations function in much the same way. If we do not know the expectations (hidden rules or unspoken codes) of the cultural setting, we may find ourselves unable to participate in the culture.

ETHNICITY, NATIONALITY, AND RACIAL IDENTITY

To many, culture refers to racial or ethnic differences. Ethnic culture results from our ancestral heritage and geography, common histories, and physical appearance (Lindsey et al., 2003). My ethnic culture is White American with ancestors who came from Western Europe. Dorothy, whose racial history is found in Chapter 3, is African American with ancestors who came from Africa and Western Europe. We share an American culture, but our lenses differ in that she views and lives her life as a Black person in this American culture, and I view and live my life as a White person in this American culture. This is our *racial identity*. Racial identity is how you perceive and name yourself racially. We share an identical *nationality*. Nationality means place of origin (Singleton, 2003). For many of us, our nationality is the United States.

Photo by Kim Anderson.

Bonnie

Ethnic Culture: W. European

Racial Identity: White

Nationality: United States

Dorothy

Ethnic Culture: African and W. European

Racial Identity: African American/Black

Nationality: United States

What is your ethnic culture or ethnicity?

_____

What is your racial identity?

_____

What is your nationality?

_____

How do your ethnicity, racial identity, and nationality differ from your students and colleagues?

_____

_____

_____

Think about the way you view your world. What factors contribute to the lens you wear as you view the world?

_____

_____

_____

CULTURAL FACTORS

Below are several major factors that influence the way we see our world and contribute to the many cultures we weave in and out of each day:

- Family
- Gender
- Racial identity
- Ethnicity
- Nationality
- Age
- Sexual orientation
- Language
- Friends
- Religion
- School
- Geography
- Income of family or social class
- Political views
- Electronic media
- Social organizations
- Ableness
- Others

When we interact with our students or colleagues, we bring the baggage of our past experiences, our prejudices, and our preferences, as well as those of our families, and other factors that influence the lens through which we view the world. Those we face bring the same.

Examine the list above. Which factors do you share with your students and colleagues? For example, your district may be composed largely of Protestants, and you are Protestant. Therefore, you share religion with your staff and students.

_____

_____

_____

In which ways do you differ from your students and colleagues?

_____

_____

_____

The more differences you find, the more bridges you may need to build to reach those in your daily work life.

What have you learned as a result of defining your culture?

_____

_____

_____

One effective way to build bridges to cultures that differ from ours is to use a framework for when we interact with others. Using a framework focuses our thinking and gives us a blueprint for taking the journey of cultural awareness leading to action and change. We can embark on this journey to meet the needs of each student by acknowledging, respecting, and accommodating the culture and value system of the family (Artiles & Ortiz, 2002).

How do we do this? Even though there is no magic formula, the change can occur when we collaborate and work together with a common goal of supporting our students' personal and academic success. We begin this journey by learning about ourselves. A book study is one tool to do that. Professional development that examines issues of equity in your school is another. The exercise that follows might be used in a staff meeting or professional development opportunity as a tool to learn about other staff members. Each time we have used this activity with students and adults, the results have been overwhelmingly positive. The result always has been that any two individuals find that they have more commonalities than differences. This simple exercise underscores our humanity, makes each participant visible within the group, builds community, gets every voice into the air, and gives us feedback about our peers that is useful for future collaboration.

SUGGESTED EXERCISE

- Pair off with another staff member.
- Use a Venn diagram.

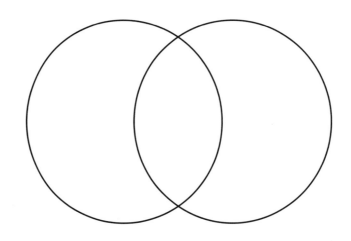

- Write your name above one circle of the Venn diagram; your partner writes his or her name above the other.
- Fill out the Venn diagram with your similarities and differences. For example, if you are of different genders, your gender would go in the separate part of your own circle. If you share gender, your gender would be in the overlapping part of your circles. Fill in your Venn diagrams with as many aspects of your lives as time allows.
- Share with the larger group. You tell about your partner. Your partner tells about you. Share your similarities however you choose. Adults and students find creative ways to share during this exercise as it creates a community of learners.

CULTURAL HOMOGENEITIES

If you are fortunate to have different cultural groups as part of your staff, check for cultural homogeneities. Cultural homogeneities are similarities that exist *within* cultural groups. For example, Deborah Tannen's (1990) work in communication styles finds that women's and men's communication styles differ because of gender. Each gender possesses its own culture.

You may find that your different cultural groups share cultural homogeneities about which you were unaware. Learning about the cultural homogeneities of other groups in our school setting increases our awareness of culture. Female appearance is one example of where you can observe cultural homogeneities. In some female cultural groups, long fingernails painted in elaborate patterns are the rage; in others, short, unpolished nails are the norm. Tattoos are a popular homogeneity of some groups. These are current fads or practices, but it is possible to find cultural homogeneities that span generations and demographic areas. During a diversity workshop, African Americans and an

Afro-Haitian (who said she learned the shared cultural homogeneities growing up in Haiti) found that they shared the cultural homogeneities of some terms unknown to the White participants. These terms included *my kitchen* for describing a place on their heads and *the hawk* for describing the wind, as well as others. Two books that offer specific information about cultural homogeneities of Blacks and Whites are the following:

- *It's the Little Things: Everyday Interactions That Anger, Annoy, and Divide the Races* by Lena Williams (2002), an African American who is a 25-year veteran of the *New York Times.*
- *Afraid of the Dark: What Whites and Blacks Need to Know About Each Other* by Jim Myers (2000), a White man married to a Black woman, who was the chief writer for a *USA Today* series on race.

If you plan to use these books in a book study with staff, consider using a facilitator skilled in cultural proficiency to lead the groups.

WHAT STRATEGIES DO WE NEED TO LEARN?

What strategies do we need to use? When I do workshops, I ask educators participating in the workshop what they are most interested in learning about—the cultures of their students, how to build relationships across cultures, or instructional research-based strategies. Even when the workshop focuses on "students who don't look like you," invariably, educators tell me by a show of their hands that they most want to learn instructional research-based strategies. Why would teachers vote they most want to learn instructional research-based strategies when they are participating in a workshop focusing on student cultures?

What do you think?

_____

_____

_____

Why *do* educators want to learn about strategies more than ways to build relationships across cultures and learn more about student cultures? Educators often want to learn "fix-it" strategies, yet the answers often are not found in simple fix-it strategies. Instead, the answers often lie elsewhere. After thinking about this for a long time, I had an "a-ha" one day. I came to the conclusion that learning about the cultures of our students and learning how to build relationships across cultures *are strategies!* If we learn strategies to build better relationships with students who don't look like us, we are learning strategies to improve student engagement and support learning. Learning about the cultures of our students and learning how to build relationships across cultures are strategies to support classroom instruction. This book includes all three: instructional strategies, strategies for understanding cultures, and strategies for building relationships across cultures.

The following is not a list of research-based instructional strategies (that comes later in the book); however, it is a small list of powerful strategies we can use to show respect and honor for our students' cultures. Our students are the future, and unless we can understand what respect means to them and show them that respect, we diminish our abilities as effective teachers supporting all students to achieve at high levels.

HOW-TO STRATEGIES

Try the following strategies and don't forget to share them with your students.

Level: Elementary/Middle/High School/Adult
Subject: Cross-curricular

- Attend art events given by or about people of other cultures. Great art is found in every culture, and art is a great equalizer.
- Become friends with people of other cultures.
- Live in integrated neighborhoods.
- Enroll your children in integrated schools.
- Read the literature of other cultures.
- Build a culturally responsive learning climate in your classroom that respects diversity.
- Use language daily in your classroom that values diversity so that your students can begin to model your language. For example, talk about the important contributions of cultural groups, such as the contribution of the Africans to mathematics.
- Bring in newspapers and magazines of diverse cultures and have them out and available for students to peruse.
- Read newspaper articles to your class that foster positive portraits of diverse groups.
- Post simple phrases in multiple languages throughout your classroom and school.
- Post role models of diverse people throughout your school.
- Share the poetry of other cultures in your classroom. You could begin class by reading a poem by a culturally diverse poet. Before class, privately ask a student who shares that culture if he or she would like to read it to the class in his or her first language.
- Study a foreign language.
- Ask your students to write about their family customs and discuss them in your classes.
- Ask your students to do the Venn diagram exercise with members of the class.

- Ask your students to bring in a family dish to share on a special day.
- Don't privilege one culture above another. For example, privileging one group occurs when a teacher calls more often on one group of students, uses examples from the lives of one cultural group more than others, and so on. In the 1950s, in the culturally homogeneous elementary school classroom, we called these "teacher's pets."
- Respect the traditions of other cultures.
- Don't make assumptions about the rituals or practices of other cultures.
- Always ask yourself how you would feel if the cultural situation were reversed. For example, what if schools decided not to honor Christmas. How would you feel if you were Christian? How would you feel if you were Jewish or Muslim? What if nearly all members of our U.S. Senate were women? How would you feel? What if your entire central office administration were a different cultural group from yours? How would you feel? Often, we take for granted the cultural dominance of a group without thinking about how it might feel if a different cultural group held that domination.
- Travel, travel, travel—forgo the tours and travel so that you have the opportunity to meet and talk with the locals, wherever you go.

Think about what you have read and reflected upon in this chapter. Write below what you consider most important.

_____

_____

_____

This first chapter examined our personal lens in preparation for learning about and understanding the lenses of our students. Since each of us "sees" the world in a unique way, the more we can learn about the cultures of others, the more we can understand the reasons why our students make the choices they make and do the things they do in our classrooms. Chapter 2 offers you reflective questions to assess your current frame of mind as you continue looking inside yourself.

❖ ❖ ❖

SUGGESTED READINGS

Gay, Geneva. _Culturally Responsive Teaching: Theory, Research, & Practice_ (New York: Teachers College Press, 2000).

Nuri Robins, Kikanza J., Delores B. Lindsey, Randall B. Lindsey, and Raymond D. Terrell. _Culturally Proficient Instruction: A Guide for People Who Teach_ (Thousand Oaks, CA: Corwin, 2012).

Saifer, Steffen, Keisha Edwards, Debbie Ellis, Lena Ko, and Amy Stuczynski. *Culturally Responsive Standards-Based Teaching: Classroom to Community and Back* (Thousand Oaks, CA: Corwin, 2011).

Tileston, Donna Walker, & Darling, Sandra K. *Why Culture Counts: Teaching Children of Poverty* (Bloomington, IN: Solution Tree, 2008).

SUGGESTED WEB SITES

African-American Experience and Issues of Race and Racism in U.S. Schools (www.ithaca.edu/wise/race_african_american/)

Boston College (www.bc.edu)

Teaching Tolerance (www.teachingtolerance.org)

University of New Mexico College of Education (coe.unm.edu)

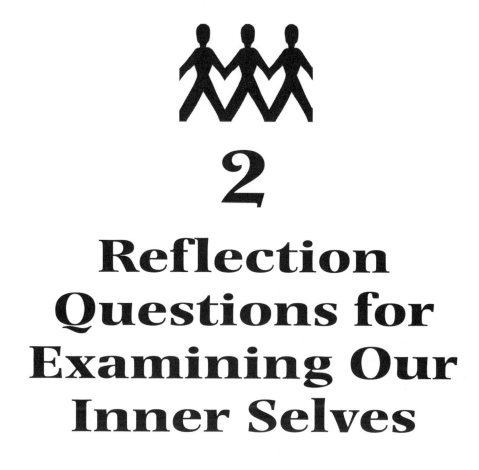

2

Reflection Questions for Examining Our Inner Selves

Before we begin to listen to and learn from others, consider the questions in this chapter. Here, you are invited to think about important questions in *your* professional and personal life. In *The Courage to Teach: Exploring the Inner Landscape of a Teacher's Life,* Parker Palmer (1998) asks this question about our inner selves: "How can the teacher's selfhood become a legitimate topic in education and in our public dialogues on educational reform?" (p. 3). Our selfhoods must become legitimate dialogue if we wish to reach across cultures and support the academic excellence of our diverse learners. As Palmer says, "As long as we inhabit a universe made homogeneous by our refusal to admit otherness, we can maintain the illusion that we possess the truth about ourselves and the world—after all, there is no 'other' to challenge us!" (p. 38). However, when we open ourselves to the "other" and admit that they (the other) have different life experiences and perspectives, the "truths we have built our lives on begin to feel fragile" (p. 38). Ultimately, the more we know about ourselves and what truths we hold true, the more courage we may develop to be open to learning from others and the better we can reach and support our diverse learners.

REFLECTIVE QUESTIONS

What questions do you ask yourself as you reflect on your work? The following questions offer you an opportunity to reflect on basic things that make a difference in working with diverse learners: your heart, your body, and your interactions with students and colleagues. These questions address the *who* of your teaching, a piece that is just as necessary, if not more so, than the *what, how,* and *why.*

- Do my students leave my classroom at the end of the school year liking more the subject I teach them than when they entered? For example, an English teacher would ask, "Do my students like to read and write more in June than they did in September?" Such a simple question, yet how many of us preassess and postassess to find out if we are truly building proficient readers and writers who enjoy using these skills?

_____

_____

_____

- What does my body language say to my students? Do I lean in to some children but lean away from others when I communicate with them? Is there incongruity between my body language and my spoken words? Do I understand the body language and social cues of each of the cultures represented in my classes? Some teachers have confessed they don't even know which Asian cultural group one of their students belong to, therefore assuming all Asian cultures have the same cultural norms.

_____

_____

_____

- Do my interactions with my colleagues model the kinds of interactions I expect among my students? If not, how can I change my interactions with colleagues?

_____

_____

_____

- Do my interactions with my students model the kinds of behaviors I expect back from them? If I scream at them to sit down or scowl at them, can I expect to see the same behaviors mirrored back to me?

_____

_____

_____

- Do I know about the cultures of my students? If I were going to teach in France, I would learn about French customs, language, and so on, yet I may be teaching children from Bosnia and know nothing about their culture.

_____

_____

_____

- Do I read professional books in both my content area and areas of pedagogy and cultural awareness?

_____

_____

_____

- Do my school environment and my classroom reflect the kinds of achievement I expect from my students? Do I post images of diverse role models, in addition to sports and entertainment figures, clearly in view for my students? What are the subconscious and hidden messages we send students when they do not see people who look like them portrayed in their place of learning? Try this at your school. How many steps must you walk into your school before you see a picture posted of a culturally diverse person? Does it matter? A local university has an office where more than ten White men's pictures hang on the wall with no pictures of women or culturally diverse individuals. The assistant in the office, a culturally diverse middle-aged woman, shared how working under their stares each day saps her energy. Ask yourself this question again, after you read the story of Dorothy, an educator and administrator, in the next chapter: Does it matter?

_____

_____

_____

- Do I love my subject content? Am I a voracious reader? Do I regularly cut out articles from journals, newspapers, and magazines about my subject matter to share with my students? Do I connect my content to the lives of my students?

_____

_____

_____

- Do I have a deep and broad understanding of my subject content? Do I make my subject matter explicit? Do I talk about how I learn and what I must do to learn?

_____

_____

_____

- Do I use the CCSS for standards-based instruction? Do I use research-based instructional strategies to support learners in my classroom?

_____

_____

_____

- Do I practice my subject content? If I teach literacy or English, am I a writer and reader? If I teach physical education, do I keep myself physically healthy and fit? Students pay attention to what I *do,* not what I say, so do I practice what I preach?

_____

_____

_____

- Do I take care of myself? Do I eat healthily, exercise, and care for my mental, physical, and spiritual self? If I don't, how can I expect to be the best teacher I can be for my students?

_____

_____

_____

Consider using the above prompts for your personal or professional journal. You may want to select one a week to address in your journal as you journey through your school year. You may want to begin your department meetings with one set of questions and discuss them in the group for the first fifteen minutes of the meeting. You may want to use these at the onset of each book study meeting in your professional learning community. Using these prompts, you may find common ground with colleagues as you work together to examine your inner worlds. As the year progresses, we experience periods of fatigue and stress, perhaps even burnout. In Chapter 18, you will find suggestions for combating these. Be good to yourself, take time for yourself, and choose what fits your needs.

We each know thousands of people and have listened to countless life stories. What have you learned from the stories of others? In the next chapter, we focus on the racial histories of three women: Dorothy, who is African American; Brenda, a Latina; and Bonnie, who is White. We read these so we can expand our understanding of racial life experiences even as we understand that these three women do not represent all women in each of their racial groups. At the same time, learning about the racial experiences of others gives us the opportunity to reflect upon our own racial experiences and how they affect our cultural lens as we teach students who don't look like us. So it's still all about you—looking inside yourself!

❖　❖　❖

SUGGESTED READING

Parker, Palmer. *The Courage to Teach* (San Francisco: Jossey-Bass, 1998).

3

Exploring Our Racial Identity Through Our Racial History

In the first two chapters, you examined your cultural lens and answered questions about your practice and interactions with your colleagues and students. Those chapters prepared you to continue our journey and delve deeper into the impact of race on our students' lives and on our own lives. In this chapter, we explore our racial identity through our racial histories. In order to understand ourselves more deeply and, I submit, to bridge better the cultural gap between culturally diverse learners and ourselves (if you are a White teacher), we must explore our racial identity. When we read the racial histories of others and share our own in writing and conversation, we expose ourselves. As we share with others who don't look like us, we learn that their experiences, though similar in many ways, also differ in many ways. This chapter offers us the opportunity to reflect on the impact of one's racial history on student achievement.

We educators are good people. We work really hard, and our focus is on the children we teach. As a White teacher, I want to believe that I treat all students the same. Yet my students do not all come to me with the same needs and experiences; students who don't look like me come with different racial experiences, experiences that I can never truly understand. However, if I look inside and examine my own racial identity, I can better equip myself with strategies to meet the needs of students who face different experiences.

We live in a racialized society, and race impacts us 100 percent of the time, no matter our color, according to Singleton and Linton (2006) in *Courageous*

Conversations About Race. One way to understand better how race affects us is to write our racial histories and share and compare them with others, especially those who differ from ourselves. It is not easy to talk about race. As White educators, we may be worried about being perceived as or being called a racist. In my experience, this is a real fear. Yet, when I accepted that I had been socialized in a society that is racialized, it became far easier for me to accept that I may have racist thoughts. My challenge is to ensure I do not act out on those thoughts. Do they come to my mind? Of course. But I try not to act out on them and not to judge others based on the color of their skin.

Following are three racial histories. In no way, however, are these representative of whole groups or cultures. Instead, they are the individual histories of three women, one who is the author of this book, one who is her close friend, and one who is the mother of her only grandchild. By sharing our histories with each other, we learned more about how our past experiences often dictate our motivations, reactions to incidents, and the decisions we make in our daily lives. We also found that our histories sparked conversations between us about the impact of race in our lives.

The first is my racial history. I concentrate on events in my life that deal specifically with racial issues. The second is Dorothy's racial history. We have been close friends since 1983, but it was not until I read her racial history that I learned of many of the childhood (and, I might add, horrific) incidents she experienced that I was spared simply because I am White. Our skin color barely differs, since I am an olive-skinned White person and she is a light-skinned African American person. Yet in this racialized society in which we live, our life experiences have differed greatly and continue to differ today simply because she is Black and I am White. The third racial history is Brenda's. Brenda is a young Latina who works in education at the national level. She brings young, newer eyes to the conversation, yet her racial history is still filled with discrimination even though she was born thirty years after I was.

The prompts following our racial histories offer you an opportunity to examine your own racial identity. By exploring our racial identity and personal experiences related to race, perhaps we can understand better the challenges of race our diverse Learners of Color confront in their lives.

My story may be typical of other small-town White women who experienced childhood in the 1950s, went to college in the 1960s, and began teaching during a time of great unrest in our country. These women may have been active in the civil rights movement or the women's movement, or perhaps they were spectators to these events, yet deeply involved with teaching the children who would enter this changing world. Not until the 1980s did I began to realize how these prior years shaped my thinking and my need to understand the world from more than the myopic lens of my past. In no way do I believe that I understand all perspectives; in fact, the more I learn, the more I understand that the "I don't know what I don't know" continues to expand rather than diminish in my life.

Histories are important. Recently I shared with two young women teachers that we women teachers were not allowed to wear pants to work when I began teaching in 1967. It was not until 1971 that we were allowed to wear a pantsuit, which meant pants with a top that covered our bottoms. Also, we could not get a credit card or purchase a house in our name alone. These women were stunned and stared in disbelief, yet they looked like me, White women in the United States. When we don't know our histories and the barriers faced in the past (and in the present), we limit our ability to reach and teach others.

MY STORY

Childhood

I was born a White female in 1946 to middle-class parents in a small town on the Mississippi River. My young world was divided into the cultural groups of Catholics and non-Catholics, with Catholicism being the normative value and all else being the "non" or "other" in my experience.

When I was in eighth grade, a Black male joined our class during the basketball season. One night after a victory, the coach took the team and the class supporters to the Southern Café. When they would not serve our star player, the coach stood up and marched us out the door. This experience was my first recognized encounter with discrimination, and I recall being upset and my mother reflecting my feelings.

Adulthood

During college I married my first husband, and while planning our wedding, I observed racial discrimination for the second time. I had made friends with a Black girl from St. Louis and wanted to invite her to my wedding. My mother objected, saying my grandmother would not enter the church with a Negro inside. This was my first awareness of discrimination in my family, since I had never heard my parents make a negative comment about race.

Soon I entered graduate school at the University of Mississippi in Oxford, Mississippi. There I mixed with many Blacks on the streets, and even now I remember the signs at the ice cream drive-in that said "Colored only" and the two separate waiting rooms at the dentist's office, one carpeted with nice chairs for White patients, the other bare floored with beat-up furniture for Black patients. Even though Black students were allowed to register for classes in 1967, I did not have a single Black person in any of my graduate classes over the period of five summers. That same year, I entered teaching and taught in a junior high school in the suburbs of St. Louis. The school was all White, and the haves and the have-nots consisted of those who lived a middle-class existence and those who eked out an existence on the banks of the small river that ran through the area. They were referred to by some staff and students as the "river rats."

I lived in the White suburbs of St. Louis for the next several years, returning to Ole Miss each summer. My daughter was born in Oxford, Mississippi, the same week that the first man walked on the moon. She entered her parents' world where our church was White, our schools were White, our neighborhoods were White, and our lives were White.

Another Culture

It was not until after a divorce in 1975 that I entered another world. On my thirtieth birthday, I met the man who would become my second husband. When I wrote my mother that I was dating a man and that, "by the way, he is Black," she wrote me a letter telling me I had ruined my father's fifty-sixth birthday with this news. Perhaps naively, I was shocked at my parents' response. I really hadn't thought that they were prejudiced. By this time, my grandmother had died, and I thought their reservation had disappeared with her death. I married my second husband in secret, and he was not welcome in my parents' house until after the birth of our son. I faced, with the birth of my son, experiences I would have never known in my all-White world. In the hospital, the nurse marked "Caucasian" on my son's hospital information without asking. Weeks later, as I changed his diaper in a department store bathroom, a Black woman noticed the black and blue spot at the base of his spine, and like a fortune-teller foretelling his future, she whispered ominously, "He must be biracial because he has the 'mark.'" The mark disappeared, kinky hair replaced my son's straight birth hair, and his skin darkened as he grew. I was now the mother of a Child of Color in my White world.

The Voluntary Desegregation Program

In 1984 the St. Louis Voluntary Desegregation Program brought Black children to the school where I taught, a suburban high school that had previously held only White students. Partway through the year, a science teacher brought a girl to me and asked if I would proofread a letter she had written to the school board. I read her letter and wept. She wrote that the Black children bused daily to our high school were largely ignored—invisible. The words of novelist Ralph Ellison (1952), author of *Invisible Man*, echoed in my head as I thought about the cloak of invisibility African Americans often experience in our society.

After reading the letter, I knew we had to do something at our school to support our Black students. We started a multicultural club, the Organization for the Appreciation of Black Culture, and invited all students and teachers to join. For the next five years, this club offered the "transfer" students, as they were often called, a place to discuss issues and network with others.

My Journey Continues

I began to study in earnest a world that I didn't know I didn't know. Luckily, I found mentors, both Black and White, who gave me books to read, offered me opportunities, such as studying with James Banks in Seattle, and traveling to Africa to study the impact of African literature on African American literature. Traveling to Africa, I found yet another world.

The next decade brought professional change as I completed a PhD in English, focusing on the impact of race and gender in the literary canon; moved from teaching to professional development; changed districts; and eventually accepted a position with a local service center at the University of Missouri. For the past four decades, I have had the good fortune to work with educators in schools at the elementary, middle, and high school levels.

My children grew to adulthood, forever influenced by the effects of racism in our society, yet often protected from its insidiousness by their family and our middle-class stature. Their stories must come from them in *The Biracial and Multiracial Student Experience* (Davis, 2009, pp. 3–7).

For nearly thirty years, I have read and studied racism. Yet I continue to make mistakes, take my White privilege for granted, and do the "White talk" Alice McIntyre (1997) refers to in *Making Meaning of Whiteness* even when it limits others' opportunities. This journey is lifelong; however, I am fortunate to have allies along the way.

One of these is my close friend, Dorothy Kelly, who through her friendship, stories, and writings continues to provide me with opportunities to listen to one who views the world through another lens.

❖   ❖   ❖

DOROTHY'S STORY

Childhood

I was born in 1957 in a small town in mid-Missouri. I attended public schools, K–12, and most of my role models before adolescence were older people. I lived in a rural African American community, so I can be classified as what some African Americans call "country." I lived there with my maternal grandparents during my early childhood. After leaving the country, I lived with my paternal grandmother and spent most of my childhood between two mid-Missouri towns. Although segregation was the law in my early years, by virtue of the size of both towns, we always lived in close proximity to White people. As a child I knew and understood that White people were in charge of everything outside of my home, but I was also taught that White people were not better than Black people.

My first lesson in understanding what being an African American meant was taught by my grandmother. She drove to the poor White section of town to show me impoverished White people, and she told me not to be ashamed of being a Negro, because White people had a hard time in this world too. She told me that no one was any better than anyone else, but you had to work hard in school because some White people would keep Negroes from making a good living. I learned most of life's lessons from my grandmother.

Outside of my home life, I was encouraged by other strong Black women and men to be an independent thinker. My neighbor across the street, who was the secretary of our local NAACP and the mother of one of my friends, used to send me and her daughter to the local Rexall drugstore every Saturday to sit at the counter to order milk shakes or cherry sodas. At that time I didn't know that we were being sent there as an act of civil disobedience. We were instructed to sit there until we were served and report back everything that was said to or about us. Luckily, we were served with no incidents. This was in the mid-1960s when I was in first through third grades.

One of the more fun times of my childhood was playing softball. One of the White community members started a girls' softball team. Everyone, Black and White, thought he was very brave, because he recruited mostly Black girls to play on his team. A few White girls joined, but the majority of the players were Black. We ranged in age from ten to sixteen years old. Our club sponsor was the local Dairy Queen. We traveled to small local towns and communities to play, and we won most of our games. Sometimes we could not play in the towns after dark or had to leave right after the game ended. Rarely were we allowed to even get drinks at the water fountains. Sometimes we would purposely go to the fountains when the coach told us that we were not allowed. One summer we won the league championship. We had been warned that we would be run out of town if we won. As soon as the game was over, we got out of town. It was a very scary and fun time for us, and we laughed about the situation, but the older girls were ready to fight if we had to defend ourselves. Interestingly, our parents did not go to the out-of-town games; it was just us and the coach. He was the bravest White man of my childhood.

My elementary school officially integrated—that is so much the wrong word—officially desegregated when I was in the fifth grade. We had to walk across town to a school that housed the fifth and sixth grades from the entire town in order to comply with the 1954 *Brown v. Board of Education* ruling. The local high school had been desegregated since the early 1960s. When we walked through the White neighborhoods, all the White residents came out and stood along the roads as the Black kids walked to the newly "integrated" school. We were scared and embarrassed because they thought we were going to do something to them or their property. Eventually, they stopped coming out, and we walked to and from school without incident.

My first real understanding of being racially desegregated came at this school. I had been with most of these students in one classroom for five years; we simply moved together to the next grade. But now my class was separated. We had never known that kind of separation, but it was very clear where you stood in society after the implementation of court-ordered integration.

I still have flashbacks of racially charged incidents during my childhood. Racial slurs and being banned from playing with White students was pretty much an everyday activity. There were times of civic unrest when a Black girl was selected homecoming queen or band majorette, and the Black community members were worried about violence at the high school because, invariably, the White students and parents would become angry. I also remember when one of those young ladies was the first Black person hired by a local financial company as a clerk. The local NAACP and a united group of church elders had many meetings before those kinds of employment decisions were finalized. There were many "first" Blacks, and there was always backlash from each hiring or selection.

Adolescence

As I entered junior high, I encountered what it was like to be the "first one" or the "only one." My junior high years spanned Grades 7 to 9. I was the first

African American cheerleader at my junior high school. Because the Black girls knew there would be only one Black chosen, the predicament made us act mean toward one another. After being selected, I was very excited and happy, but that soon ended, and the reality of being the first Black cheerleader at my junior high consumed me. It was extremely odd always being on the outside of the White cheerleader clique. When we were making decisions about uniforms, hairstyles, or cheering stunts, they would whisper among themselves to agree on who would try to explain to me how to be a cheerleader. I felt odd and they felt odd. I was almost relieved when I became ill and had to have surgery and couldn't be a cheerleader. Once again, I was on the outside looking in as the rest of the Black girls again became competitive and divisive as they vied for that one spot. Some girls argued over who would be the best person to take my place, while others made bets on who might get selected even though they were not good at cheering. Some of the White parents and their daughters became outraged because only Black girls could try out as my replacement—that's desegregation. I was glad to be through with the whole mess.

In my second year in junior high, I was the first Black student council member, which was an exciting time for me because I felt like I was able to make a difference and I wasn't selected because of my race. I got to see the kids in my social studies class hold their hands up, both Black and White, and I knew I was legitimately voted in because the kids wanted me.

I felt a sense of independence; it was a racially uplifting time—my early adolescence. But as I entered my high school years, I moved to a neighboring larger university town. Although I knew my relatives who lived there, this town presented my mid-adolescence with a host of new friends, and acceptance was tenuous. Perhaps because I was considered a nice, friendly young lady and easy to talk to, I made friends with White students. Along with these friendships came a price. The price was being exposed to their racial history. I had a really cool White girlfriend, who had a Volkswagen, and we would hang out together. One day we were getting into her car and a good White friend of mine made this remark: "I don't ride nigger." (This was a local expression sometimes voiced by a White person who did not want to ride in the back seat.) She immediately apologized. I told her I don't consider myself to be a nigger. We got through it, and we are still friends. Once, with another group of friends at a park, we observed a Black family having a reunion. A girl in our group burst out laughing and said, "Hey, there's a coon reunion!" Whenever I heard *nigger* or *coon*, I didn't hesitate to remind my White friends that I didn't put up with that talk and they shouldn't use it around me.

One of my high school sweethearts was a White guy, and he found himself often berated and called "nigger lover" by some of the White boys. My boyfriend lost some White friends along the way, and he also kicked butts because he would get so upset at racism. However, just like many other adolescents in the 1970s, we saw ourselves as righting the world and being together because we wanted to be together, not because we were a Black and White couple. We selected our friends based on how they treated us, not because of race.

I still resent how I was treated by my high school counselor—I believe that to him I really did not matter. Prior to leaving high school, everyone met the high school counselor, whom we looked to for guidance on how to go to college. It never occurred to me that I wouldn't go to college. I was excluded from the Upward Bound program that most Black students participated in at my high school. The program was designed to acclimate Black high school juniors and seniors to college life. I still don't know why I was excluded from the program other than the fact that we did not receive social aid from the government or live in government housing.

My guidance counselor did not give me any encouragement, ideas, or suggestions about going to college. So, as a result, I had no idea that you could get financial aid, what college would cost, or how one got into college. I walked to the local university and found the office of admissions. The receptionist told me what I had to do in order to get into college. By the end of my summer, I had taken and passed the ACT, then began classes in the fall. Without any guidance, I selected the wrong classes and did not have a good experience in my freshman year.

Adulthood

As I entered college in the late 1970s, my world expanded to encounter other People of Color from all over the world. I had come to experience the world from a multicultural perspective. I spent a lot of time with foreign students and learned about their lives and how they were affected by race and racism. I majored in history and eventually decided to become a teacher because I wanted all students to feel that they were special. I believed that I could help my students to understand the world and accept others and not practice prejudice, discrimination, or racism. I also believed that their understanding of the world would come from learning about everyone's history. It wasn't until my early 30s that I began to understand that matters of race and racism were paramount to understanding how people relate to others in their families, in their communities, and even worldwide. I also believe that until this idea is truly explored, we educators will continue to perpetuate racism and misunderstand issues of race.

❖   ❖   ❖

Dorothy states that until matters of race are "truly explored, we educators will continue to perpetuate racism and misunderstand issues of race." In what ways do you agree or disagree?

_____

_____

_____

Next, Brenda shares her racial history.

BRENDA'S STORY

I'm the product of a Mexican mama and a Puerto Rican papa. I like to say I'm Mexi-Rican or a Borimex. I always thought that since I was made up of two ethnic groups I would be in a position of large-scale acceptance amongst my people. However, when coming of age, this combination proved to be damaging to my self-perception.

My parents separated when my mama was two months pregnant with me. As a result, I grew up listening to her talk about how Puerto Ricans aren't nice people, how I should never bring a Puerto Rican kid to the house and, more importantly, I shouldn't tell people I'm Puerto Rican. My mama wasn't the only one who told me to stop telling folks I was Puerto Rican, but my brother as well. One day, my brother heard me tell a group of neighborhood White kids that I was Puerto Rican. He immediately called me into the house. As soon as I walked in, he grabbed me by the shoulders and with tears in his eyes said: "Don't be telling people we're Puerto Rican! Don't you know White people don't like Puerto Ricans?!" As a little brown girl I never realized that other brown people belonged to other ethnic/racial groups.

Negative comments about being Puerto Rican were not just in my home, but in the playground as well. At school, Mexican kids had no qualms about calling me a spic. In fact, one day, a White kid called my girlfriend a spic. Her response to him was "I ain't no spic. I'm not Puerto Rican." She then went on to explain to me that Puerto Ricans are spics and Mexicans are wetbacks. I remained silent.

I carried this silence with me for years. Instead of telling people to go to hell, I accepted their word as truth. I began to loathe the very idea of my Puerto Rican blood. I felt wrong. I felt negative. Soon enough, I stopped telling people I was Puerto Rican. Puerto Rican kids weren't as offensive. They were just less inclusive because I didn't speak like them, I didn't live in a predominantly Puerto Rican neighborhood or I didn't "look" Puerto Rican.

During my junior high and high school years I stifled my voice because I didn't know where I belonged. However, I eventually rediscovered myself during my late college years. I exposed myself to not just Puerto Rican culture, but to all cultures. The more I stepped outside of my comfort zone, the more I was able to close the gap of my identity crisis. I eventually capped my insecurities after a trip to the island where I met my papa. After 24 years, the mystery of who and what made me was sealed the instant I set my eyes on his face.

I now look at the whopping eyes of my five-month-old daughter, Eva Salomé Álvarez Davis. She is Mexican; she is Puerto Rican; she is White; and she is Black. Yet, when I look at her, I don't see any of this. All I see is a little girl who has the potential to enjoy life and to develop her own thoughts; I see a little girl who will be confident in her skin regardless of ethnic and racial backgrounds; and I see a little girl who will benefit from being multicultural and who will cross all boundaries despite color and language.

I'm excited to be her mama. (Davis, 2009, pp. 8–9)

❖   ❖   ❖

We three women experience life in different yet similar ways. What differences and what similarities did you find in our histories?

_____

_____

_____

As you work with students who don't look like you, consider their racial narratives. How can you learn more about their life experiences? Below is a list of how-to strategies for meeting that need.

HOW-TO STRATEGIES

- Have your students write about themselves and share in class.
- Have your students create self-portraits and display them in the class.
- Ask your students to bring in photographs of themselves and their families to display in the classroom on a "family wall."
- Ask students to write an oral history in English and social studies classes.
- Post family pictures on a school Web page (when appropriate).
- Highlight a family of the week in your classroom.
- Share family histories as a way to build community in your classroom.
- Read biographies of people who do not share your racial identity.
- Read histories of groups who do not share your racial identity.
- Stay abreast of current racial issues in newspapers. Read opposing viewpoints of the controversial cases centered on race and consider the different perspectives.
- Write your racial past. Write a history that includes the interactions that you have had with people of a different color from yourself. You may choose to draw a time line rather than write your racial history.
- Share your racial history.

In your professional learning group or with the entire staff:

1. Divide into smaller groups of four or five colleagues.

2. Find a comfortable space with no table or obstruction between any of the group and sit in a circle facing each other.

3. Decide upon a timekeeper.

4. Discuss protocols: the speaker has four minutes of uninterrupted speaking time; no questions at the end of each individual's sharing; listeners offer positive body language and good listening skills, such as looking the speaker in the eyes and affirmatively nodding the head.

5. Begin with one colleague (perhaps the person whose first or last name is closest to the end of the alphabet).

6. Speak for four minutes about your racial history, either reading what you wrote or just saying what you feel.

7. Go directly to the next person when the four minutes ends, and if the speaker finishes before the time is up, stay silent in the group (this is the hardest part of the exercise).

8. Finish all sharing and then give your group time to share openly with each other with any comments or questions they may have.
- Discuss racial histories with others.
- Hold courageous conversations about race with your professional learning group and a trained facilitator.

What compelling similarities and differences do you find in your racial history and the racial histories of others? What other power dynamics, such as those related to ethnicity, class, and gender, were shared in the group? Considering all that was shared, what have you learned as a result of your participation in this exercise?

_____

_____

_____

_____

_____

THE ONGOING JOURNEY

Having close friends who possess different racial pasts helps me understand better my own myopic view. Each day I learn something new; often I am embarrassed by my ignorance; seldom do I feel smug. Usually I feel humbled and wish knowledge didn't hurt so much. Even assuming I can understand the life experiences of People of Color illustrates my thought processes of privilege. Of course, I can't understand, but I am more willing to listen and, hopefully, honor our differing experiences.

Reflect on your "fatigue level" upon completing this chapter. Do you find it tiring to think about your racial past and others' racial identities?

_____

_____

_____

If you are White, have you considered how tiring it must be to have to deal with your racial identity all the time? Even though we each are affected by our race 100 percent of the time (Singleton & Linton, 2006), I can choose to walk away from it and not have to think about it as I move about in our White-dominated society until I encounter a Person of Color.

❖   ❖   ❖

SUGGESTED READINGS

Delgado, Richard, and Jean Stefancic. *Critical White Studies: Looking Behind the Mirror* (Philadelphia: Temple University Press, 1997).

Landsman, Julie. *A White Teacher Talks About Race* (Lanham, MD: Scarecrow Press, 2001).

McIntyre, Alice. *Making Meaning of Whiteness: Exploring Racial Identity With White Teachers* (New York: State University of New York Press, 1997).

Singleton, Glenn, and Curtis Linton. *Courageous Conversations About Race* (Thousand Oaks, CA: Corwin, 2006).

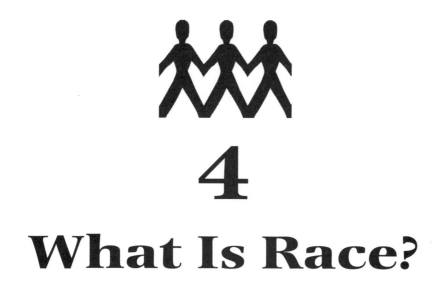

4

What Is Race?

In the previous chapter, we shared our racial histories and strategies for learning the histories of our students' families. With our histories as a basis for understanding the racial lens through which we see the world, we can move on to an examination of race.

What is race? This question has haunted me for decades. Even though I used to identify people as fitting into different races, I never understood exactly why or how. I always wanted to better understand exactly what race is and how the concept of race evolved. Originally, I thought it had only to do with physical appearance. Not until I began to study the phenomenon of race did I learn about the anthropological, economic, and political aspects of race. The concept of race is so complicated, and I continue to search for better definitions and more understanding.

What is your understanding of race?

_____

_____

_____

Originally, I thought of race as a simple classification system that put humans into distinct categories based mostly on their skin color and a few other physical features. In geography class in elementary school, I learned about the races of the world. But as I grew older, simple observation about skin color caused me to realize that it could not be a determiner of race since skin color varies tremendously within every racial designation. And certainly, when I have a tan, my skin color is darker than many people who self-identify or are identified by others as being People of Color. So if it is not skin color, I wondered if there were another physical feature that is distinctive to a race. The answer is no. There is no distinctive characteristic that defines one as belonging to a certain race.

THEN WHAT IS RACE?

People hold varied beliefs about the definition of race. Some believe race is a biological reality attached to a variety of physical features (phenotypes). Others believe race is the socially constructed meaning attached to a variety of physical features (phenotypes). Still others say race does not exist at all but is rather the *belief* in either of these.

Are any of these correct? What do you think?

_____

_____

_____

The American Anthropological Association (AAA) has been studying race for some time, and it issued a statement on race in the 1990s to help clarify erroneous definitions.

American Anthropological Association's Statement on Race

The AAA's *Statement on "Race"* (1998) says that "we have been conditioned to viewing human races as natural and separate divisions within the human species based on visible physical differences" (p. 8). However, this is simply not true. Due to the scientific expansion of the 20th century, it has "become clear that human populations are not unambiguous, clearly demarcated, biologically distinct groups" (p. 2). So the AAA says that there are *no* distinct biological groups we can define as races.

Do you agree or not? Explain.

_____

_____

_____

Phenotypes

How does the AAA know there is no such thing as distinct biological groups we can define as races? The AAA says it knows this because physical traits—such as hair texture, skin color, and physical features—are inherited independently. These physical traits are known as *phenotypes*. Phenotypes are the visible characteristics of an organism resulting from the interaction between its genetic makeup and the environment.

Interestingly, one trait does not predict the presence of others. Dark skin may be associated with kinky hair or wavy or straight hair. All of these combinations are found among indigenous people in tropical areas (AAA, 1998). Since phenotypes are inherited independently, they can't be bound together to be indicators of distinct groups of people, known as racial categories. Yet they are bound together when used for *racial profiling*. Racial profiling, the practice of categorizing individuals based on phenotypes associated with particular racial categories, continues today even with scientific evidence to the contrary. For example, racial profiling occurs when we target persons who *appear* to be members of the same race. Remember how persons who looked Middle Eastern to some people may have been profiled as terrorists following the September 11, 2001, terrorist attacks in the United States. And more recently, in the 2012 case of Trayvon Martin, he was racially profiled based on his skin color and what he was wearing—a hoodie.

Lack of Physical, Scientific Basis

In *Philosophy of Science and Race,* Professor Naomi Zack (2002) underscores the lack of evidence for the existence of race. She states, "Differences in skin tone are gradual, not discrete; and blood-type variations occur independently of the more visible phenotypes associated with race, such as skin color and hair texture" (p. 88). There are not different blood types associated with different races. The same blood types run through all our veins, no matter our racial categories. Furthermore, Zack states that "essences, geography, phenotypes, genotypes, and genealogy are the only known candidates for physical scientific bases of race. Each fails. Therefore, there is no physical, scientific basis for the social racial taxonomy" (p. 88).

All Humans Are One Species

If there are no distinct biological groups we can define as races, then what are we? The AAA states that we are truly a *human race,* not distinct races. So there are no biological races. We all belong to the same species with innumerable variations in genetics, including phenotypes. The AAA says we have continued to share genetic material that has maintained all of humankind as a single species, not distinct races. In the late twentieth century, the human genome project revealed that humans can't be biologically classified into races. *Newsweek's* December 4, 1995, issue explored the topic thoroughly. PBS has a three-part series that can be previewed at www.pbs.org/race/.

Educator and former high school advanced placement social studies teacher Donna Beard puts it this way: "To my granddaughter and all other humans, I say welcome to the 21st Century. Embrace it. Get to know yourself; reject the category of race as a way of defining who you are. Know that life is difficult for all us humans. Enjoy the many good days ahead of you that you will have when you are in control of who you are" (Davis, 2009, p. 17).

Learning this was a huge *a-ha* for me. I assumed that brown and black people, because of their skin color, belonged to a different race than I, a white person, belonged to, but I now know we all belong to a single race: the human race.

Reflect on this information. What are your thoughts?

_____

_____

_____

HOW DID THE CONCEPT OF RACE EVOLVE?

If we agree with Donna Beard, then how did the concept evolve? Race evolved as a mode of classification linked to colonization that was used to rationalize attitudes and treatment by those in power (AAA, 1998, p. 4) and for economic power. In the United States, leaders among the European Americans linked "superior traits with Europeans and negative and inferior ones to blacks and Indians" (p. 4), thereby institutionalizing and deeply embedding these beliefs in the American psyche. There was a need for the belief in race, for how else could we enslave fellow human beings? If we believed they belonged to an inferior race, it justified the treatment. Unfortunately, we still see the beliefs in and assumptions about race played out on our national scene and in our neighborhoods, schools, and families.

MULTIRACIAL INDIVIDUALS

An additional assumption about race may occur when human beings, who identify as belonging to different races, have children who identify as biracial, multiracial, or mixed. If biological race is not a reality, then their children are not biologically mixed race, but race is still real for them. They may self-identify and be seen by others as biracial, multiracial, or mixed, or they may choose a monoracial self-identity such as Black American. In our society, these individuals have the freedom to self-identify and choose their "racial" category on the Census. It is important for educators to recognize this group, for this population is large and growing, especially among school-age children. In the 2000 Census, 6.8 million people, 2.4 percent of the U.S. population, reported more than one race (Jones & Smith, 2001, p. 4). The self-designated multiracial population is diverse and young. About 42 percent, or 2.9 million, were under eighteen years of age, with nearly 70 percent of all multiracial people being younger than thirty-five years of age and only 5 percent of the multiracial population reporting being sixty-five or older. About 25 percent of the population who reporting one race was less than eighteen, and 12 percent of the population reporting one race was over age sixty-five (p. 5). Clearly, more younger people than older people are self-designating multiracial identities. The 2000 Census was a historical census in self-reporting, and it was followed by a historical election in which a man with a mixed-race heritage was elected president of the United States (Davis, 2009, pp. 88–89).

Multiracial students often hunger to find others who share their experiences, just as the rest of us seek those who share our experiences. At a hotel where I have stayed for the past three years doing work in a nearby school district, there is a desk clerk who is a young, biracial woman who shared with me how hard it is to work there with no one else who is mixed like her. After our conversation, I gave her my book, *The Biracial and Multiracial Student Experience: A Journey to Racial Literacy,* and she began showing it to the other desk clerks. To her surprise, one of them was biracial, and the two young women were delighted to learn this and communicate about their racial experiences. Our multiracial students need opportunities to talk about their experiences, just as other Students of Color. If you want to learn more about students who experience life as biracial and multiracial learners, read *The Biracial and Multiracial Student Experience* (2009). It includes more than forty narratives, nearly all written by teachers and students, and they give us a personal and poignant glimpse into the experiences of race these individuals encounter.

CULTURAL BEHAVIORS

If there is scientific proof that race does not exist, why do we still treat others based on our perceptions of what race they identify with? Well, as the concept of race evolved as a worldview, behaviors were attributed to different groups and culture was implied to be genetically inherited. What we might label as *race* is really cultural behavior. So the judgments we often make about others that we attribute to race are really cultural behaviors. Their cultural behaviors are being misdefined as racial behaviors. Race is implying biological designation, and culture is something else. Cultural behaviors are learned, and "it is a basic tenet of anthropological knowledge that all normal human beings have the capacity to learn any cultural behavior" (AAA, 1998, p. 7). We learn the cultural behaviors of the groups in which we were socialized.

Think about cultural behaviors that you learned as a child. Write about them.

_____   _____

_____

_____

I learned the cultural behaviors of Catholicism as a child, and I mastered the practice of being a Catholic. If all Catholics had green hair, would I have been classified as belonging to a race of Catholics? Yet, this happens with race.

Mali, a young man whose mother is of Mexican heritage and whose father is African American, shares that he is often told, "You don't act Black" or "You don't act Mexican." He understands that his peers are referring to cultural behaviors, not racial designations, but it irritates him when others assume he should act a certain way because of his skin color.

While teaching, I found that I had to fight not to assign racial labels to cultural behaviors. Students from different cultural groups may behave differently than students from other cultural groups. Yet it is so easy to group students based on skin color rather than culture, too often forgetting that Students of Color come to our classrooms from hundreds of different cultures, not as homogeneous races.

Have you assigned racial labels to cultural behaviors? Is there something you might do because you "don't know you don't know"? Reflect below.

_____

_____

_____

CULTURE OR RACE?

Race is sometimes used interchangeably with _culture,_ and the confusion deepens. According to Singleton and Linton (2006), in _Courageous Conversations About Race,_ culture describes "how we live on a daily basis in terms of our language, ancestry, religion, food, dress, musical tastes, traditions, values, political and social affiliations, recreation" (pp. 169–170). What we may call _race_ when we observe individuals acting a certain way may be behaviors they learned within a cultural framework. Race, for the most part, is the meaning "affixed to the melanin content found in the skin, hair, and eyes." Therefore, persons with a lot of melanin are defined as being "of color," and those with little are defined as white (p. 170). Race both "_exists_ and _does not exist_" in the United States and throughout the Western world, and "racial issues are not about physical skin color but rather stem from the meaning and value people assign to skin color" (p. 106). The meaning people assign to skin color is based on a system of power and superiority. Race as a biological reality does not exist, but as stated above, race both exists and does not exist in our everyday lives because people assign meaning and value to others based on phenotypes. Therefore race is based on power and superiority, and culture and ethnicity are based on common heritages.

The AAA concludes that "present-day inequalities between so-called 'racial' groups are not consequences of their biological inheritance but products of historical and contemporary social, economic, educational, and political circumstances" (AAA, 1998, p. 8). These present-day inequalities can impact students and may affect their perceptions of themselves and how they fit into the culture in which they live.

Think about what the term *race* means to you. Does the above information challenge or change your thinking? Share below.

_____

_____

_____

Race may not exist, but racism does exist. *Racism* can be defined as "beliefs and an enactment of beliefs that one set of characteristics is superior to another set (e.g. white skin, blonde hair, and blue eyes are more beautiful than brown skin, brown eyes, and brown hair)." A *racist* would then be anyone who "subscribes to these beliefs and perpetuates them intentionally or unconsciously" (Singleton & Linton, 2006, p. 39).

Our challenge then—if you choose to take up the challenge—is to examine our inner worlds for behaviors and thoughts that could perpetuate racism while continuing our journey to learn what we don't know we don't know.

Next, we examine racial identity. Educator Graig Meyer has studied racial identity development for years. He is the father of an African American daughter and two White sons, and part of his interest in the topic stemmed from his personal connection. Graig shares below.

On Racial Identity Development

I am a white man, a social worker, and an educator. I'm also the parent of three children. My eldest child is adopted and black. My two youngest are biological and white. Through their experiences in school, I've learned a lot about the way one system works differently for people from two different races (even within one family).

My daughter had internalized the belief that white kids are smarter than black kids by the time she was in sixth grade. My sons are younger than that still, but I'm sure they'll learn the same thing. My fear is that when they wonder why their sister ended up going to college, their answer will be because she came from a white family. To me that would be a sad answer and create a divide between my own children. I want all of my children to succeed in school, and I want them to learn that kids of all races are intelligent and successful. That's my personal motivation to run a program that ensures every single Student of Color goes to college.

We know from research[1] that having a positive racial identity is a precursor for the academic success of Students of Color. Many educators are surprised to hear this because they assume that it's academic success that leads to positive identity development. However, if the positive racial socialization must come first,

---

[1]Mary Stone Hanley and George Noblit. 2009. http://www.heinz.org/programs_cms.aspx?SectionID=233

(Continued)

(Continued)

then schools must consider what it takes to support this process if they want to eliminate racial achievement disparities.

Since schools are a primary socialization milieu for all young people, there are a multitude of ways that they help students through various identity development processes. In the case of racial identity development, the first step is that schools must be willing to talk openly about the issue of race, and then second they must be able to show examples of intelligent and successful People of Color that counter the dominant narratives that connect beliefs about intelligence with racial stereotypes. To be blunt, we have to teach black and brown kids that people who look like them are smart and that they are smart too.

What I love about working on racial identity development with students is that it is something that they respond to quickly with deep internal motivation. I've never seen a student be lazy or disengaged in the work we do around this topic. Another exciting element is that one of the best ways to approach this topic is through the arts. When we engage students in self-reflective artistic processes that are connected to other curricular content, there is deep engagement, meaningful learning, and powerful results in student identity formation and academic performance.

On Black Identity

Many black students struggle with social pressures for them to conform to some singular African American identity. Part of White racism seems to be leaving a very small opening for variation in the ways people can be Black. This is perhaps felt most strongly by students who are racially Black but have cultural identities that are not African American.

My students who are Black immigrants (usually Caribbean or African) are often quite confused by how they are related to U.S. Blacks, and their identity development process can be quite painful as they struggle to figure this out. They need a lot of help in exploring this, and often their parents just don't know what to tell them. I also have found this to be true with Black students who are Muslim. In both cases, they acutely feel the label of being Black, but they struggle to fit in with Black peers. One of my Black Muslim students said something that unintentionally showed how he stands apart when he tried to show how normal he is, telling his peers: "I'm just a Black kid who likes alternative rock music like Audioslave."

Similarly, I think all non-Black Students of Color need guidance on where they fit in a society that is often stuck in a Black-White racial paradigm. For Latinos, Asians, and Native Americans, there is a common experience of being left out of the dialog about race. When students from these races try to assert their identities, they are often reminded that they are not White nor are they Black. Unfortunately, they are not often enough offered assistance in learning what they are and where they fit in.

Race is something we create to categorize people and relate to them. It is solely based on the color of their skin and other phenotype markers. We also create racism based on the categorization around race. Saying we're all one race will not make racism go away. (e-mail message to the author, April 22, 2012)

❖   ❖   ❖

Graig shares the conundrum of race with us: race doesn't exist but racism does, and we have to do more than just say we are all one human race. We must act on that knowledge. As we learn about the impact of race, we build a repertoire of resources on which to draw when we interact with students who don't look like us to respect their experiences with race and racism.

WHAT I LEARNED WHEN I EXAMINED THE CONCEPT OF RACE AND RACIAL IDENTITY

Share your thoughts below.

_____

_____

1. There is no such thing as different races, according to the American Anthropological Association. All human beings belong to one race: the human race.

2. Race does not exist as a reality, but racism does.

3. There is no separate multiracial species of people. Multiracial individuals are people who self-identify as such or are viewed by others as such because they possess a blending of the phenotypes that are stereotypically applied to different groups of people, artificially called "races" in the United States.

4. People who identify as first generation biracial are using biological race as the basis for that definition—whether they understand this or not.

5. Color, hair, and other phenotypical genes do not bind together. Therefore, within a single family, there is a variety of skin colors, hair textures, and other physical features. There is no fixed racial phenotype because there is no such thing as race.

6. Race was created to give economic advantage to its creators and provide a rationale for enslaving human beings.

7. Having a positive racial identity is a precursor for the academic success of Students of Color.

8. Many Black students struggle with having to conform to a singular African American identity.

Reflect on the following statements.

- Americans are multiethnic.
- Confronting the impact of race and ethnicity in our classrooms includes knowledge of White people who have their own stories of struggle, even if they often overlook the advantages of their skin color.

- Race as a biological construct does not exist, but the consequences of it being a political tool do. Race isn't real, but racism is.
- When discussing oppression, we must avoid the tendency to rank "who suffers most."
- Personal racial histories, or *identity narratives,* offer the opportunity to examine how race is embedded in personal lives and what it means in the broader context.
- Individuals can self-identify differently from others' identification labels for them.
- To work to end racism, we can allow individuals to self-identify, recognize ideologies of racial superiority, and commit to ending systems of racial privilege.

Circle the statements with which you agree. With which statements do you disagree? In what ways do you disagree? Reflect below.

_____

_____

_____

This chapter examined our definitions of race, with an attempt to clarify the question What is race? Why is it important to be clear in our understanding of race and its impact on our students?

In the next chapter, you will read about a day in the life of three educators: Dorothy, Bonnie, and Keith, an elementary school counselor who is the White male father of two Asian children. Once again, these examples are not representative of entire groups but rather illustrate the diverse experiences each of us lives. The more we know and understand about the diversity of others' daily experiences, the more equipped we are to understand their perspectives. This, in turn, builds understanding for the diversity of students who enter our classrooms.

❖   ❖   ❖

SUGGESTED READINGS

Davis, Bonnie. *The Biracial and Multiracial Student Experience: A Journey to Racial Literacy* (Thousand Oaks, CA: Corwin, 2009).

Pollock, Mica. *Everyday Antiracism: Getting Real About Race in School* (New York: New Press, 2008).

Obama, Barack. *Dreams From My Father: A Story of Race and Inheritance* (New York: Times Books, 1995).

Root, Maria. *Racially Mixed People in America* (Thousand Oaks, CA: Sage, 1992).

Singleton, Glenn, and Curtis Linton. *Courageous Conversations About Race* (Thousand Oaks, CA: Corwin, 2006).

Winters, Loretta, and Herman DeBose. *New Faces in a Changing America: Multiracial Identity in the 21st Century* (Thousand Oaks, CA: Sage, 2003).

5

A Day in the Life . . .

This chapter discusses White privilege. If you are reading this as a White person, do you possess privilege denied to educators and students who are not classified as White? This chapter examines this issue by describing Bonnie's, Dorothy's, and Keith's days and compares the experiences of a White woman, a Woman of Color, and a White man's sons of Asian culture. Prompts follow to give you an opportunity to reflect on your experiences.

If I, as a White educator, am not aware of what my Whiteness brings to my classroom full of culturally diverse learners, I lack needed information. If I fail to understand the power dynamics of White female culture, I lack needed information. What does it mean to be White in the United States? When I bring up the concept of White privilege during workshops, most White people are surprised with this concept. As a White person, I live with a freedom from negative experiences based on skin color, unless I find myself in a minority position. I don't have to think about my skin color unless I choose to put myself into a minority position or am forced into one. Yet People of Color don't have that option. Glenn Singleton states that each morning he looks out the window as a Black man, while I, as a White person, look out the window as just a person (Singleton, 2003).

WHITE PRIVILEGE

In "White Privilege and Male Privilege," Peggy McIntosh (1998), women studies professor at Wellesley College, defines White privilege as an "invisible package of unearned assets which I can count on cashing in each day, but about which I was 'meant' to remain oblivious" (p. 291). McIntosh cites fifty-four privileges that Whites use daily as "an invisible weightless knapsack of special provisions" (cited in Delgado & Stefancic, 1997, p. 292). In this White-dominated society, I wear my Whiteness as an invisible protection each moment of my life.

Think about your day. Do you daily receive privilege due to your skin color? Or do you daily confront the challenges outlined by Dorothy, a Woman of Color? Dorothy, as an African American, does *not* represent *all* persons of cultures who are not classified as White. However, her experiences hold a mirror up to White privilege. Let's examine the invisible privilege package that I, a White woman, wear in a typical day in my life.

A DAY IN BONNIE'S LIFE

I awake. I read the paper and watch the television news, where I see White men portrayed as the authority, full of confidence, with a vocal style that matches mine. My speaking patterns are reinforced—they refer to their mothers as "Mother" or "Mom," not "Mama" or "Mum." Their vocabulary, even their accent, matches my middle-class, White, midwestern self. I drive to work.

Mostly I pass Whites driving cars as I drive from a suburb up a superhighway that stretches through the middle of St. Louis to the University of Missouri. I see passengers of my own color in the majority of the cars.

At the building where I work, there are approximately twenty-five people. Four are African American women, three of whom are support personnel. None is Asian. None is a Black male. None is Hispanic. I am reinforced throughout my day that my culture is in charge, correct, and successful.

After work I drive to a fitness center where I work out. Usually one or two African Americans work out too, but the interesting thing is that all of the cleaning people and the service people in the coffee shop are Black. The only Black person in the spa section is the receptionist, a light-skinned woman with long, flowing hair. My subconscious mind sees that Blacks clean the toilets at the fitness center, Whites and one Asian do the massages and the nails.

I drive home to a neighborhood block that is 80 percent White. There are a few neighbors who are People of Color. One biracial woman is married to a White male; others are Asian and Hispanic. One is a Black male.

I watch the 5:00 p.m. news. The anchors are White; the important news usually revolves around Whites, usually males. Stories of violence mostly depict Blacks.

My friends are mostly middle-class White women like me. My significant other is a White male. I don't have to worry about being followed by security at the local shopping mall; I don't have to worry about being stopped by the police because of my skin color. I don't have to worry about being invisible in my community. I am acknowledged when I walk up to a counter, whether it is a fast-food place, the cleaners, the video counter, or the local school.

I am White. I have unearned power and freedoms because of my skin color.

❖   ❖   ❖

If you are White, in what ways is your day similar to mine? If you are an Educator of Color, in what ways does your day differ?

_____

_____

_____

_____

_____

Think about your Students of Color. In what ways might their days differ from yours?

_____

_____

_____

Dorothy's day differs from mine in many ways. As you read her account, think about the differences.

A DAY IN DOROTHY'S LIFE

In this "White" or "dominant culture" society, I feel like I wear my Blackness as an offense to some people. I do not have just one typical day, because for me the days are a continuum of responses to race and racism. I do not have any protection against what I may encounter—I simply have the wisdom of a warrior.

When I wake up, I view the news and hear what seem to be endless accounts of Black-on-Black crime. I see sad mug shots of Black folk, mostly males, and always there is commentary from a family member or bystander. I often cringe, hoping not to hear the name of a former student or one of their family members. I have recognized several over the past twenty years.

Despite how my day starts, I manage to make it to the neighborhood coffee shop, pick up coffee, and drive to work pretty happy about what I might encounter. Although I live in an integrated community, I rarely see any People of Color at the coffee shop, not any Asians, Latinos/as, or African Americans—just White baristas and customers. Currently, my workplace has 14 People of Color: 12 African Americans and 2 Chinese. The remaining 100 employees are White. I am one of two African American administrators in the school district. Previously, I worked as the first and only African American administrator for over ten years, and I was the single African American employee in my building for the duration of my tenure with the district. I presume now I work with an ethnically diverse staff.

I am challenged on personal and professional levels by issues of race and racism. The challenges do not happen every day, but I have been challenged so many times that there is no doubt to me, and to whoever is privy to the "onslaught," that it is indeed about my being African American and it is undeniably about race or racism. My decisions may be questioned or second-guessed by the staff members whom I supervise. My ideas sometimes seem to be dismissed or not perceived as legitimate explanations surrounding matters of African American student achievement by my fellow administrators. White parents comfortably insult Black students or me by using racial slurs and blatant stereotypes when discussing matters of conflict between their child and a Student of Color or Teacher of Color. In turn, Black parents comfortably challenge my racial identity or Blackness when they disagree with a decision I have made about their son or daughter who is involved in a conflict with a White student or White teacher.

Another insult that I occasionally encounter is that I'm called "nigger" by a White parent who is angry. I have encountered racial slurs numerous times: "nigger," "Black bitch," "jiggaboo," "you're just one of them." Equally disturbing, I'm also called some of these racial slurs by African American parents. I have been told by an angry White parent after I suspended her son for fighting that the KKK is watching how I treat White kids. I have been told by a White teacher that I would not be allowed to observe her or I would be sued. I have been told by a White teacher that I better not come into her room or she would report me to the board of education. I have been jokingly told by a White teacher that when the desegregation program started, she had to take down a sign in her room that said "No administrators and no niggers allowed." While sitting with a group of Black employees at my current job, I have been teased by a White teacher that we are planning a conspiracy together, yet White teachers sit together all the time without fear of being alluded to as conspirators. As an administrator, I try to be professional, friendly, and respectful to everyone. I walk a balance beam because of my supervisory role, and I have to hold back on a personal level because by being a Black supervisor, you are always in fear of being removed from your job. This is a common belief among African American administrators or supervisors in most fields. You have an uneasy feeling that others, especially White people, believe you were hired because you are Black, and you fear you will be fired (laid off, phased out, downsized) because you are Black. I also find in talking with other African Americans that we get the "Black" problems whether they are one of our students or not. And no one wants to admit to that particular phenomenon.

The best encounters during my days are with the students. At times it is hard for students to put their feelings of discrimination into words—they just know they were treated unfairly. A teacher may scold them for disruptive behaviors that White students are not reprimanded for by the same White teacher. They may fail classes even though they have completed all the assignments and received passing grades on all those assignments but fail or achieve low test scores. They cannot find any other explanation for the F, nor can their parents. African American students and other Students of Color complain of racism when a White teacher or a White student makes a racially insensitive remark or joke and no one intervenes. I understand that I'm working with middle school students, and their sense of fairness is skewed at times, but I also understand when issues of race or racism are present. In turn, I understand that many White teachers are uncomfortable, untrained, and unable to talk about matters of race and racism.

My Day as an African American

My day as an African American runs on a continuum to the degree that I encounter race and racism—not because it's one day, one morning, or one afternoon; it is ongoing, day after day and year after year. Even in my personal life, I have endured humiliating racial incidents, such as not getting served in a restaurant or standing at a counter for several minutes when a White male or female butts in front of me and gets immediate service. I can be smartly dressed or casually dressed and I'm somehow still invisible. It makes me wonder who really is ignoring me, the person who butts in front of me or the service person who is supposed to be waiting on me. Perhaps the worst is when, for some unknown reason, a White person will drive by and holler out a racial slur at me—I can only pray that a physical attack does not take place next. Sometimes I keep track of this by marking the date it occurred, but eventually I get discouraged, and I think to myself: Don't keep a record of racism, because it only increases the tension and stress that goes with being a Black person.

As my day ends and as I mature in my career, I appreciate the drive home and entering the safe place where I can momentarily think of things that are not about race and racism.

❖　❖　❖

A DAY IN THE LIFE OF KEITH AND HIS SONS

Keith's day differs from Dorothy's in that Keith is a white male who has adopted Asian children. He writes about his journey to understand the impact of race in his children's lives and, ultimately, in his own life.

Think first about your own children or a favorite niece or nephew. How would you feel if they were ridiculed, bullied, or made fun of because of their phenotypes—their skin color and facial features? Write your feelings below.

_____

_____

_____

On October 23, 2008, my family officially grew from five members to seven with the adoption of our two sons from Vietnam. When we stepped off the plane at 10:30 that night, I felt that I was prepared to be the parent of the two brothers that looked completely different from me. I had experienced the comments from others of "why are you adopting from there," or "why not Russia, they will look like you?" I had handled these with as much calm grace and patience as I could muster and felt the better for it. Less than a year after getting Sam and Eli home, we decided that Sam would attend first grade at the school where I am the guidance counselor. Over time I watched Sam handle questions from his peers about why he looked different from me with more grace than I could have imagined.

At the beginning of Sam's third-grade year (Fall 2011), we made the decision to move him back to our "neighborhood" school. Eli, Sam's younger brother, was beginning first grade and my wife, Gina, and I felt that would be the best time to make a move. Our rationale being, that now Sam was through the adoption transition he could start developing friendships with kids in our neighborhood. The school is in walking distance in a very White, traditionally Catholic and Lutheran community, where families' parents and grandparents still live.

Eli had always been a kid that didn't particularly like going to school and he let us know this. Because he has speech and language deficits, I always assumed that school was just hard for him. Getting him dressed and fed before school was no picnic, but I accounted that to him not being a morning person. The school year progressed for all of our family. It was a year of transition for all of us. Sam and Eli were together at school for the first time, our oldest daughter would be getting married in less than a year, and our second-oldest daughter left home to start her first year of college. This left our youngest daughter, Sam, and Eli at home with Gina and me. Every day I would ask the boys, "How was school?" and I would get the obligatory "Fine." I, again, told myself, "standard answer; everything must be good."

Then in January of 2012, while at my school's parent-teacher conferences, things dramatically changed. My daughter, Susie called to say that Sam was very upset and crying after school. The dam had broken and his emotions came pouring out. He sobbed that nobody at school liked him, he was bullied, often-times overtly with kids calling him names and some with racial innuendos. He was left out or ridiculed for following the directions of the class (singing in music class). I rushed home to talk to Sam and get to the bottom of the problem. Sam reiterated everything he had told Susie and asked, "Can I please just go back to school with you?" I immediately shifted into counselor fix-it mode. I made phone calls, talked to my building principal, and filled out forms. In less than a week, I had received permission to immediately transition both boys back to school with me.

In the fall of 2010, the staff at my school began a book study on Courageous Conversations by Glenn Singleton and Curtis Linton. When we started, I remember saying that my goal was to have a better understanding of race and how I could use that understanding to better myself, in particular for my sons. It was in the moment, sitting in my office after I had received word that the boys would be able to move schools, that I realized just how deficient I truly am in the understanding of race. I am a White man, the parent of two Vietnamese children, and I had completely disregarded the effect race had on the treatment my sons had received. A flood of emotions washed over me at that moment. Initially I had felt relief that "I had fixed the problem" for my sons. However, this slowly gave way to a sense of humility and then anger, frustration, and sadness. My relief that the boys would be close, so I could protect them, gave way to the realization that I never could. Their skin color would always identify them as "different" from the White majority. And living in that overwhelmingly White community, they would always be seen this way. As their father, I could no longer bury my head in the sand and deny that race played a part in their experiences. I could no longer stand behind my White privilege that permitted me to deny that not only was race a part of my sons' treatment at school, but that it always would be. It is a part of our community. As a White male I could say, it's because Sam is new, they just don't know him yet, or Eli has language processing delays so he must just not have understood or he got confused. But this implies that not only is this something I, or they, can fix, but somehow they played a part in. If they did something differently, the outcome would have been different. And if I could have this mentality with two people who I love unconditionally and definitely have "mother lion" protectiveness over, how was I viewing and treating the students, parents, and fellow staff members at my school. To continue in this perspective minimizes and discredits their perspectives, beliefs, feelings, and experiences.

Although, as a White male, I can never completely understand the perspective of those of color, including my sons, I must do a better job of listening. I must allow them to share their perspectives, feelings, and emotions, and work diligently to empathize with them. This is how I will better myself and become a better father, counselor, and person.

❖   ❖   ❖

UNDERSTANDING PRIVILEGE

What differences did you find in Bonnie's day, Dorothy's day, and Keith's day?

_____

_____

_____

_____

_____

In what ways might you examine your own freedoms and privilege in every decision that is made in your educational setting?

_____

_____

_____

_____

_____

In what ways might you examine the privileges of White children in every decision that is made in your educational setting?

_____

_____

_____

_____

_____

_____

Do you understand how and when *privilege* is used as a verb in your school setting? For example, when a tuxedo business asked six senior boys to model tuxedos for the students during their lunch periods and not one young Man of Color was asked to participate, I went to the administration and complained. The administrators understood, and that is all it took to remedy the situation. Sometimes we just need a set of eyes to call to the attention of well-meaning folks what they do not see. Unfortunately, if a Person of Color had complained, they might have been judged as being overly sensitive.

Learning about race and its impact on those in our society is a lifetime journey. I strongly reject the notion that some White people "get it" and others don't when it comes to understanding issues of race and racism. I think we continue learning until we die, and I think labeling a person as someone who "gets it" does a disservice to that person, just as labeling someone as a person who "doesn't get it" is not fair to them. We are all at different places in a lifetime journey, and labeling people only divides us. We can be better colleagues for each other when we listen to others and give them a break instead of judging them.

I truly don't think I will ever understand the power of race and racism, and I've been studying it since 1986. But I have never lived it—I've never been a Person of Color in this country. I don't get it; I just work to learn more.

After reading this chapter, what are your thoughts?

_____

_____

_____

_____

_____

This chapter has examined three educators' days in an attempt to add another dimension, that of White privilege and personal freedoms, to our understanding of what educators bring to the classroom. In the next chapter, we read about the richness and diversity culturally diverse learners bring to the classroom.

❖ ❖ ❖

SUGGESTED READINGS

Delgado, Richard, and Jean Stafancic. *Critical White Studies: Looking Behind the Mirror* (Philadelphia: Temple University Press, 1997).

Landsman, Julie. *A White Teacher Talks About Race* (Lanham, MD: Scarecrow Press, 2001).

McIntyre, Alice. *Making Meaning of Whiteness: Exploring Racial Identity With White Teachers* (New York: State University of New York Press, 1997).

Singleton, Glenn E., and Curtis Linton. *Courageous Conversations About Race* (Thousand Oaks, CA: Corwin, 2006).

PART II

Listening to and Learning From Others

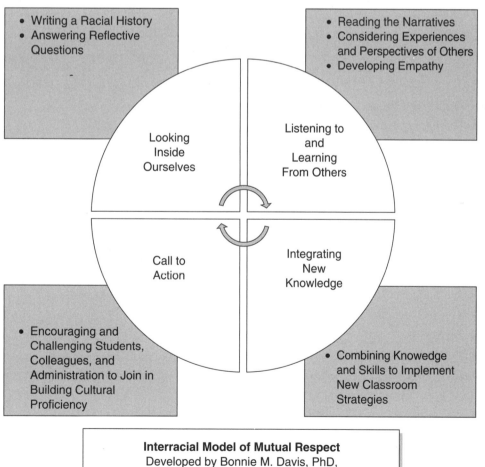

- Writing a Racial History
- Answering Reflective Questions

- Reading the Narratives
- Considering Experiences and Perspectives of Others
- Developing Empathy

Looking Inside Ourselves

Listening to and Learning From Others

Call to Action

Integrating New Knowledge

- Encouraging and Challenging Students, Colleagues, and Administration to Join in Building Cultural Proficiency

- Combining Knowedge and Skills to Implement New Classroom Strategies

Interracial Model of Mutual Respect
Developed by Bonnie M. Davis, PhD,
and Kim Anderson, MSW, LCSW, ATR-BC. © 2010

6

What Do We Need to Know About Culturally Diverse Learners?

Learners enter our classrooms with a diversity of experiences. They may differ from you and each other in ethnicity, race, socioeconomic status, gender, learning modalities, cognitive development, and social development (Tileston, 2004; Tileston and Darling, 2008). This chapter examines some of these differences and offers strategies to use in your classrooms. In no way can we cover comprehensively every cultural group of students; however, we offer cultural homogeneities, or norms, for student cultures you may most likely encounter in your classrooms. Included also are strategies suggested in this chapter and throughout this book that are cited in the research as effective for these students.

Our job as teachers is to reach and teach all learners. What might seem an overwhelming task can be better accomplished through understanding ourselves, as well as understanding the cultural practices of the learners in front of us. Experts on culture, such as Sonia Nieto, share with us that culturally diverse students often practice different communication styles from the dominant culture (Nieto, 2000). As a result, we know we may need to use additional teaching strategies from those we have been using with the dominant culture (Marzano, 2004). In addition, our culturally diverse students may require a relationship with us, their teacher, before they decide to learn from us (Haycock, 2001), and they may be confronting personal issues about which we are unfamiliar.

Some of the differences culturally diverse learners experience are common to *all* learners, and some are specific to culturally diverse groups and individuals. Peer pressure is an example of one experience that occurs in all groups, including students of the dominant culture, but it also varies from group to group. Communication style is another.

The more you know about the cultures of your diverse learners, the better equipped you will be to teach them. One of the best ways to bridge cultural gaps to your diverse learners is to find out as much as you can about them.

HOW-TO STRATEGIES

Level: Elementary/Middle/High
Subject: Cross-curricular

- Begin with students' names. Ask students to share what their names mean. Teach the class to pronounce each name correctly, and then display them in the classroom in several ways. Introduce the topic by reading "My Name" in Sandra Cisneros's book *The House on Mango Street* (1984, pp. 10–11). This book is available in English and Spanish. Ask for a student volunteer who speaks and reads Spanish to read "Mi Nombre" in the Spanish version (1994, pp. 10–11). This honors the cultural capital of the Latino/a student and allows the student to shine in front of the class. Ask students from other cultures if they have poetry or literature in their home language they can share with the class.
- Ask students to bring in a family item and share it with the class.
- Ask students to draw self-portraits and then display them in the classroom. This allows you, the teacher, to observe how the student "sees" his or her skin color.
- Ask a general question at the beginning of class, such as "What is your favorite food?" "What do you enjoy doing in the evenings after you finish your homework?" Have students each share round-robin.
- Invite parents into the school to interact with staff and students.
- Begin your year by having students write personal narratives about themselves. If you are teaching content other than English in middle or high school, you can tie this assignment to your subject matter and classroom goals. Ask students to write their "math history" or their "science history" (or whatever subject you teach) and tell you how math or science has been a part of their lives. Have them end their history with goals for your class.
- Call each student's family before the year begins and introduce yourself, expressing how excited you are to have their child in your class. Although this is time intensive, the payoff is immense.

CULTURALLY DIVERSE LEARNERS' COMMUNICATION STYLES

Think about your classroom communication style. How would you describe it?

_____

_____

_____

Keep your communication style in mind as you read the following. How does your style compare with the communication styles of your culturally diverse learners?

Communication styles differ among groups and within groups. Understanding student communication styles is critical. When we don't understand our students' cultural communication style, we may be contributing to their school failure. Some of the things that make up communication style are our nonverbal gestures and our preferences for interacting with others. Even the traditional seating arrangement of our classrooms is not necessarily the best for all students. Some cultural groups tend to learn better in groups and nontraditional seating patterns (Nieto, 1996).

Simple instructional strategies we use may conflict with some students' cultural communication styles. For example, teachers who use short wait times (the time a teacher gives a student to think of an answer after the teacher asks the question) can put some students at a disadvantage, because their cultures may teach them to think deliberately and respond more slowly after considering all options.

When you ask a question of the group, count aloud: 1001, 1002, 1003, 1004, 1005, 1006, 1007. Tell the students you are doing this to give all students an equitable amount of time for their brains to process the answer. Do not use a student's name in your question. When the seven seconds are up, have the students either write their answers on white boards or paper, share with a partner, or raise their hands for you to call on them. Use a stack of index cards or Popsicle sticks with student names on them as you call on students. Draw one and call on the student whose name appears on the card or stick. You will get a response from someone if you allow enough wait time. Consider role playing the first couple of times, answering questions, sharing with students the types of questions that require more thought and those simply needing a simple answer. (Of course, if you are asking many lower-level questions, you may want to examine why you are spending your time at that level.)

Cooperative learning is one strategy worth exploring with Latino/a, African American, and some American Indian students, as well as other cultural groups who tend to focus on cooperation rather than competition (Gonzalez, Huerta-Macias, & Tinajero, 1998).

USE OF RHYTHM

Another instructional tool, the use of rhythm, may vary between the culturally diverse learners' culture and that of the dominant teacher's culture. For example, African American adults and children may use a "contest" style of speech, based on the call-and-response patterns found in Black music (Nieto, 1996) and preaching. Teachers who are aware of this can incorporate it successfully into their lessons. You might ask students to create a study guide using a call-and-response mode and create opportunities for students who respond to this cultural mode to use their oral skills as often as possible in your classroom. They can do this through oral presentations and performances. Capitalizing on student cultural capital is one of the best ways to improve achievement and reduce behavior issues. Warning: remember, every student who self-identifies as African American may not know and respond to call-and-response patterns, so don't assume you can implement a one-size-fits-all strategy for any cultural group. First and foremost, each learner is an individual brain, and we must get to know the individual child.

HOW-TO STRATEGIES

- Use upbeat music to welcome learners into the classroom. Stop the music at the bell. Play calming music at a low volume while students complete a "Do Now" activity.
- Use music as a mental break at intervals throughout the class. Give students thirty seconds to stretch to music.
- Teach call and response. Use it to go over factual material before a quiz.
- Use music for "thinking" breaks or quiet meditation. Teach students how to breathe deeply and relax; then play soothing music and give learners a two-minute mental break to recharge their brains.

MISREADING CULTURAL COMMUNICATION

Misreading cultural communication cues can result in behavior issues and incorrect feedback about learning. One EL teacher misread the nonverbal cues of her Puerto Rican students. When they exhibited a "wrinkling of the nose," she did not know they were signifying they did not understand the material. In some Alaska Native cultures, a wrinkled nose often means no and a raised eyebrow often means yes (Nieto, 1996). Not knowing the nonverbal cues of your students might cause you to assume they are acting in a disrespectful manner or not paying attention, rather than simply following your instructions. In addition, when we do not understand the communication cues of our culturally diverse learners, we may be telling them (unintentionally) that we don't care enough about them to learn about them. Consider asking students about their nonverbal communication and their latest slang. They usually enjoy sharing what is important to them and playing the role of the expert in the classroom.

In addition to asking the students, another method to learn about cultural communication cues, especially those ELs with special education needs, is to assess students in their homes and communities. By involving parents as participants in these evaluations, educators can "minimize misdiagnoses and inappropriate special education placements" (Garcia, quoted in Artiles & Ortiz, 2002, p. 23). When the values of the educators and the parents differ, there may be cultural discomfort. If educators learn and understand the cultural, linguistic, and socioeconomic influences of their students and families, they probably will experience improved communication.

HOW-TO STRATEGIES

- Ask learners to write about and share one nonverbal communication their culture deems important. This can be a folding of the hands in prayer, a friendly gesture, a family gesture to get attention, and so on.
- Ask learners how they signal to others when they want to communicate the following: praise, displeasure, a greeting, boredom, and so on. Make it a fun activity where you and students laugh but learn about each other.
- Have students choose a culture not present in the classroom and share its communication styles.

CLASSROOM BEHAVIORS

Culturally diverse learners bring with them expectations for classroom communication with their teacher and classmates, especially how they are expected to answer questions in class. Does the student expect to give an individual answer in front of peers, use eye contact, guess an answer, or volunteer in class? These behavior expectations vary among diverse learners. Students also vary as to the amount of teacher guidance they expect (Cloud, quoted in Artiles & Ortiz, 2002). It is up to us to clearly explain when and why we offer individual guidance and help. Once again, unless we make our expectations clear and model them for students, we may be placing our culturally diverse learners in an uncomfortable classroom situation. For the past three years, I have worked in six urban high schools with a large number of culturally diverse students. As we sit in these classrooms and observe the patterns of classroom behavior, we see cultural differences among groups of students. Some tend to be more boisterous; some tend to be quiet; some tend to interact just with peers. Strong teachers in this environment have mediated this situation by using a group structure comprised of different cultural groups. By doing this, we don't see all the Asian students sitting in one area of the room, the African American students in another, and so on. Of course, you must teach students how to work with each other and include a reason for them to do so. Creating a positive classroom culture where students know and like each other supports this process, and rotating students in the groups throughout the school year eliminates most student objections. The more the students complain, the more feedback you have for the necessity of working on your class culture.

Time on task is another way that culturally diverse students often differ from the dominant culture. How do you expect students to begin class work? Do you expect them to listen to your directions and begin immediately? Or do you take into account group styles? For example, your African American students, because they "have expressed an orientation toward collective responsibility and interdependence" (Hale-Benson, 1986, p. 16), may first interact with others, rather than immediately beginning academic work. If you are a teacher whose style is "Get to work NOW!" you may find yourself frustrated and assume that the students are attempting to avoid doing the work. Being aware of this style difference allows you to make the necessary accommodations that best fit all the students in your classroom. Begin class before class begins to alleviate this issue. Stand at the door, no matter how busy you are, and greet each student with a smile and a welcoming sentence. Allow students to talk until the bell rings; then add your own nonverbal signal. This can be music playing that you stop at the bell or a gong you use to call students to attention. At this time, students begin a "Do Now" activity you have on the board—one they know must be done in total silence. After a five-minute Do Now, begin a general activity to focus the class. One way to do this and incorporate talk and socialization at the beginning of class is to give a question to the class and allow the students to answer one at a time with the option of saying "pass." This builds community and gets each student's voice in the air, thus eliminating some of that need to socialize among friends during class time. You will find more examples of how to begin class in the next section of the book.

CULTURALLY DIVERSE STUDENTS' LEARNING STYLES

In a culturally diverse classroom, you will find every learning style, yet students from particular ethnic cultures may respond more willingly to the kind of instruction that is reinforced by their culture. For example, African American learners tend to be multimodal (Hale-Benson, 1986). Their involvement with classroom instruction is cognitive, emotional, and physical, all at the same time. If you are a teacher who learns cognitively, not needing the emotional and physical modes, you may have trouble understanding why some African American students may need emotional and physical connections to the material in order to learn it. You can capitalize on students' multimodal needs by assigning tasks to students. Active students might get the classroom ready for learning. You might have a student who is a "greeter" and makes sure everyone is relaxed and ready to learn. You might have another who is a "materials" student who gives out textbooks and other materials, and so on.

In her book *The Power of One: How You Can Help or Harm African American Students,* Gail L. Thompson (2010) states that African American learners say that boredom is one of the main reasons they disengage from class. They want to learn, but they too often feel bored and not challenged. She suggests interviewing your students and asking them what they would do if they were in charge, and then allowing them to create lessons and actually teach them to the class (pp. 90–91). Capitalize on student strengths and embed their strengths into your procedures as well as your content instruction.

In contrast to many African American learners, a newly arrived Vietnamese immigrant learner might feel uncomfortable in an informal classroom where students are expected to ask questions and work together, so you must find ways to respect that student and offer support for becoming part of the classroom culture. Once again, the secret is to know the cultural homogeneities of cultural groups while keeping in mind that each student is a unique brain and may not adhere to his or her cultural norms, as well as learning about each student as an individual.

It is obvious the quiet, traditional classroom in which many of us learned, quietly seated in rows of desks and raising our hands to answer the questions the teacher posed, does not match the cultural communication styles of many of our culturally diverse learners. What can we do?

In *Educating Latino Students*, Gonzalez and colleagues (1998) suggest developing a "learning context that is multiculturally sensitive, where differences are acknowledged and appreciated and where opportunities do exist for learning in nonmainstream patterns" (p. 31). The following are aids for learning about the communication styles of our culturally diverse learners.

HOW-TO STRATEGIES

- Observe your students' cultural group in your classroom and throughout the school.
- Adapt your instruction and the curriculum to meet the needs of culturally diverse learners. Instruct them using a range of different modalities and include examples from all the cultural groups in your classroom when you tell stories, use metaphors, and teach the histories of your discipline. To teach math without sharing the contributions of Africans to mathematics misses an opportunity to build awareness of cultural capital.
- Hold meetings at school for parents so you can interact with and learn from them.
- Read books on body language and cultural communications.
- Hold professional workshops about diverse learners in your school.
- Ask your students about their communication styles.
- Ask students' parents to share their professions with a class.
- Attend conferences that include workshops on your student populations.
- Talk with educators from culturally diverse cultural groups.
- Do home visits and observe your students with their families.

In addition to these suggested strategies, Tharp (quoted in Artiles & Ortiz, 2002) developed several guiding principles for effective pedagogy when working with ELs with learning disabilities in general education, suggesting we work collaboratively with students; incorporate language and literacy across the curriculum; connect classroom learning to students' lives; and teach higher level thinking through conversation (p. 140).

PEER PRESSURE

Even when we understand the communication patterns of our culturally diverse learners, we still face the effects of peer pressure, both positive and negative, in our classrooms. There are many peer pressure challenges in cultural groups that I, as a White female teacher, may be unaware of, and yet I often succumb to peer pressures of my cultural group—White females. For example, as a White female, I am acculturated and encouraged to

- Not "rock the boat"; to avoid conflict and maintain the status quo of my dominant culture
- Not say what I really feel in public but rather talk behind others' backs or in the parking lot
- Not be too loud, bold, challenging, or confrontive
- Be *nice* at all times

Of course, these messages have changed from the 1950s to the present day. However, when I work with school staffs, I hear complaints about "bossy" White women, as well as the quiet "niceness" of school staffs during faculty meetings who then eviscerate their administrators afterwards rather than speaking up about their needs. Unfortunately, also, I still see White girls who do not assert themselves academically for fear of being labeled by peers.

IMPACT OF PEERS ON STUDENT ACHIEVEMENT

In "The Canary in the Mine: The Achievement Gap Between Black and White Students," Mano Singham (1998) writes of the impact of peers upon student achievement. Examining college students, Singham, using the research of John Ogbu and others, found that Chinese students often studied together and shared tips and strategies for success. African American students, on the other hand, partied together but seldom studied together. Black students often had no idea where they stood with respect to others in the class, and they usually were surprised when they received poor grades, thinking they had done exactly what was expected of them. In addition, Kunjufu (1988) examines negative peer influence on Black students who exhibit "acting White" behaviors. They may be ridiculed by their peers for buying into the dominant culture if they choose to listen in class, do their homework, and make good grades. At the runaway shelter where I taught, young men had to hide their schoolbooks from the neighborhood gang members or risk getting beaten up or killed for "acting White." To these students, acting White meant they adopted the cultural norms of White culture if they achieved in school. One young man related that he had to sneak down the back alley to attend the GED program for fear of his life.

Often, students lack the understanding of what it takes to make As and Bs in a rigorous academic setting. Students need to hear that in order to make As and Bs in high school, they must study hours a night, limit phone calls, texting, time on the computer, and television, and set up a schedule for homework. Some students are unaware of what honor roll students actually do in order to make the honor roll. Once again, there are "hidden rules" of academic achievement that must be taught to our children if we want them to achieve academically.

SKIN COLOR PREJUDICE

Another negative peer culture pressure is skin color prejudice. Why is skin color so important? It is important because it has assigned value and affords privilege to those with White skin (Singleton & Linton, 2006). When my son was growing up, I used to try to figure out just what it was that made others see him as Black. Was it the shape of his nose, his hair, or his skin color? I'm not sure of the answer in his case, but the fact that his skin color is darker than what most define as White makes a difference in the ways others categorize him. And since skin color is an external, physical attribute, we can use it to classify others into groups of the powerful and the not so powerful (Davis, 2009, p. 87).

What color is your skin? Does it give you power?

_____

Has skin color ever robbed you of power?

_____

Have you been stopped by the police because of your skin color? Refused service in a restaurant? Passed over for a position? I know none of these things has happened to me.

Others have stories that differ. In St. Louis, where I live, African Americans share stories of the "paper bag" test. They share they were placed into certain public schools based on their skin color. If someone was "light" enough—lighter than a paper bag—they went to different high schools than those with skin darker than a paper bag. They also relate that the test was used for certain sororities and other social groups, and even mate selection. This is a phenomenon many Whites know nothing about, yet my adult African American female friends share stories of how they were included in social groups they can name because their skin was light enough (my friend Dorothy, whose story is told in Chapters 3 and 5), or they were excluded from social groups they can name because their skin was too dark (my friend Roberta, who shares information about her student group in Chapter 17). Unfortunately, families (and society) may still give favor to lighter-skinned children and are more critical of darker-skinned children.

What decisions, knowingly or unknowingly, are made based on skin color? Do I tend to favor lighter-skinned Students of Color because I find them more attractive? Are blond-haired White children preferred over dark-haired children? Is inclusion in particular groups, whether they be cheerleaders or social clubs, ever based on skin color? Educators may deny this occurs, but we need to examine our own preferences and biases and ensure we do not act out on them.

Skin color tension in our schools tends to be more prevalent among females. Prejudice is more prevalent in females because the worth of a female is tied to her physical appearance (Rockquemore & Laszloffy, 2005). You only have to look at the magazine covers at the nearest store to see that light skin is valued over dark skin in our society, as evidenced by the sheer quantity of covers featuring light-skinned women. Hopefully, First Lady Michelle Obama and other Women of Color will change this as they grace the covers of popular magazines. Yet presently, it is no surprise that we have internalized the racist message that White skin is superior to dark skin, and the ideal beauty is still one who possesses White skin, blonde hair, and blue eyes. As a result, if we possess White skin or blonde hair and blue eyes, we may feel a false sense of superiority to those with darker skin. This false sense of superiority may translate into our body language and cause hostility from those with darker skin with whom we interact.

COLORBLINDNESS

Often in workshops, I hear educators, who are good people, talk about how they "don't see color" and consider themselves "colorblind." They see this as a strength, and they believe it speaks to their equitable treatment of all children. I believe they mean well. However, at the same time, Children of Color see color because of the meaning attached to skin color in this country. Because of their personal experiences and probable incidences of discrimination based on their skin color, they bring that history with them into your class. If you do not recognize they have experienced life differently from the White children in the room, then you deny the Students of Color the truths of their experiences. They look at me, a White teacher, and see I am White. They see which peers are White and which are Students of Color. A very simple strategy for a White teacher to use when working with Students of Color is to acknowledge one's Whiteness early on in the relationship. That tells the students you know who you are. Skin color carries power and meaning in our society. If you are White and you don't believe that it does, then shadow an African American teacher for a few days and notice the different experiences she encounters, even though she is an educated woman, just like you.

Skin color as a descriptor is used differently in cultures. With my White friends, we usually use the terms *light, medium,* or *dark* to describe a White friend's tan, and that is only when we are talking about tans, not part of our usual description of a White person. However, among Students of Color, there are scores of words to describe varying shades of the color of one's skin. Another interesting phenomenon is that my Latino/a and African American friends often describe another's skin color when talking about them. My son does the same thing. For example, "Sonia has skin the color of mine," my son announced when telling me about a college friend. Think about the last time you heard a White adolescent describe another White person. Did she or he add a descriptor of the shade of that person's whiteness? Listen to your Students of Color when they talk about other Students of Color. What do you hear?

HOW-TO STRATEGIES

You can fight against skin color prejudice by doing the following.

- Educate yourself about this phenomenon.
- Post pictures of people of all different skin shades in your classroom.
- Build a classroom library of books with Students of Color on the covers and inside the books.
- Post self-portraits of your students on the walls of your classroom.
- With older students, consider discussing racism in its externalized forms and internalized forms as it centers on the issue of skin color. (You may want to show the video of the doll experiment posted on the Web that deals with internalized racism.)
- Continue to reflect and question yourself on your own perceptions of skin color.

If you choose to change a negative peer culture at your educational site, you may want to find students who will work with you (see Chapter 17 for info on student support groups). The key to building the critical mass of students goes back to relationships. If you have a good relationship with your target students, you can begin to build a critical mass of students to focus on achievement goals. The research (Singham, 1998) presents the idea of a "critical mass" of students who need to buy into the idea of academic achievement and who, therefore, create a *positive peer culture* for achievement. Creating that critical mass in your classroom provides a supportive peer network for diverse learners. How do you do that? (See the box.)

Level: Elementary/Middle/High
Subject: Cross-curricular

- Call on all students equitably.
- Ensure that your lessons include role models from the cultural groups represented in your classroom.
- Use student names in your examples.
- Impress upon students the necessity of book knowledge so they can't be cheated in their lives.
- Use cooperative learning.
- Emphasize cooperation and de-emphasize competition.

(Continued)

> (Continued)
>
> - Use a "We're all in this together" classroom approach.
> - Build a classroom community that expects excellence from each student and allows a flexible time frame for achieving excellence.
> - Talk explicitly about the negative effects of peer pressure and how students can counteract them.
> - Sponsor clubs (see Chapter 17 for a model) that support academic excellence and offer a support group to students willing to fight negative peer pressure.

The negative peer culture exists because of perceptions and belief systems; a positive peer culture can exist because of perceptions and belief systems too. You and your colleagues can find the ways that work best for you. When you put your plans into action and see the results, you will begin to see the changes in the perceptions of students, as well as changes in the perceptions of the staff.

Describe the peer cultures at your educational setting.

_____

_____

_____

What strategies might you employ to create a critical mass of positive peer support in your classroom or in your school?

_____

_____

_____

THE STEREOTYPE THREAT

Have you ever been stereotyped? For example, if you are a woman, did others assume you could not change a tire, fix a leaky pipe, or run a business? If you are a male and an elementary teacher, did others assume that you would not be as adept at the job as the females in your building? Think about a time you were stereotyped by others.

_____

_____

_____

When you performed under this stereotype, how did it affect the outcome?

_____

_____

_____

Stereotypes are perceptions, and perceptions create our reality. Just as our cultural lens largely determines what we see and how we interpret it, our students' perceptions of themselves may affect their academic achievement. Claude Steele (1999) defines the *stereotype threat* as "the threat of being viewed through the lens of a negative stereotype, or the fear of doing something that would inadvertently confirm that stereotype" (p. 46). Exploring the impact of the stereotype threat on Black college students, Steele found that when students were presented with a difficult verbal standardized test as a test of ability, Black students performed "dramatically less well than White students," even though the groups were "matched in ability level" (p. 47). But when they presented the same test as a laboratory task that was used to study how certain problems generally are solved, the Black students' performance equaled that of the White students. Steele suggests that "race consciousness" brings about impaired achievement (p. 47).

Steele and Aronson (Steele, 1999) went on to test their hypothesis with a group of White males. They told the group that they were taking a math test on which Asians usually scored higher than Whites. The result? White males who heard this comment scored less well than the White males who did not hear this comment (p. 48).

The stereotype threat most affects the academically able students. On tests, Black students tried too hard, rereading the questions and rechecking their answers more than when they were not under the stereotype threat. Searching for solutions, Steele (1999) found that Black students who participated in discussion groups in an informal dormitory setting improved their grades and reduced their feelings of the stereotype threat. Steele suggests that we educators might spend more time in developing the trust in our schools with our African American students if we hope to see the academic achievement that our students are capable of demonstrating (p. 54).

You can help students diminish the stereotype threat in their lives by beginning academic support groups to support them by building a peer support network to diminish the stereotype threat. In Chapter 17, you read how these groups teach students how to "do" school in order to academically achieve. You can also discuss with your colleagues ways to build safe spaces for students to discuss these issues in the context of some classes or school forums.

THE "MODEL MINORITY" STEREOTYPE THREAT

Asian Americans suffer a different stereotype threat. They often are perceived as the "model minority" and depicted as diligent, quiet, intelligent, and academically able, and they are often seen as immigrants or foreigners, rather than minorities (Ogbu, cited in Singham, 1998). Stacey J. Lee (1996), in *Unraveling the "Model Minority" Stereotype,* finds that the stereotype silences the voices of low-achieving Asian students and denies the complexity of higher-achieving student experiences. In addition, the stereotype reinforces the "racial order by focusing on Asian American success and redirecting attention away from Whites" (p. 99). Lee argues that African American students' failure to "challenge White success is related to the silence that surrounds Whiteness in general" (p. 99). Since the model minority stereotype consists of a comparative and competitive nature, Lee found many African American students in his study who believed Asian American students were a threat. Some even believed that Asian American success was achieved at the expense of African Americans and that they were one more group who had climbed over African Americans to pursue the American dream. Moreover, Lee found a direct link between a "racial group's perceptions of their own position and their attitudes toward Asians/Asian Americans and Asian American success" (p. 121).

Interestingly, most groups of Asian-identified students blamed themselves for the challenges they faced and did not expect the dominant group to accommodate them. Of all the Asian-identified groups Lee studied, only Asian Americans challenged the dominant group. Ultimately, the model minority stereotype has been used to "support the status quo and the ideologies of meritocracy and individualism" (Lee, 1996, p. 8).

While acknowledging that being seen as a model minority carries with it a kind of privilege, Lee states that the dangers exceed the privilege. This stereotype is dangerous because of the way it has been used by the dominant group to silence Asian Americans and their experiences and against other minority groups to silence claims of inequality (p. 125). The research clearly points to the dangers of the stereotype threat experienced by some of our diverse learners.

HOW-TO STRATEGIES

The following are strategies to support students in combating the stereotype threat.

Level: Elementary/Middle/High
Subject: Cross-curricular

- Learn about each student as an individual.
- Do not lump students into one ethnic group. Korean students differ from Chinese students. Puerto Rican students differ from Mexican students. Immigrant children face different issues than second-generation Asian Americans or Mexican Americans. The list continues; do not assume all children of any one ethnic group are alike.
- Talk about stereotypes with your class.
- Have students share their cultural experiences.
- Do a daily check of your perceptions. Have student behaviors reinforced stereotypes? Negated them? We tend to see that which reinforces our stereotype, so we must be vigilant in doing daily perception checks.

- Include a variety of role models from the cultural groups of your students, continuing to emphasize that not all Blacks are alike, not all Whites are alike, not all Asians are alike, and so on.
- Share the literature of each of your students' cultures. Poetry, short stories, folk tales, and novels are wonderful ways to learn about cultures and to support positive dialogues.
- Encourage student forums to discuss the issues of stereotypes.
- Invite the Anti-Defamation League's World of Difference presenters to work with students and staff.
- Encourage students to write their stories and share them in a writers' showcase (see Chapter 13).
- Use cooperative learning to allow students to get to know each other as individuals.
- Create classroom projects that allow students to get to know each other as individuals.
- Start an academic achievement group for students (see Chapter 17).

This research has profound implications for our school settings. It offers a wonderful vehicle for staff discussion and problem solving. Consider using the Claude Steele (1999) article in a whole-staff discussion (you could also use this in a senior high contemporary issues class, or English or history class). Encourage staff to reflect on times when they felt a stereotype threat. Encourage them to share this with their high school students and ask their input. Discussions about this article with groups of students might encourage an honest look at this dilemma and provide opportunities for problem solving.

Understanding the communications styles of our diverse learners and the effects of peer pressure and the stereotype threat upon them allows us to become more culturally proficient.

HOW-TO STRATEGIES

The following are strategies to reach diverse learners.

Level: Elementary/Middle/High
Subject: Cross-curricular

- Place value on students' home languages and cultures.
- Acquire a basic command of the language of your diverse learners. This may seem extreme, but learning to speak only a few words to your diverse learners in their native language usually will bring smiles to their faces.
- Integrate the culture, experiences, and language of diverse learners into your classroom lessons.
- Set high expectations for all diverse learners.

(Continued)

(Continued)

- Communicate these expectations to your diverse learners.
- Include professional development focusing on the cultures of your diverse learners.
- Check your instruction to see if you are following the suggestions found in *Educating Latino Students* (Gonzalez et al., 1998): Are you using a learning context that is multiculturally sensitive? Are you acknowledging and appreciating differences among your diverse learners? And are you creating opportunities for learning in ways that differ from the mainstream?

Which suggestions in this chapter might you consider for your classroom?

_____

_____

_____

Set a goal to implement one to three suggestions or strategies you found in this chapter.

_____

_____

_____

In this chapter, you read about many influences on our students' lives, from peer pressure to the stereotype threat. In the next chapter, we closely examine one family's experience with education. Brenda Alvarez, a Latina, shares her family's powerful struggle with acculturating to the educational system in the United States.

❖   ❖   ❖

SUGGESTED WEB SITES

Principles for Culturally Responsive Teaching (www.alliance.brown.edu/tdl/tl-strate gies/crt-principles.shtml)

Supporting Linguistically and Culturally Diverse Learners in English Education (www .ncte.org/cee/positions/diverselearnersinee)

Why Is Culturally Relevant Pedagogy Important? (www.tolerance.org/tdsi/crp_why)

7

Latino/a/ Hispanic Learners

A Personal Story

Ten years ago I knew very little about Latino/a/Hispanic learners. But today my only grandchild and my daughter-in-law, Brenda Alvarez, are Latina. In addition to a deeply personal reason for learning what I don't know I don't know about Latino/a/Hispanic culture and learners, I have worked with Latino/a/Hispanic students for the past several years in school districts across the country. In this chapter, you will learn factual information about these students. More important, you have the opportunity to read a first person account about a Mexican family's experience with the educational system in the United States.

LATINO/A OR HISPANIC

In the earlier edition of this book, I discussed the terms *Latino* and *Hispanic* and admitted I used whatever term the school district in which I was working preferred me to use. For example, in a district in Texas, I was told to use *Hispanic*. In a district in California, I used what everyone else used and that was *Latino/a.* But because how people name themselves is so important and I wanted to respect that, I felt a need to learn more. I asked Brenda, my daughter-in-law, which term she prefers, and she shared she uses both, as does the National Education Association (NEA), her employer. I consulted Kim Anderson, my colleague and co-author of *Creating Culturally Considerate Schools: Educating Without Bias* (2012), and she shared her research from her earlier book. In *Culturally Considerate*

School Counseling: Helping Without Bias (2010), Kim writes, "Words are powerful. They matter" (p. 7). Understanding the power of words, she researched the use of *Latino/a* and *Hispanic* and found that "the federal government considers race and Hispanic origin to be two separate and distinct concepts, asserting that Hispanics and Latinos may be of 'any race.' In fact, there is disagreement within Hispanic/Latino communities and between generations and gender about which term is preferred" (Hede, quoted in Anderson, 2010, p. 6). Furthermore, Kim writes that Dotson-Blake, Foster, and Gressard (2009) state that many regard the term *Hispanic* as being "inadequate for use as a total population descriptor as it neglects to address unique identities of individuals from Mexico, Central and South America, and Spanish-speaking Caribbean. Immigrants from these areas often identify more strongly with their nationality than with their language. The terms 'Latino'/'Latina' have become more widely accepted in an effort to establish an identity with Latin cultural roots rather than those founded in Spanish colonialism" (p. 6). The word *Hispanic* appears to be "more accepted by younger generations, while older Latinos view it as a more pejorative term originating from colonization" (pp. 6–7). After learning the above, I continue to use both terms throughout this book. Once again, I realize I have much to learn from others about their cultures. As a result, I need to listen and learn from our students and their families so I can learn how to best show respect and use what terms they prefer as we build relationships across cultures.

FACTS ABOUT LATINOS AND HISPANICS

In my current search to learn more about what I don't know I don't know about Latino/as/Hispanics, I began a search of government sources. Wanting to share current statistics on Latino/as/Hispanics, I checked the following government Web site: www.census.gov. From there, I searched *Hispanic* and found the U.S. Census Bureau's definition of the term. The definition of Hispanic or Latino origin used in the 2010 U.S. Census is the following: "'Hispanic or Latino' refers to a person of Cuban, Mexican, Puerto Rican, South or Central American, or other Spanish culture or origin regardless of race" (Humes, Jones, & Ramirez, 2011, p. 2). The government Web site uses both terms, *Hispanic* and *Latino/a,* to record statistics; therefore, I am using the terms as used on the Web site, which vary throughout the information provided.

Hispanics are one of the largest and fastest growing ethnic groups in the United States, and they are a diverse group that varies in national origin, immigration, and migration patterns. They have settled in diverse communities across the United States. In 2010, there were 47.8 million Hispanic/Latino/as in the United States, or 15.5 percent of the total population. Out of that 47.8 million, more than 15 million are children under the age of eighteen. By 2020, the Hispanic/Latino/a population will reach nearly 60 million (projected at 59.7 million), or 17.8 percent of the U.S. population. The Hispanic/Latino/a population comes from twenty countries in Central and South America, Spain, and the Caribbean.

Between 2000 and 2006, Hispanics accounted for one-half of the nation's growth, and the Hispanic growth rate (24.3%) was more than three times the growth rate of the total population (6.1%). The top five states by Hispanic populations are California (13,074,156 persons); Texas (8,385,139 persons); Florida (3,646,499 persons), New York (3,139,456 persons); and Illinois (1,886,933 persons). Approximately 60 percent of Hispanics are native born to the United States and 40 percent are foreign born (U.S. Census Bureau, 2006). Government Web sites offered valuable information for my understanding of statistical information about Hispanic/Latino/as. Learning the "big picture" statistics laid a foundation for examining Hispanic/Latino/a schoolchildren.

TODAY'S KINDERGARTEN LEARNERS

Today around one-third of kindergarten learners are Latino/a (Rong & Preissle, 2009). With Latino learners entering schools from origins in twenty different countries, we educators *cannot* afford to lump all Latino/a learners into one group. We must honor their diversities and learn what we can about the Latino/a learners who sit in our classrooms.

RISKS LATINO/A LEARNERS FACE

In schools, Latino/a learners are a population that faces many risks. Latino/a youth participate at a high rate in health-risk behaviors, "including attempted suicide (10%, a rate 32% to 86% higher than that of Black or White youth), unprotected sex (42%, a rate 12% to 26% higher than that of Black or White youth), lifetime cocaine use (11%, a rate 47% to 600% higher than that of Black or White youth" (Centers for Disease Control and Prevention, quoted in Kuperminc, Wilkins, Roche, & Alvarez-Jimenez, 2009, p. 213). Latino/a gangs make up 46 percent of all gangs in the United States (p. 213). These statistics show us how important it is for us to support our Latino/a learners so they can avoid these risks and experience success in our classrooms and in life.

LATINO/A LEARNERS' COMMON LEGACIES

The above statistics are frightening, yet Latino/a learners share common legacies that can support them in finding success in school. They possess a "common legacy of language and cultural values, such as personalismo, espiritualidad, and familismo. These cultural values refer to the importance of social support, trust in spiritual support systems, and the extended family, respectively. Latinos/as also share the value of interdependence, in which the family and interpersonal needs are favored over the individual" (Bernal, Sáez, & Galloza-Carrero, 2009, p. 310). When I asked Brenda what cultural norms she felt reflected her Latina culture, she told me that the "group always takes care of its members." She said that when socializing, no one is allowed to be ostracized or feel left out. She agrees that the family and interpersonal needs are favored over individual needs. In addition, there are other important cultural constructs particular to the Latino community, such as "respeto (respect), confianza (trust), fatalism (fatalism), controlarse (self-control), and aguantarse (putting up with)" (Bernal et al., 2009, p. 311). These important cultural constructs offer us entry points for creating culturally responsive instruction. Knowing that family and interpersonal needs are often favored over the individual helps us understand why some Latino/a learners don't want to stand out in class but would rather be part of their cultural group, and also why they enjoy working on group projects, unlike some majority students who may prefer to work individually on projects. Of course, we have to remember not every Latino/a shares the same learning needs, so we must still learn each of our students as an individual brain. Yet collectivistic cultures share a common goal of acculturating their children to place family well-being as their ultimate priority (Trumbull & Rothstein-Fisch, 2008, p. 51).

With all of these definitions and facts swirling around in my head, I asked Brenda if she would share her story. She was willing to share her knowledge and her family history. Understand that her family history does not represent all Latino/a families, but because of who she is and what she does, she can share firsthand some commonalities about the Latino/a experience. Brenda is a public relations person for the National Education Association and a teacher-advocate who is passionate about securing the best education for all children, including my grandchild, her daughter. By reading Brenda's story, we learn about the world of one Latino family as they emigrated from Mexico to the United States. Even though their story does not represent all families originating in Mexico or Latin America, it does serve to illuminate cultural norms and offers us a narrative to use for collaborative conversations and for learning about what we don't know we don't know.

BRENDA'S FAMILY HISTORY

When growing up in Chicago, it was common for White people to ask, "What are you, Mexican?" This type of question immediately put me on the defense, and I would become dismissive toward the person. The poor efforts to genuinely engage me tangled with the assumption that because I'm brown, speak Spanish, and live in a predominantly Mexican city were offensive. As it turns out, I am Mexican. However, a better approach would have been, "What is your cultural background?"

Words have power, and generalizations and assumptions can dangerously hinder a Latino student's potential for high achievement. However, a wonderful opportunity exists for America's educators to revive the national ideal of a quality public education for every student by having faith in human equality, political democracy, and high faith in the benefits of a rigorous education.

Data

I begin with data. Everyone loves statistics, right? Maybe not everyone, but here's something to get you thinking: The U.S. Census reports that Latinos are the second-largest ethnic minority group in the United States, making up 16 percent

(50.5 million) of the population. This figure represents a 43 percent spike, compared to just twelve years ago when the Latino population stood at 35 million. By 2050, the number of Latinos in America is expected to increase to 30 percent.

When it comes to student achievement, Latino students have seen gains in math and reading scores throughout the years. However, they still lag far behind White students. The most recent 2009 scores from the National Assessment of Education Progress (NAEP) show Latino eighth-grade students are 26 points below White students in math and 24 points behind in reading. This means, according to NAEP's definition, Latino students are two grade levels behind their White counterparts.

A growing Latino population coupled with a double-digit student achievement gap is a bad combination. Keeping America strong will require educating Latino students to compete in a global economy—a critical piece for the future of the United States, especially since the Latino population is only going to continue to grow.

Educators don't have an easy task, especially when cuts in education spending threaten quality public education and inherently flawed policies are being widely promoted without much proof of success. Moreover, Latinos come with their own distinct set of cultural norms that are often viewed as problematic instead of an additional resource to bridge Latino culture to the American experience. But, it can be done. Latinos can succeed, and they need your help.

Father Rudy

Take my father, Rudy. He made his trek to the United States in 1968. He was nineteen years old. Before leaving Mexico, he had finished high school and would be characterized as a good student. He liked history and was great at math. When Rudy arrived to Chicago, Illinois, he enrolled himself as a senior at his neighborhood public high school, thinking he could quickly thrive in an American education setting.

"I enrolled in school because I wanted to continue to learn. I was interested in learning English and the history of this country," he recalled, adding he felt his math skills were equal or better than his new American classmates so he wanted to focus on areas where he needed help.

The day Rudy enrolled in school everyone was friendly. The school staff wrote down his name; told him about his classes, coursework, and the materials he would need; and they told him the names of his teachers. Rudy was excited about his new life in the United States and the opportunities he knew an education would afford him.

His first day of school curbed that enthusiasm. "When I arrived to class my first day of school, the teacher blurted out 'this is your seat,' and that was it. No one ever paid any attention to me—no one bothered with me," Rudy said. When homework assignments were given, Rudy would submit them to his teachers, but he never received any feedback. And, like a lost memory that unexpectedly surfaced, Rudy revealed, "I don't even remember getting a report card! It was difficult. It felt like I didn't exist," Rudy said. "Teachers didn't dedicate any time to me. What I learned, I learned on my own." Communication between Rudy and his teachers was nonexistent because they perceived he didn't understand, which led to the idea that Rudy couldn't learn.

His teachers had low expectations for him. However, he expected a lot from his teachers. "I wanted them to pay attention to me. I wanted them to say, 'This is your class and this is what I want you to learn.' I desired to learn English. I wanted to learn how to read and write. I wanted to learn the details of American grammar." He concluded, "I would have wanted them to tell me what they could have taught me. But it wasn't like that." Rudy was enrolled in school for one year before he dropped out.

At first thought, one might wonder why Rudy didn't just speak up or assert himself more. That would be a legitimate expectation in the United States, except it's an important distinction because culture often dictates different responses and actions. My father is quiet in nature. His quiet manners were misconstrued as lack of effort. His respect for teachers and authority muffled his irritation to question those who ignored him. His illegal status created angst in bringing any kind of attention to himself. And yes, language did impede Rudy's abilities to communicate, but it was neither a barrier nor a shortfall in his ability and desire to learn.

Sister Erika

Then there is the case of my sister, Erika. She came to the United States in 1976. Erika was five years old and she immediately entered kindergarten. "I was traumatized. Before leaving Mexico, my school elected me 'Queen of the Class,' which was a big deal. I was bought a big dress and felt honored," Erika fondly remembered. "I went from a warm loving school to a place where they ignored me."

Erika shared that her first-grade teacher ignored her to the point where she peed in her pants. "It may have been part of the language barrier, but I wanted to be respectful and I waited to be called on to go to the bathroom. I raised my hand and waved it in the air. She never called on me. So, I peed in my pants—that haunted me for a long time." The next three years were unpleasant for Erika. Her teachers would mispronounce her name and say in a frustrated tone, "Eureka? What kind of name is that?" Also, Erika's school didn't have a bilingual education program. She learned English by listening. "Learning English felt more like a survival mechanism," Erika said. "Kids would tease me and the teachers wouldn't acknowledge me. I had to learn to survive," adding that on occasion she would repeat words she had heard from other students, which would lead to teachers washing her mouth with soap or hitting her with a paddle because she unknowingly used profanity.

Despite Erika's best efforts to fit in with other kids, they would bully and tease her because of her accent and long hair. It even went as far as fighting. She recalled, "Connie had told her older sister I had hit her. It wasn't true. But during recess Connie convinced me to go behind the field house. Her sister was there. While one held me down, the other hit me." Erika never shared any of this with her mother because she didn't want to risk getting in trouble. The thinking behind this was that any phone call from school was bad news and equated punishment.

Erika's outlook on school changed in the third grade. Her teacher was Latino, and he was the first to push Erika to excel. "Mr. Hernandez encouraged me to do well. He even wanted to promote me to the next grade level," Erika said. "And, Mr. Hernandez would make a big deal about my knowing Spanish and being able to translate better than he." From this point forward, Erika stopped trying to fit in with her classmates and began to focus on her academics. When asked how teachers had helped her stay focused on her academics, Erika explained, "I had teachers who believed in teaching kids regardless of background. They were aware of diversity and knew more about it.

There was a cultural shift within the school and I felt my teachers were encouraging me instead of dismissing me." Erika concluded, "I got smart and wanted to prove everyone wrong. So, I became more involved in academics. I won science fairs and poetry contests. I was a first chair violinist and had solo performances. I felt I had more help and opportunities than in years past. Before, I was just this crazy little girl, getting her mouth washed out with soap." My sister went on to being the first person in our family to go to college. She earned a master's degree in finance and is currently charged with providing financial information to hospital leaders for good patient outcomes.

My Experience

My experience in school was different from both my father and sister. I was born in the United States. I started school in the early 1980s. By this time, more minorities were becoming teachers and most of my classmates looked like me. Language wasn't an issue for me, either. My first language is Spanish, but I had learned English from my siblings before I entered kindergarten, making me fully bilingual. My teachers were hit or miss. I remember my third-grade teacher, Mrs. Thoreau. She reprimanded us for saying "salud" to a boy who sneezed. She thought we were saying "salute," and found it offensive. When we explained to her that it meant health, she said, "Oh! I didn't know that," and allowed us to continue to say it whenever someone sneezed. She also allowed one of my classmates to help me with my math work in Spanish. I didn't understand the material, but when it was explained to me in Spanish, it became clear. Cultural celebrations were normal in elementary school. We would research flags, foods, language, and dances that represented our culture. We would write essays about everything we learned. It made me proud to talk about my ethnicity.

In high school, I had an excellent history teacher, Mr. Tuten. He pushed us to do better and allowed us to question his teachings. For example, one of his lessons dealt with Christopher Columbus, the great explorer and discoverer of America. I respectfully disagreed. I called Columbus a degenerate who was lost, stumbled onto America, and conquered and killed thousands of people. I explained to him that Columbus was not looked on favorably in the Latino community. Mr. Tuten called me cynical. Nonetheless, he allowed me to make my point. Giving me the space to share my ideas based on my culture was important to me and critical to my continuous learning. I felt empowered. Although I didn't win awards in science fairs, like my sister, I did win awards for writing, which led me to a master's in communications.

And, you would think I've forgotten about my mother, Yolanda, who hails from Mexico City. Her educational experience started in 1955 when she entered primary school. Primary school ends in the sixth grade, and it was considered a great accomplishment to graduate since, according to Yolanda, many students leave primary school in the third grade. "Receiving your elementary school diploma was a big deal. But [in the United States], when you tell someone you finished the sixth grade, they think you're uneducated and a dropout—the system is just different." Yolanda shied away from her children's education, saying she didn't feel comfortable or confident to speak with any of the educators because of the language barriers. "I knew it was difficult for my daughter because she didn't know English, but neither did I," Yolanda said. "I didn't have a relationship with her teachers since they knew I didn't speak English and so they never invited me to anything."

My Brother

Yolanda's son was different. She admits to spoiling him and allowing him to stay home from school whenever he complained of not feeling well, which was often. She would follow up with his teachers and ask about his behavior, but found it difficult to remain engaged. The advice from his teachers would be to speak with him or take away television privileges. "I would talk to my son about making an effort. He would never say 'no' or push back. He would say 'yes,' but still do whatever he wanted," Yolanda said, adding that it was difficult because she couldn't sit down with him to figure out his homework. Yolanda concluded: "His teachers were friendly, but I don't remember having meaningful conversations with them. After some time, they stopped telling me about his bad behavior, and I would find out only during report card pick up day, which was four times a year."

My brother eventually dropped out his third year of high school. Growing up, he had less responsibility around the house. My parents focused their attention on his ability to play baseball, and not on his academics. I would venture to say that because my brother was coddled at home, he carried that expectation into the classroom setting. When his teachers resisted, he acted out. When asked the question, "Why did you spoil your son?" Yolanda responded: "I don't know. I spoil him to this day because he's the one who needs the most nurturing." This is where culture can betray you. I'm sure you've heard the adage of "Mothers love their sons, but raise their daughters." This was the case with my brother, and it's important for educators to recognize how culture dictates different responses among boys and girls.

When it came to my education, my mother's involvement was nonexistent, especially as I became older. I would ask my mother to help me with my homework, but I remember her saying she didn't understand and how I needed to pay attention in school to master the material. She would say, "Do the best you can," and walk away after kissing me on the head. It was my sister who helped me with my homework. She would pick up my report cards and talk with my teachers. And, whenever a teacher needed to speak with a parent, they called my sister.

During my freshman and sophomore years of high school, I wasn't performing at high levels. Through my own volition, I forged my mother's signature and transferred myself out of school and into a smaller high school that I thought was better for me. It wasn't that my mother didn't care. She knew education was important. She just couldn't get over her own fears, and there wasn't a welcoming bridge to connect her to the school. Both our parents worked a second shift, so when it came time for homework during the week we only had an older sibling to help us.

I share our stories to illustrate real-life examples of what Latino students often encounter: neglect, low expectations, cultural insensitivity, misconceptions, humiliation, mistreatment, and bullying. Parents often feel excluded and unable to form a meaningful partnership with teachers and schools.

Given what we know today about culturally responsive pedagogy, as well as social justice and cultural competency trainings, teachers today have more resources and support to help them become culturally responsive teachers. The National Education

Association's CARE (Cultural, Abilities, Resilience, and Effort) Guide (see www.nea. org) on strategies for closing the achievement gaps states, "effective teachers of low-income and/or culturally and linguistically diverse students find ways to connect school to their students' lives every day" by

- *Contextualizing or connecting to students' everyday experiences; and*
- *Integrating classroom learning with out-of-school experiences and knowledge of life inside the community.*

The guide also showcases ways to improve a teacher's practice. Some of the suggestions include the following:

- *Design lessons that require students to identify and describe another point of view, different factors, consequences, objectives, or priorities.*
- *Integrate literature and resources from Latino students' cultures into lesson plans.*
- *Provide instruction that helps to increase the consciousness and valuing of differences and diversity through the study of historical, current, community, family, personal events, and literature.*
- *Engage Latino students and form a meaningful relationship while pushing them to excel academically.*

In the case of Erika, the day Mr. Hernandez encouraged her academically was the day she became self-aware of her intellect and passion for learning. For Rudy, it could have meant recognizing his existence and providing him with rigorous curricula in math. For my brother, it could have meant forging a strong relationship with Yolanda to get her son motivated and engaged, as well as encouraging Yolanda to move beyond her own fears of culture and work together toward a common goal. The latter would apply to me, as well.

What Educators Can Do

Educators need to look at Latino culture as an asset, not a deficit. For example, language in the past was seen as a hindrance. Today, there are ways to move students from their first language to dual-language programs that emphasize cross-cultural learning.

I would also encourage educators to help create a support system with other Latino students to help lead learning as a group (family). Additionally, encourage Latinos to step out of their own comfort zones to take on leadership roles. It's important to recognize that teachers can't do this work alone. It takes a collaborative effort between parents, teachers, and the community to educate students. Latino parents care deeply about their children, but language often impedes their confidence to become involved, as was the case with Yolanda.

Latino parents often bring their negative experiences into the academic lives of their own children. In the past, phone calls from school usually meant bad news; however, more and more teachers are reversing this attitude by calling parents to share good news. They're also visiting the homes of their students, which provides an opportunity to forge meaningful relationships with parents and learn about a student's hidden strengths and how to work best with families.

Gone should be the days of Latino students feeling neglected, humiliated, or stereotyped because of culture, language, gender, sexuality, or economic standing. Opportunities exist to have open and honest one-on-one conversations with parents to improve student learning. From my personal and family experiences, teachers have made improvements. And though our stories span the course of four decades, many Latino students today face similar problems to that of my father, sister, and brother, especially, when Latino families move to areas that had never before experienced influxes of Latinos.

According to a 2003 study by the League of United Latin American Citizens, Latinos are no longer moving to the large urban cities of years past—like Los Angeles, Houston, Chicago, or Miami. They are also moving to the suburban outskirts of large cities, including states not traditionally familiar with receiving clusters of Latinos, such as the Mid-South and the Great Plains. It's imperative to the future of the United States to break the cycle and close student achievement gaps within all minority groups, especially Latinos since they (we) will be the majority in the next three decades.

—Brenda Alvarez, National Education Association Public Relations

Reflect on what you read. What did you learn from Brenda's story?

_____

_____

_____

❖   ❖   ❖

Brenda's family history helped me understand many things about Latino/a culture. I know I must not lower my expectations for Latino/a learners, and I must take an extra step toward forging a relationship with both the students and their families. As I build this relationship, I need to understand there may be a cultural disconnect between a Latino/a family's values and my own Western European White cultural values. Elise Trumbull, coauthor of *Managing Diverse Classrooms: How to Build on Students' Cultural Strengths,* conducted research that helped me understand this disconnect. She found that a "cross-cultural conflict in values between Latino immigrant families and the schools was the heart of the problem of formal education for the families' children" (Trumbull & Rothstein-Fisch, 2008, p. xi). Working with Trumbull, teachers learned that

> [P]arents had different goals for child development than they did. For example, they learned that helping one another was a very high priority for Latino immigrant parents, whereas, in the same situation, teachers favored independent achievement. Before that, most had assumed that there were right and wrong ways to do things at school

and with the school. They had never realized that what was right from the school's perspective could be very wrong from the parent's perspective. (pp. xi–xii)

Trumbull and Rothstein-Fisch operate using the premise that "cultural values and beliefs are at the core of all classroom organization and management decisions" and "students' responses to teachers' strategies and of students' own attempts to engage in and influence interactions in the classroom" (p. xiii). They understand that Latin American cultures tend to be far more collectivistic than the dominant, European American culture (Hofstede, quoted in Trumbull & Rothstein-Fisch, 2008, p. xix), and that African American culture is also more collectivistic; however, it has strong individualistic elements, too (Boykin & Bailey, quoted in Trumbull & Rothstein-Fisch, 2008, p. xix). In their book, Trumbull and Rothstein-Fisch offer a framework for working with students who belong to a collectivistic culture. The group orientation is at the core of this cultural lens. Group work embraces the family core value of placing the "group before the individual." Successful teachers use group work with support structures to ensure each individual member of the group is successful.

Having a strong family unit and ethnic identification supports Latino/a learners as they come to school ready to learn. What can we do to support them? A young Latino and Latina share their suggestions.

Mani Barajas-Alexander, a Mexican and African American college graduate, tells teachers to

approach teaching in a variety of different ways. Everybody in class learns differently, so teachers should diversify their techniques. Do the same thing for all races and classes. Be open minded to students' personal backgrounds and what they have experienced. Have the teacher create an environment where everybody feels comfortable because students are not going to share the truth about anything if they're not comfortable in class. The result is that other people miss out on hearing all the perspectives in the classroom, and everybody's learning suffers. (Davis, 2009, p. 135)

Christina Amalia Andrade, Latina and White teacher, shares that she uses Spanish to reach her Latino/a learners. While working in a kindergarten class with approximately 20 percent Latino/a learners, she asks the "kids to come to attention in Spanish. When teachers take the time to cross that language, it really means something." She adds:

I suggest teachers do the following: make an attempt to learn the language, approach the students, and ask how they as a teacher can support them. Connect lessons to the kids in class. I had a chip on my shoulder about that because my ethnic literature experience was not varied. Why not use a piece of literature by Sandra Cisneros? Holden Caulfield is a character that speaks strongly to teen males; even today that's their favorite book, but I haven't had a single experience like that.

Understand the audience you're teaching to and tailor your content to that. Bring in short pieces; give everyone something different to talk about. Even if there are no Hispanic kids in class, using Hispanic literature is a valuable perspective to give to other students. High school students are the center of their own world; bringing in multicultural fiction and asking questions such as, "What would that be like?" and "Is that like something I'm doing now?" are important for students. It allows them to step outside of themselves, and I think that's very valuable and gives [them] a perspective. (Davis, 2009, p. 133)

HOW-TO STRATEGIES

- Learn about the countries of origin of your Latino/a learners.
- Do not assume all Latino learners share the same learning style.
- Ask Latino/a learners to share their cultural heritage.
- Remember that your Latino/a learners may be more communally oriented than individualistically oriented.
- Find out how your students want to be identified.
- Learn to speak some Spanish.
- Be explicit when you give directions. Do not rely on subtle signals that Latino/a learners may not understand.
- Post pictures of Latino/a role models in your classroom and around the school.
- Ask the students to share information in Spanish, such as poetry, the days of the week, numbers, and so on.
- Post Spanish words in your classroom along with the language of your other learners.
- Learn about the holidays and holy days of your Latino/a learners.
- Learn about how race is viewed differently for many Latino/as from other countries than for Whites in the United States; educate yourself on racial identity and ethnicity.
- Establish learning partners in class.
- Use collaborative learning in "family groups."
- Hold class meetings to emphasize the goals of the groups.
- Give students weekly responsibilities to contribute to the group.
- Do class projects; perform authentic assessments of projects.
- Use a class cheer that all students have contributed to in order to begin class.
- Have students write "class books" and share with their families.
- Establish a class code of conduct, emphasizing group goals, not individual goals.
- Include class activities that do not showcase the individual but rather spotlight the group.
- Make a positive call home each night to a different family—one a night.
- Consider implementing home visits.
- Post cultural artifacts and language throughout the classrooms and school.

- Stand out in front of the school in the morning and welcome families.
- Speak individually to each student each day, sharing something positive.

Choose one to three strategies you will implement and write them below.

_____

_____

_____

Rosalinda Velazquez, a sixth- and seven-grade teacher at Volta Elementary School in Chicago, shared the following with me, and it nicely sums up this chapter.

> One thing I have learned from working with Latino/a . . . Asian . . . etc., . . . learners is not to lump them all together. I had [worked with] a teacher from Cuba and three students from Mexico. OIL AND WATER! They were all annoyed with me when I thought, "Well, they are all Latino/a!" NOPE! So when suggesting posting Spanish words or other things, recognize all Latino/a cultures are different and the language is sometimes different. (e-mail message to the author, May 1, 2012)

Rosalinda drives the point home: Learn about each student as a unique individual and treat him or her accordingly. And above all, don't assume all Hispanic students are the same.

In this chapter, we learned about Latino/a/Hispanic students through the lens of an individual who lives the culture. The next chapter looks at new immigrant learners and suggests strategies for learning more of what we don't know we don't know, as well as how to best support these students.

❖   ❖   ❖

SUGGESTED WEB SITES

The Crisis in the Education of Latino Students (www.nea.org/home/17404.htm)

Educating Hispanic Students: Obstacles and Avenues to Improved Academic Achievement (www.cal.org/crede/pdfs/epr8.pdf)

Overview of Race and Hispanic Origin: 2010 (www.census.gov/prod/cen2010/briefs/c2010br-02.pdf)

Teaching Tolerance: A Project of the Southern Poverty Law Center (www.tolerance.org)

8

New Immigrant Learners of the Twenty-First Century

This book is not intended to be a compendium of information about culturally diverse students. Instead, it offers limited background about culturally diverse students while focusing on how-to strategies for you to use in your classroom. However, learning the histories and cultural information about the groups of students in our classrooms is necessary, and a good place to begin learning about immigrant students of the twenty-first century is with the book *Educating Immigrant Students in the 21st Century: What Educators Need to Know* (Rong & Preissle, 2009). Easily accessible, this book compares the demographic, social, economic, language, and academic characteristics of immigrant learners, aged five to eighteen, from twenty-eight nationalities with significant numbers of immigrant children. It also includes a chapter on children from the Middle East and addresses the difficulties faced by Middle Eastern immigrants due to recent events.

Xue Lan Rong and Judith Preissle state in the book that an "estimated 17 million immigrants entered the United States between 1990 and 2005, and the number of immigrants and their children reached more than 70 million, accounting for more than 20 percent of the U.S. population" (p. ix). A third of these people are from Mexico, and these immigrants came mostly from rural areas and earn minimal wages in the United States.

We can't describe here each of the 28 immigrant nationalities. However, we can focus on the authors' recommendations and how we can apply them in the classroom. What can we do in the classroom to support the academic achievement of our immigrant learners? Understanding the motivation of new immigrant families is a start, and Rong and Preissle point out that immigrant children may do better educationally than nonimmigrant children for several reasons:

- Many recent immigrants were professionals and were well-educated in their home countries, and their children reap the benefit of having educated parents;
- Immigrants on the whole have "higher educational and occupational aspirations than indigenous groups and are reportedly more determined than nonimmigrants of comparable class backgrounds to overcome difficulties and achieve upward social mobility";
- Immigrant children are more likely than nonimmigrant children to come from intact families with close connections to their ethnic communities; and
- Voluntary immigrants consider education to provide a better life for their children. (Rong & Preissle, 2009, pp. 160–161)

Understanding these factors helps provide a positive attitude when meeting and working with new immigrant learners in your classroom. These beautiful children come, for the most part, wanting to learn. Knowing this, what do Rong and Preissle recommend?

RECOMMENDATIONS FOR EDUCATORS WORKING WITH IMMIGRANT CHILDREN FROM ASIA

- Understand the stereotype of the "model minority" and the negative ramifications it can have for Asian learners.
- Realize that immigrant children from Asia are heterogeneous.
- Be aware that immigrant children from Asia are more likely than other students to be physically and verbally harassed by peers. (Kiang & Kaplan, 1994; Rosenbloom & Way, 2004)
- Understand that racial prejudice plays out in a different form. (Rong & Preissle, 2009, pp. 160–161)

Knowing the above, educators can support immigrant learners from Asia in building self-esteem since Asian learners report the lower levels of self-esteem and the highest grade point averages (Barringer, Takeuchi, & Xenos, 1990). Schools can set up structures to identify Asian children who are experiencing psychological problems. In addition, structures must be in place to identify and work with disadvantaged Asian children.

Recommended for every immigrant group is the necessity of developing and implementing culturally responsive curriculum and instruction. Throughout this book are suggestions and strategies for doing that.

Finally, we need to recruit and retain Asian-American teachers. Asian students account for 4.5 percent of precollegiate students, but Asian teachers make up less than 2 percent of the teaching profession (Rong & Preissle, 2009, pp. 165–166).

HOW-TO STRATEGIES

- Solicit university students with Asian heritage to be mentors in your school.
- Solicit parent volunteers with Asian heritage to work in the schools.
- Ask authors with Asian heritage to present to the student body.
- Do a book study on a book by an Asian author.
- Offer language study in Asian languages.
- Don't assume all Asians belong to one ethnic group. (When I worked with a panel of Asian teachers in Los Angeles Unified School District, this was their number one pet peeve—each panelist said, "Don't assume I'm . . .")
- Have students complete self-portraits and bio-poems.
- Ask students to share personal narratives.
- Post pictures of Asian role models.
- Rotate groups in your classroom so Asian students are placed with students of other ethnicities.
- Incorporate Asian literature into your curriculum.
- Share news from Asian countries.
- Give Asian students roles that counter stereotypes.
- Learn about each student as an individual.
- Understand that Asian learners face bicultural challenges in ways both similar and different from Latino/a and African American learners.
- Look for instances of harassment toward Asian students. (Read Keith's story about his sons in Chapter 5.)

BLACK IMMIGRANT CHILDREN FROM AFRICA AND THE CARIBBEAN

Only one of eight Black Americans was an immigrant child or child of an immigrant in 2005. That is changing, however, and Black immigrant learners face different challenges from American Black learners and others. The foreign-born Black population constitutes 8 percent of the entire Black population, and 4 percent are second generation (Rong & Preissle, 2009, p. 169). More Black persons have migrated to the United States from Africa between 1990 and 2003 than in the two preceding centuries combined. For the first time in history, more Black people are arriving in the United States from Africa than during the slave trade (Roberts, quoted in Rong & Preissle, p. 169). Many of these are refugees, and since 2000, around 20,000 African refugees have come annually (Arthur, 2000).

While the White majority population often considers these populations as simply "Black," Black immigrants come from a number and variety of African and Caribbean countries and may have "quadric-disadvantaged status"— being Black, foreign, poor, and refugees (Rong & Preissle, 2009, p. 172). However, not all Black immigrant children live in poverty. In fact, Black immigrant children (26 percent) are less likely to live in poverty than U.S.-born Black children (31 percent) (pp. 179–182). Black immigrant children coming from

Africa and those coming from the Caribbean are different in the following ways: most current Black immigrants from Africa don't have a family history of enslavement as the Black immigrants from the Caribbean do. And most Caribbean Black immigrants come to the United States for economic reasons, while most from Africa come to escape wars, genocides, and ethnic cleansing (p. 173). Black immigrant children are more likely to speak English than other immigrant children, and they have lower dropout rates than all U.S. immigrant children (p. 193). They are less likely to live in poverty and more likely to live in affluence, with two parents, and with parents who are college graduates (p. 194).

RECOMMENDATIONS FOR EDUCATORS WORKING WITH BLACK IMMIGRANT CHILDREN

- Adapt curriculum and instruction to a culturally responsive model.
- Create a caring and culturally supportive school environment.
- Work with families and communities.
- Enhance preservice and inservice teacher training so teachers may recognize cultural differences in acceptable school behavior, cultural norms and expectations, and so on.
- Have training on how to work with immigrants with pronounced and unfamiliar English accents.
- Have training on why there may be animosity between African Americans and Black immigrants.

HOW-TO STRATEGIES

- Include stories and literature from African and Caribbean countries in the curriculum.
- Invite families into the classroom.
- Post pictures of Black role models from African and Caribbean countries.
- Where appropriate, show films by African and Caribbean filmmakers.
- Learn the history of the country of your Black immigrant children.
- Share positive news about the countries of your Black immigrant children.
- Do not assume Black immigrant children will gravitate toward Black American children for special friends.
- Rotate students in groups so each student has a chance to work with others.
- Do not assume Black immigrant children live in poverty.
- Do not assume Black immigrant children understand Black English or African American cultural norms.
- Interview Black immigrant learners about school structures in their country of origin. They may have experienced a very different learning environment.

- Explicitly teach the cultural norms you expect from the learners in your classroom.
- Warmly greet Black immigrant learners into your classroom.

IMMIGRANT CHILDREN FROM THE MIDDLE EAST

Even the definition of what constitutes the Middle East is debated, and immigrant children who come from the Middle East arrive from a variety of countries, such as Egypt, the Palestinian territories, Israel, Jordan, Lebanon, Syria, Turkey, Saudi Arabia, Yemen, Oman, the United Arab Emirates, Bahrain, Qatar, Kuwait, Iraq, and Iran. Along with indigenous religions, the Middle East is home to five major world religions: Judaism, Christianity, Islam, Baha'ism, and Zoroastrianism. Arabic has become the dominant language (Rong & Preissle, 2009, p. 263). Two additional dimensions that affect the identity experiences of Middle Eastern immigrants to the United States are class and gender. The population of Middle Eastern children immigrants, aged five to eighteen, was 400,000 in 2000, with Iranian children comprising the largest group (p. 267).

Middle Eastern immigrant families have parents who are generally better educated than average U.S. parents and with more high school and college graduates. However, immigrant parents are less well-educated than general Middle Eastern American parents. The exceptions are the Iraqi immigrant families, who were the least likely to be high school graduates, but the general Iraqi parent population had higher rates of college graduates than all U.S. parents.

Middle Eastern immigrant children are more likely to speak a language other than English at home than all U.S. children. In addition to being bilingual, Middle Eastern children are less likely to be either physically or learning disabled than U.S. children, with immigrant children more likely than the general population of Middle Eastern children. They are twice as likely as other immigrant children and the general population to be enrolled in private schools. The following are three differences between Middle Eastern immigrant children and other children that educators need to understand: (1) Middle Eastern children are more likely than others to have highly educated parents; (2) the six groups described are diverse in culture and languages, yet similar in educational attainments; and (3) the variations across Middle Eastern children are less pronounced, with the exception of Iraqi children (Rong & Preissle, 2009, pp. 287–288).

RECOMMENDATIONS AND HOW-TO STRATEGIES

- Challenge stereotypes.
- Acknowledge children's religious diversity and learn about the religions of the learners in your classroom.
- Consider gender influences and differences.
- Recognize influences of individualism and collectivism.
- Hold workshops for staff on Middle Eastern history.

- Be aware of learners who come with traumatic war experiences.
- Self-assess for your biases.

The cultures described in this chapter emphasize the need for us to build relationships with our students from other cultures and to provide opportunities for them to learn about each other and share with others while working together in a classroom community that respects all cultures and works to better understand them. In the next chapter, we examine the reasons behind the learning gaps that exist in many of our schools.

❖ ❖ ❖

SUGGESTED READINGS

Gay, Geneva. "Designing Relevant Curriculum for Diverse Learners." *Education and Urban Society* (August 1988): 327–340.

Gonzalez, Maria Luisa, Ana Huerta-Macias, and Josefina Villamil Tinajero. *Educating Latino Students: A Guide to Successful Practice* (Lancaster, PA: Technomic, 1998).

Lee, Stacy. *Unraveling the "Model Minority" Stereotype: Listening to Asian American Youth* (New York: Teachers College Press, 1996).

Rong, Xue Lan, and Judith Preissle. *Educating Immigrant Students in the 21st Century: What Educators Need to Know* (Thousand Oaks, CA: Corwin, 2009).

Tileston, Donna Walker. *What Every Teacher Should Know About Diverse Learners* (Thousand Oaks, CA: Corwin, 2004).

SUGGESTED WEB SITES

Advocates for Children of New York (www.advocatesforchildren.org/pubs/imrights guide.html)

Educational Intervention With New Immigrant Students From Ethiopia at the Caravan Parks "Hatzrot Yassaf" and "Givat HaMatos" (www.icelp.org/files/research/LPAD NewImmigrantStudents.pdf)

The New Immigrant Students Need More Than ESL (www.eric.ed.gov/ERICWebPortal/ recordDetail?accno=EJ740555)

9

What the Research Says About Learning Gaps

During the last century, you probably had not heard of the "achievement gap." Yet today, talk about the achievement gap, in many ways now a cliché, abounds in faculty meetings, educational journals, and political speeches. Standards, high-stakes testing, and disaggregated data have dropped the challenge to close the achievement gap at our school doors. Successes and failures have given way to the need for consistency in standards, and we now have the Common Core State Standards (CCSS), a new hope for today's schools.

In this chapter we examine causes for low student achievement and learning gaps, both those outside of our control and those over which we exert control. Included in the chapter are strategies to mediate learning gaps in your classroom and school. To close all learning gaps is much more elusive. Clearly, this is a complex and complicated issue that reaches far beyond the classroom door, for these gaps arose and continue as a result of societal issues (Linton, 2011; Noguera & Akom, 2000; Singleton & Linton, 2006; B. Williams, 1996).

What is a learning gap? The term refers to the gap in academic achievement between and among student groups. Presently, the achievement gap shows large percentages of low-income African American, Latino/a, and Native American students at the low end of the achievement ladder, and large percentages of middle- and high-income White and Asian students at the top of the achievement ladder (Johnson & La Salle, 2010).

Even though the gap narrowed among diverse groups in the 1970s and 1980s, this changed in the 1990s (Haycock, 2001; National Center for Education Statistics, 2000; Viadero, 2000), when the gap widened again.

The gaps persist regardless of economic status. By second and third grades, African American, Latino/a, and Native American students are scoring lower than White or Asian students. African American, Latino/a, and Native American students score less well on standardized tests. Gaps persist in additional levels of achievement, such as grades and class rank. Gaps persist in SAT and AP scores. African American, Latino/a, and Native American students earn lower grades in college despite similar admission test scores and earn fewer degrees (Johnson, 2002; Johnson & La Salle, 2010). In addition, African American students are more likely to be placed in special education classes and, once placed, are less likely to be mainstreamed or returned to regular classes (Johnson, 2002).

CULTURAL EXPECTATIONS

Perhaps one explanation for the learning gap is as simple as the cultural expectations for academic excellence we find in our schools, for we often wear blinders that keep us from seeing the truth. Consider the following scenario.

While teaching a workshop on the gap, I suggested that the school staffs in the upper-middle-class suburban district where the workshop took place have the ability to prepare all of their students for college, notwithstanding those with severe mental disabilities. An elementary school counselor vehemently disagreed, saying, "Not all of our kids have the ability to go to college."

I then asked the counselor the following question: "You have two children—do you expect them to go to college?"

The counselor answered, "Well, yes," in an exasperated tone.

"Then why shouldn't all your parents have the same expectations for their children?" I replied.

The next morning the counselor announced to the group that she had something to say. She told the group that she had never thought of the college question in quite the way it had been asked. She now understood that her blanket assumption that some kids don't have the ability to go to college was dangerous and potentially limiting to the students in her care, young elementary school children, ages six to eleven, who were in their early years of academic development. The research shows that the initial labels attached to first-grade students placed in high and low groups follows them throughout their elementary and middle school careers (Johnson, 2002).

To assign an assumption to any child at any level can be dangerous. Tomlinson's (2003) work in differentiated instruction tells us that children learn in different ways and at different rates of speed. Some children need more time than others to process a learning task. Our job is to find ways to support the academic achievement of all children.

In *Data Strategies to Uncover and Eliminate Hidden Inequities: The Wallpaper Effect* (2010), Ruth S. Johnson and Robin Avelar La Salle explore how to expand data use in schools and districts to "delve into more complex issues related to equity and outcomes" (p. 1) building on Johnson's (2002) earlier book, *Using Data to Close the Achievement Gap.* In these books, you find case studies investigating equity and inequities for special education students, students who are underrepresented in gifted and talented programs, and ELs. You can find additional resources and materials at www.corwin.com/wallpapereffect. Ruth Johnson's (2002) earlier research suggests that it is possible for all students to learn at grade level, and it is also possible to reverse low outcomes for children that others have given up on. The counselor in the scenario above changed her belief system, moving from a belief that some groups of children were less capable than others to a belief that what she expects for her children might be what other parents expect for their children, and that children may be capable of their parents' expectations. These questions spark powerful discussion among staff members and challenge our expectations and perceptions of what children can achieve.

My perceptions of what students were capable of achieving evolved over the years. Several experiences forced me to rethink my assumptions. The following three examples happened in my classrooms.

1. Senior high African American students with C averages were placed in the college-level composition course (in a pilot program), and they succeeded as well as White students who entered with B or A averages. Because of a previous minimum grade requirement for the college credit class, the African American students had not been given the chance to perform in an honors-level class.

2. Men in a maximum-security prison, most with only a GED certificate, not a high school diploma, were placed in a college-level writing class. On the whole, they performed as well as or better than the college students I taught on the university campus.

3. Students who did not perform well in a seventh-grade English class matriculated into honors English during their sophomore or junior years in high school. Because I taught these students both in middle school and as freshmen in high school, I witnessed their cognitive growth as they evolved into honor students. They matured cognitively at a slower rate than other students placed in freshman honors English. However, had they been judged by their seventh-grade English performance and retained in the average track, their potential to do the honors work would have been overlooked.

These three examples illustrate that learners develop cognitively at different rates and are capable of doing higher level work.

Think about a time when someone in your life did not have high expectations for you. How did you feel? What did you do?

_____

_____

_____

Think about a time when your students outperformed your expectations for them. How did that affect future expectations for your students?

_____

_____

_____

Recently, an educator shared that, although she came from a family where no one had previously attended college, she was placed in a high school where nearly everyone attended college. Because her peers assumed that they and she would be attending college, she assumed that she would be attending college. She now holds a college degree and is a teacher. But, she added, had she been in a school where the "school culture" did not support attending college, she might have accepted her family's past and made no attempt to attain a college degree.

- The school culture determines, in part, the academic achievement of its students.
- Our perceptions (our cultural lens) determine, in part, the academic achievement of our students.

If we want to raise the academic achievement of all students in our schools, we must address the school culture and the personal lens through which we view our students. We have to ask ourselves the hard question: Do we expect to find a learning gap? If so, why? Researchers suggest myriad reasons. The following five offer us opportunities for mediation and change. They are poverty, academic course work, test bias, teacher expectations, and teacher quality.

POVERTY

How does poverty contribute to the learning gap?

Approximately one in five children lives in poverty in the United States (U.S. Census Bureau, 2010). Poverty contributes to lower test scores, psychological stresses, and lack of language acquisition. In addition, poverty and ethnicity are linked. The U.S. Census Bureau shows that more than 36.1 million people, or 11.7 percent, in the United States live below the poverty line. About twelve out of every 100 people live in poverty; however, for Hispanics and African Americans, it is higher. Approximately 24.2 percent of African Americans and 24 percent of Hispanics live at or below the poverty line; for White people, it is 9.8 percent (U.S. Census Bureau, 2010). If children are born African American or Hispanic, they have more than twice the chance of being born into poverty.

In _Using Data to Close the Achievement Gap,_ Ruth Johnson (2002) states that we must kill the myth that children living in poverty and some racial and ethnic groups are "incapable of anything but low outcomes" (p. 11). In fact, Marzano's research, cited in _Building Background Knowledge for Academic Achievement_

(Marzano, 2004), indicates that "innate intelligence is not as strongly related to academic achievement as once thought" and "learned intelligence is the stronger correlate of success in school" (p. 13). Therefore, if the knowledge and skill that affluent students bring with them into the classroom is learned rather than innate, then students from poverty can learn it too.

The previous anecdote about the counselor demonstrates the myth that well-meaning educators can carry with them. Only by exposing this myth can we create the academic culture all children deserve.

There is little doubt that poverty plays a role in the achievement gap, yet many educators are aware of data that prove otherwise. In fact, Johnson (2002) finds tremendous resistance to using the data that prove poor children can achieve. She calls this unwillingness to use the data a "conspiracy of silence." However, when districts use this data with caring educators, it is possible to develop a belief that "all children are capable of achieving at academic levels for enrollment in baccalaureate degree-granting institutions" (p. xvii).

Yet children raised in poverty are more likely to demonstrate the following:

- Acting-out behaviors
- Impatience and impulsivity
- Gaps in politeness and social graces
- A more limited range of behavioral responses
- Inappropriate emotional responses
- Less empathy for others' misfortunes (Jensen, 2009, p. 18)

These behaviors can add stress to the classroom community the teacher desires to build, and they necessitate a direct teaching of the emotional responses students need for learning. All but the six hardwired emotions of "joy, anger, surprise, disgust, sadness, and fear *must be taught*" (p. 19). Even though it is the primary caregiver's job to teach the child how to act and what appropriate responses are, if that has not occurred, the school must step in and do the job. Emotions such as "cooperation, patience, embarrassment, empathy, gratitude, and forgiveness" (p. 19) are examples of those we need to teach if our students lack an understanding of them. Once again, role playing is an excellent way to teach emotional responses, as is using writing and discussion in the classroom.

Low-income students represent more than 42 percent of this country's student population, with African American, Asian, Latino, and Native American students representing 47 percent of public school enrollment. By 2020, there is an expected increase of Asian students (39 percent) and Latino students (33 percent), while White students are expected to decrease by 6 percent (Johnson & La Salle, 2010, p. 20). Due to the number of immigrants entering the United States each year and the competition for jobs, along with increased childbearing, the number of children living in poverty is forecast to increase during the next few decades (Jensen, 2009). The 1999 U.S. Census data (cited in Marzano, 2004) indicated that 33 percent of African American children live in poverty. Even though this is abominably high, we have to remember that the majority of African American children *do not* live in poverty. Yet some educators assume that because a child is Black, he or she must be poor. Many educators equate poverty with lower academic achievement.

It is true that the majority of "schools of poverty" have lower standardized test scores than the majority of schools with an affluent population. Also, fewer students attending schools of poverty attend college. However, having students in your classroom who live in families with low yearly incomes does not automatically mean that these students will not or cannot achieve. There are many additional reasons to consider when examining low student achievement. If you encounter educators who blame low academic achievement solely on poverty, suggest that they check the SAT test scores, which show that poor Whites outperform the most affluent African American students (Singleton & Linton, 2006). This fact alone indicates that other reasons in addition to poverty cause the academic achievement gap between African American students and White students.

One reason, of course, is that schools of poverty usually have fewer resources than schools of affluence. Having worked in schools where 98 percent of the students are on reduced price school meals, the disparities between these schools' resources and those of the schools in affluent districts are obvious. Some of these disparities exist in the "things" available to both students and staff; some exist in the expectations of both students and staff.

Can you and your school actually address the poverty of your students' families? Some school staffs do this in creative ways. In one school the principal bought a washer and dryer and allowed parents to clean their clothes at the school if they volunteered while their clothes were being washed and dried. If you consider that a parent may be spending more than $100 monthly at a Laundromat after paying for the soap, machines, and transportation, this could be a tremendous savings for a family. It also maintains the dignity of the parent.

Other schools provide rooms where children can be fitted for shoes and clothes. Still other schools provide free computer instruction for parents, parent rooms with resources, and so on. So there are ways that schools can mediate poverty while maintaining the dignity of all involved.

Think about the times when you needed money, perhaps when you were in college. What kinds of stress did that give you? Were you more irritable? Did you make more mistakes than usual?

_____

_____

_____

What things can you do to provide support with dignity for your students living in poverty?

_____

_____

_____

One thing we educators can do—and it is free but not easy—is to examine our assumptions about students living in poverty. When I did that, I was shocked and ashamed of what I found. I grew up in a church where we often collected money for the "poor," and I learned to pity "poor" people. These teachings seeped into my classroom instruction. For many years, my unexamined assumptions were a trap that possibly led to inequitable instruction and lowered expectations for students living in poverty.

We must consciously fight against stereotyping students as poor students, feeling sorry for them and lowering expectations for them. All students need to be held to high standards. At the same time, we know different children have different needs. One child may have a learning disability and another child may be living in poverty, but that does not mean that either deserves pity. Instead, it is our responsibility as educators to provide a rigorous curriculum, along with the scaffolding each child needs to achieve at high levels.

If you want to understand the impact of generational poverty on student behaviors and achievement, examine the schools of high poverty that are closing the gap. These schools do exist. Some poor schools in Harlem, as well as in other urban and rural areas throughout the United States, are closing the gap. These are schools that have examined their school culture, improved teacher quality and expectations, provided additional resources for students, and addressed the needs of their specific populations. Check out the work that School Improvement Network is doing: they are filming in high-poverty schools that have closed or are closing the learning gaps (Linton, 2011). After examining schools of poverty in which children academically achieve at high levels, we must conclude that "perhaps it isn't poverty, or racial/ethnic background in and of itself, but rather our response to it" (Johnson, 2002, p. 6).

HOW-TO STRATEGIES

- Teach social skills to students.
- Teach the emotions.
- Change educators' mind-sets (study Jensen's [1998] and Dweck's [2006] work on mind-sets).
- Interview students about their mind-sets and sense of self-efficacy.
- Teach goal setting.
- Gather data.
- Learn about how the brain works.
- Pair students with mentors.
- Offer students authentic assessment, provocative lessons, and meaningful tasks.
- Support students in eating healthy meals; offer healthy snacks and water throughout the day.
- Include exercise and outdoor time with students.
- Read about and study the effects of poverty.
- Take part in a poverty simulation to better understand the stressors of living in poverty.
- Shadow a student and visit a student's home.

ACADEMIC COURSE WORK

Rigorous academic course work makes a difference, and studies show that compared with White students, a disproportionately small number of African American, Latino/a, and Native American students take challenging courses. Some schools rigidly track (group students according to ability), and by high school, students in the lower track may have no possibility of taking an academically challenging class (Johnson, 2002). Some minority students opt out of academically challenging courses because of peer pressure; some students don't want to do the work. Some urban schools do not offer calculus or advanced physics or chemistry.

Even today, some educators, sadly, steer some Students of Color, particularly African American and Latino males, away from academically challenging courses, thinking that the students need to take more "practical" classes or classes in which they will not fail. My son encountered this: when transferring from a highly academic high school in his junior year to a new school, he was told by the well-meaning counselor he should take "shop" instead of continuing in the honors track where he had been placed in the previous school. The counselor told him he should "enjoy" his senior year, and not work hard on academics. Would this man have said that to a White male with a high grade point average coming into the school? I don't know. My African American and Latina educator friends have shared personal stories of how high school educators told them they did not "need" to go to college or they would not be able to succeed in college. Now they hold advanced college degrees.

Another phenomenon I find in some schools is an unrealistic notion of what rigor is. Students think they are being rigorously challenged until they are asked to compete against students from high-achieving schools or take advanced placement tests and score a 3 or below. It is so important for teachers to remain apprised of what rigor entails and to compare their students' work not only with their colleagues but with students from high-achieving prep schools in order to know what students are capable of achieving. I learned this when I changed school districts and found students working at least two years ahead of what I thought students at their ages were capable of doing. I had low expectations and didn't know it. Added to this, some high school students have expectations of becoming a "doctor" and don't realize they need to take challenging courses. When a student does not understand the pathway of classes he or she needs to meet the entrance requirements for their chosen career choice, there is a problem. If schools are not providing rigorous and advanced classes for students with quality teachers, there is a problem. I talk to too many high school students who do not understand what classes they need in order to achieve their dreams.

What can schools do to encourage Students of Color to take academically challenging courses? Try the following strategies.

HOW-TO STRATEGIES

- Take whatever steps are necessary to ensure that each child reads at grade level.

- Give each student a goal sheet for tracking the classes needed in high school to achieve his or her dream career. Explain clearly to students what they need to know and be able to do to achieve what they want.
- Offer students positive role models. Post throughout the school posters of minority engineers, scientists, writers, doctors, judges, and so on. How many steps do you have to take inside your school before you see a picture or poster of role models in a profession other than sports who reflect the ethnicity of your students?
- Hire minority staff.
- Begin "college talk" on day one. Assume each child has the ability to go to college. After high school graduation, the choice is then up to the child.
- Carefully monitor students as they progress through elementary school. Notice their strengths. Inquire about their dreams. Encourage those dreams.
- Begin to offer specialized clubs at upper elementary school levels, such as science club, math club, chess club, foreign language clubs, writers club, and academic club. Ensure that diverse learners are central participants in these clubs.
- Take students to visit local universities; start in middle school, if not before.
- Call your students "scholars" (Kunjufu, 1988) when you address them in class.
- Identify local university students who will mentor middle school students.
- Ensure that each high school student has a mentor who encourages him or her to take a rigorous academic course of study. This means one adult must continually check in with the student to encourage him or her to take honors and AP courses, and then be ready with support when students take the leap into rigorous courses.
- Find teachers who really want diverse learner students in their advanced classes and who will support their success.
- Organize a student support club (see Chapter 17 for one model) so that the students will have positive peer support.

What can you do in your own classroom or school to ensure culturally diverse learners enroll in your most academically rigorous courses?

_____

_____

_____

How can you shape your instructional practices to ensure that you offer the most academically rigorous work to all students?

_____

_____

_____

TEST BIAS

Test bias is a complex issue. Many researchers now say that test bias has been largely eliminated. Much has been eliminated, but often bias remains because of the cultures in which we live. Even though test makers scrutinize tests, the playing field is far from level.

Teachers have shared personal anecdotes about their students and the tests. Some students are tested over things they have not experienced in their lives. One teacher said a recent test had a passage about grasshoppers, but her students did not know what grasshoppers were. In addition, particular words can hold different meanings for different children, such as the word *weave*, which may mean a kind of stitchery to one child and a hairpiece to another.

Studying the language of test taking is relevant for educators. If we want all of our children to close the academic achievement gap, we must teach all children the language of test taking. If children lack knowledge of the language of test taking, they may be unable to interpret the test language.

HOW-TO STRATEGIES

To eliminate further test bias, do the following.
- Get involved in the test-making process in your state.
- Write test items for the ACT.
- Teach students to read critically.
- Use a wide variety of reading materials to build background knowledge.
- Select old test items to use as opening activities in class. Do one a day for practice.
- Teach your students the concept that language gives them power, and give them numerous examples of how language empowers their lives. Tell them that they must learn standard English in order to succeed in college.
- Work with your entire staff to determine areas of concern on state tests.
- Have your students create test passages and items.
- Teach your students the art of test taking.
- Brainstorm with your students ways to create a positive test experience.
- Do everything you can do to make the test-taking experience a positive one—several books in the marketplace provide numerous strategies to address test taking.
- Look upon the testing situation as an opportunity rather than a negative experience for you and your students.
- Use test data to improve your instruction.

Are you a good test taker? Why, or why not?

_____

_____

_____

What things can you do to improve the test-taking abilities of all of your students?

_____

_____

_____

In what ways can you use standardized test data to improve your instructional practice?

_____

_____

_____

TEACHER EXPECTATIONS

In her book _The Dreamkeepers: Successful Teachers of African American Children,_ Gloria Ladson-Billings (1994) states that successful teachers treat students as competent, use a _no-deficit_ model, provide instructional "scaffolding," focus on instruction with a sacrosanct reading period, extend students' thinking and abilities, and possess in-depth knowledge of both subject matter and the students.

What are teacher expectations?

_____

_____

_____

In the learning process, teacher expectations include teacher engagement. In _Closing the Achievement Gap_ (B. Williams, 1996), Karen Louis and BetsAnn Smith write about teacher engagement as integral to teacher expectations. Students must believe their teachers are engaged with the content and care about them as individuals. Unless this occurs, students fail to engage with the content. Teachers must believe that their students are engaged with the content. Unless this occurs, teachers do not teach at optimal levels of instruction. This creates a catch-22.

This catch-22 appears to be especially true for schools with a high concentration of lower income and minority students. Compared with teachers of more affluent children, teachers who work with students from poorer families are more likely to believe that they have little influence on their students' learning. Over the past three years, I have worked with Students of Color in six high schools in one district where there is a high poverty rate. Throughout the time, I interviewed students about their teachers' expectations of them. Time and time again, they shared that their favorite teachers expect them to do the work and help them when they need help.

Angela Estrella, a teacher at Monta Vista High School, Cupertino, California, shared that when she was in eighth grade, her language arts teacher, Mrs. Griffin, raised her expectations for her future by telling her: "I do not want you to invite me to your high school graduation; I want you to invite me to your college graduation." Angela said that this was the first time anyone had ever expressed the belief that she could get a college degree, and eight years later, she proved Mrs. Griffin right by being the first person in her family to graduate from college (Estrella, 2012). We can never underestimate the power of our words!

Think about your teacher engagement. How engaged are you?

_____

_____

_____

What influences your teacher engagement?

_____

_____

_____

What can you do to ensure that you remain engaged throughout the school year?

_____

_____

_____

Write out your expectations of your students. Do they vary, depending on which students you consider?

_____

_____

_____

Do you truly believe that your diverse learners can achieve at the same levels as White males? What proof do you have that you believe this?

_____

_____

_____

What concrete steps can you take to ensure that your teacher expectations are high enough for all of your students?

_____

_____

_____

HOW-TO STRATEGIES

How do you find out what your students are capable of achieving? Try the following.

- Use formative assessment throughout your instruction to keep track of student learning.
- Examine student work with your professional learning group to ensure your expectations are high enough.
- Examine district benchmark tests for student learning and areas where students need support and reteaching.
- Examine your state tests. They offer one standard of judgment.
- Visit a school, public or private, that graduates students who have achieved academically at top levels. Examine the curriculum and student work.
- Read award-winning student literary magazines for examples of high-quality writing.
- Attend science fairs and view winning projects.
- Attend conferences to network with educators and participate in sessions.
- Examine your subconscious prejudices and perceptions.

A book that clearly demonstrates how teacher expectations create a classroom of excellence is Erin Gruwell's (1999) _The Freedom Writers Diary: How a Teacher and 150 Teens Used Writing to Change Themselves and the World Around Them._

TEACHER QUALITY

What does teacher quality mean to you?

_____

_____

_____

For the past several years, Kati Haycock has researched teacher quality, and she asserts what she has known all along: "No matter what measure of 'quality' you look at, poor and minority students—and not just those in inner city schools—are much less likely to be assigned better qualified and more effective teachers" (Haycock & Hanushek, 2010). In searching for the causes of the achievement gap, she and her research colleagues ask adults why there is a learning gap. They hear comments from educators that the children are too poor, the parents don't care, and they come to school hungry. The reasons, she adds, are always about the children and their families. Yet, when she talks with students, she hears different reasons. Students talk about teachers who do not know their subject matter, counselors who underestimate their potential and misplace them, administrators who dismiss their concerns, and a curriculum and expectations that are so low level that students are bored.

Haycock (2001) agrees that poverty and parental education matter, but she states that we take the children who have the least and "give them less of everything that we believe makes a difference" (p. 8). High school students who take more rigorous course work learn more and perform better on tests (Haycock, 2001; Johnson, 2002). The more rigorous the courses students take, the better they perform. Also, the rigor and quality of high school course work determines success in college. By giving the honors work to all children, we create exciting, rigorous classrooms set for achievement.

The research of Haycock, Johnson, and others (Haycock & Hanushek, 2010; Johnson, 2002; Johnson & La Salle, 2010) shows that all students can achieve at high levels if they are taught at high levels. Recent research has turned upside down the assumptions previously made about why students did not achieve. Those assumptions included the belief that "what students learned was largely a factor of their family income or parental education, not of what schools did" (Haycock, 2001, p. 10). We now know that what schools do matters and that what teachers do may matter most of all.

HOW-TO STRATEGIES

- Read professional journals.
- Attend professional conferences and meetings.
- Participate in professional learning groups.
- Read professional books on rigor and teacher quality.

Do you agree or disagree with Kati Haycock's findings?

_____

_____

_____

Describe your teacher quality.

_____

_____

_____

In what ways might you improve your teacher quality? Design a plan for yourself.

_____

_____

_____

This chapter covered ways that poverty, test bias, academic course work, teacher expectations, and teacher quality affect the learning gap. The strategies listed in this chapter have been implemented in schools at every level. Consider the strategies and choose some you believe will work for you. You may also consider working with your colleagues in a professional learning community in your school to examine the gap and ways to mediate and close the gap in your district. Chapter 2 includes a list of questions to consider about your professional experiences. Those questions can be used as self-reflective tools, journal prompts, and discussion starters. They are yours to keep, think about, use, and add to as we continue our inquiry into classroom instruction and how to support the academic success of diverse learners.

Throughout the early chapters in this book, we examined culture, racial histories, the impact of race, research on culturally diverse learners, and sources of learning gaps. The remaining chapters in the book examine classroom culture and expectations for students, relationships, classroom instruction, and a focus on the strategies we can implement to improve student achievement, ending with a chapter on wellness just for you.

SUGGESTED READINGS

Jensen, Eric. *Teaching With Poverty in Mind: What Being Poor Does to Kids' Brains and What Schools Can Do About It* (Alexandria, VA: ASCD, 2009).

Johnson, Ruth S., and Robin Avelar La Salle. *Data Strategies to Uncover and Eliminate Hidden Inequities: The Wallpaper Effect* (Thousand Oaks, CA: Corwin, 2010).

Linton, Curtis. *Equity 101: The Equity Framework* (Thousand Oaks, CA: Corwin, 2011).

Tileston, Donna Walker. *Closing the RTI Gap: Why Poverty and Culture Count* (Bloomington, IN: Solution Tree, 2011).

10

How to Build Relationships With Culturally Diverse Students and Families

Have you noticed that students just love some teachers? What is their secret? What do these teachers do to build relationships with individual students? This chapter offers you an opportunity to ponder your relationship-building skills and suggests numerous strategies based on the research to build relationships with your students.

When is the last time you learned something new outside of your comfort zone? Perhaps you bought a new cell phone, installed a new computer program, or adopted a new curriculum. What did you notice about yourself as you tried to learn to use the new material? Were you often frustrated or even angry? Did you need time to practice the new material more than once? Did you need someone who knew more than you and who would give you uncritical support? Was there a guidebook with clear directions?

Learning something new gives us the opportunity to reflect on the challenges and fears our students face daily: the stress and threat of failure, peer or teacher criticism, material presented outside of student learning styles, and grades given before the material is mastered. In addition, if you are a student who often experiences failure, you may lack the self-confidence in your ability to master the new task.

CLASSROOMS THAT WELCOME STUDENTS

Therefore, students need classrooms where there is a strong sense of community and no fear of ridicule, and where the teacher not only cares about them but refuses to allow them to fail. Students need to be welcomed to class. Recently, I observed in a class with a young, new teacher who sat behind her computer as students entered her high school English classroom. Her first eight comments to the students were commands or reprimands; not once did she offer a welcoming invitation to the students. I listened as she hollered: "Sit down; the bell is going to ring." "You know what you're supposed to be doing." "Get away from the computers." And so on. Even when she began the lesson, she failed to say "hi" to the students and welcome them. Hopefully, this is rare, yet I observe far too many teachers in classrooms across the country who jump into their lessons without acknowledging the learners in front of them, much less welcoming them at the door. How do you feel when someone begins a meeting without acknowledging you? How different is it when someone looks you in the eye and simply says hello before beginning the work?

In your classroom, it might look like this: You welcome each child, each day, into your classroom. You may do this with a hello at the door, using the student's name or a variation of it.

Consider this strategy: Give each student a 4" × 6" index card. Have students print their names on the cards. Laminate the cards, if possible. Each day, lay out the cards in alphabetical order on a table inside the room. Students enter the room, pick up their cards, and greet you with a "Good morning, [teacher's name]" while shaking your hand. You reciprocate with a "Good morning, [student's name]" as you look into the student's eyes. After you enter the attendance, you recycle the cards to the table, ready for the next day. The young teacher who shared this strategy said that using this procedure has cut down on tardies, built classroom community, and allowed her to learn quickly a large number of students' names. Her students were ninth graders, but this strategy would work with students once they were old enough to recognize their names, as well as with graduate students.

However you decide to welcome your students, this initial contact with them sets the tone for the class. Until you acknowledge the visibility of each student, you may find that particular students refuse to acknowledge your lesson. They may not care about what you are teaching until you demonstrate that you care about them.

Some classrooms use a strategy for students who are tardy that alleviates the stress and tension of the moment. There is a sign-in sheet right inside the classroom door and students sign in, marking the date and time. A local preschool uses this procedure beginning at age three, so our older kids can surely do this. It eliminates the dreaded question "Why are you late?" Instead, the student can quietly enter the classroom and take his or her seat. Questions about tardies can happen at the end of class. This respects the learning, the teacher, and the student.

Write below how you welcome students to your class.

_____

_____

_____

If you are not satisfied with your procedure, reflect on and create a new positive welcoming ritual.

_____

_____

_____

Welcoming Every Student

When we belong to a group that makes us feel welcome, these are some of the behaviors the members exhibit toward each other:

- They greet each other warmly with a big smile and eye contact.
- They ask questions about what has happened in each other's lives since the last time they saw each other.
- They listen intently with both their minds and their body language.
- They ask probing questions to demonstrate they really care.
- They share their personal lives.
- They sit as if they want to be in each other's presence.
- They warmly say goodbye and let each other know how happy they will be to see each other again.

How does your list compare?
These seem like simple things:

- Greet
- Listen
- Share
- Engage
- Respect
- Give feedback
- Say goodbye

When educators do these things with students each day, they create an inclusive and powerful learning environment. When educators

- Greet students at the door;
- Listen to their stories;

- Share something about themselves with them;
- Keep close to them as they learn;
- Respect their brain's functioning by allowing time for thinking, talking, writing, and processing;
- Listen to their learning output;
- Give feedback to their learning; and
- Tell them goodbye, letting them know they are anxious to see them again, they are responding to learners' needs.

Child or adult, we would respond to this paradigm of learning. Brain to brain, we would feel safe in this environment if the teacher and the other students all responded in kind.

In addition to being greeted, we need to see images of ourselves in the environment. Do you see images of yourself in your educational setting? If so, what kinds of images do you see?

When walking into a school, students need to see themselves. Ideally, they will see themselves reflected in their teachers. However, if there are no teachers who look like the students who need role models, there are other ways to provide images for the students. There might be images posted throughout the school; persons from different cultures can volunteer in the school; role models from diverse ethnic groups can be part of the student lessons; students can take field trips to businesses, neighborhoods, or campuses where there are members of diverse cultural groups. This is not to say that role models can't come from a different cultural group than the students; nonetheless, all students need to see themselves projected visually in some manner in their school setting.

Post pictures of your students in your classrooms and school. You can take a class picture and post it on your classroom wall. You can ask students to bring in their favorite pictures and post them in the room. You can have students draw self-portraits and post them on the walls. When a group of struggling ninth graders were asked what would tell them that their teacher cared about them, one young male said, "My teacher would have a picture of me as her wallpaper on the computer screen." This young male was serious about wanting to see himself projected in the classroom where he needed to learn. Educators have the power to project their students' images in their classrooms and throughout the rest of their schools. An inclusive environment is one where all students succeed at high levels within an equitable school culture.

RESPETO

Gary Howard (1999), author of *We Can't Teach What We Don't Know*, suggests we show our students *respeto*—a Spanish word that goes beyond respect. It means that I, as an individual, will deeply honor you both as a person and as someone different from myself. It is often translated to mean deference and esteem, in addition to simply respect. In practice, because I respect you, I will change who I am to become connected with you, despite our differences. As teachers do this, they overcome difference and ensure that all students achieve because they have built a foundation of respectful relationships with their students. With *respeto*, educators truly engage the equity framework, holding high expectations, implementing rigor, creating relevancy and building powerful relationships.

Here are some strategies to help you learn about and develop *respeto* for other cultures:

- Attend art events given by or about people of other cultures.
- Truly listen to what persons from other cultures have to say.
- Become friends with people of other cultures.
- Live in integrated neighborhoods.
- Read the literature of other cultures.
- Travel to other countries.
- Place value on students' home languages and cultures.
- Invite persons from other cultures into your home.
- Study a foreign language.

You can use these strategies in your classroom to develop *respeto* for other cultures:

- Talk about the important contributions of cultural groups.
- Bring in positive articles about people of different cultures to share with students.
- Post simple phrases in multiple languages throughout your classroom and school.
- Post positive pictures of people from other cultures throughout your classroom and school.
- Schedule home visits and observe your students with their families.
- Include class projects that allow students to get to know each other as individuals.
- Ask your students to write about family customs and share with the class.
- Respect the traditions of other cultures and don't make assumptions about their rituals and practices.

BODY LANGUAGE

Once you have welcomed your students and connected with them, does your body language continue to connect with your students? Is your body language congruent with the words that come out of your mouth? A professor at UCLA, Albert Mehrabian (1990), did research on how people communicate their feelings and concluded that 38 percent of the meaning communicated is based on how it sounds—tone, volume, and speed. With that knowledge, think about your classroom tone. Is your tone appropriate and congruent with the words you say? To demonstrate the importance of tone, try this exercise: Stand in front of a chair and pretend it is a dog. Pet it lovingly as you say something like this: "I hate you; you are evil and I don't want you." What would the dog do? Wag its tail and nuzzle up to you. Now kick the chair and scream these words in anger: "I love you, you sweet doggy." What would the dog do? Recoil in fear. The tone conveys your message (and notice how much more difficult it is to say nice things in anger than to say mean things in a pleasant tone). Think about your students. Does your tone of voice often communicate displeasure, disappointment, or frustration as you say something such as "We are going to try this again"?

Ask a colleague to give you feedback on your tone of voice after he or she observes you teaching a challenging class. Does your tone of voice work against you? Perhaps you were socialized to ask rather than tell, and this plays out in your classroom management. Do you tell students to do something by asking a question? For example, "Mary, are you ready to start your work, Sweetie?" If Mary is an English language learner, she may hear the tone of your voice asking her if she "wants" to do something rather than hearing the direction you think you are giving. Mary's mind may think she has a choice to either do the work or not, and no, she does not want to. She needs to begin her work. Check how you give directions. Make sure you are using declarative or command sentences, not questions, and use strong nouns and verbs, cutting out the adverbs and extraneous words when speaking to learners' brains.

Once you are convinced that your body language conveys an assertive, caring teacher, you may want to examine how you continue to build relationships throughout your school day. Students often come into class wound up or tired, certainly not focused on the lesson you are ready to teach. Yet the opening moments of class are tremendously important and offer countless opportunities to build classroom community and relationships. Think about your opening class procedure. How do you effectively begin your time with students?

GREETING YOUR STUDENTS

Have a colleague videotape your morning welcomes several days in a row so that you are unaware of it after the first few days. If you can't videotape, ask a colleague to observe you and provide feedback.

- Do you lean in to some students as you greet them and lean away from others?
- Is your smile more genuine with certain students?
- Do you joke around with some and not others?
- Do you tend to compliment the same students day after day?
- Do you privilege some students and slight others?

It is usually necessary to have outside eyes help with the monitoring of our body language. Body language is often unconscious, so we may not know what subtle cues we are sending to our students. After you have been observed by a colleague or by using a camera, examine what you see. Do you notice you tend to give more attention to the students who look like you or the students who perform better? Do you tend not to use small talk with your "trouble makers" or students failing your class? Self-examination is a courageous thing to do; you can learn so much from the feedback.

A middle school teacher did an action research project with her students, greeting one class at the door, and then observing changes in their behavior and class work. Within days she saw changes in both classroom behavior and student engagement. Her other classes remained the same. Consider trying this with one of your classes. Stand at the door. Make eye contact with each student, greet them, and make a pleasant comment to them.

Describe your perception of the body language you use with your students.

_____

_____

_____

Think about a person you enjoy being around. Probably that person's body language is welcoming. Can you articulate what she or he does to make you feel welcome? Describe the person's body language.

_____

_____

_____

What changes might you make in your body language?

_____

_____

_____

THE EMOTIONAL CLIMATE

Assess the vibrations of the class. This may make no sense to you, or you may be a person who knows exactly what this means. But look at each of the students as they walk into the room. Look at their faces. Are they relaxed? Are they angry? Is the tenor of the class anticipatory? Is it belligerent? Assess the tenor of the class as a whole. In the book _You've Got to Reach Them to Teach Them_, educator Mary Kim Schreck (2011) writes: "Educators must take seriously the fact that how a student _feels_ about a learning situation will determine how much attention and effort that child will expend" (p. 26). When learners enter our classrooms, we need to do a quick assessment of how individual students feel and use a strategy to connect all students to the learning. If you use a check-in question at the beginning of the class (discussed later in this chapter), you will have the opportunity to check the emotional state of each student.

If a fight has just occurred in the hallway, students may come into class in a heightened emotional state and be physically unable to begin class work without transition time. Some students take much longer to transition than others. Consider allowing kids transition time. If you need quiet in your classroom immediately for behavior control, use writing in a journal as a transition. You can write a prompt on the board or overhead and have students respond to it in their journals. You can tie the prompt to the material to be studied in the class, or not. You can choose several avenues for sharing: students can share with a class buddy, with the whole class, or with the teacher.

If you have a class that can talk without losing control, let them talk a minute while you take attendance, assess their feelings, and move throughout the classroom addressing students and making connections.

LEVEL: ELEMENTARY/MIDDLE/HIGH

Rituals

Some teachers have an opening routine that functions as a positive ritual. A ninth-grade teacher begins each class hour with a Venn diagram on her board. Over each section of the diagram is a word from the ACT/SAT vocabulary lists. When students enter, they go to the board and write their names in the section of the Venn diagram that best describes them. For example, if the words are *loquacious* and *reticent*, they decide which terms best describe them and write their names in the appropriate space. The teacher then uses the words throughout the lesson that day and incorporates them into the word bank of the class. You can also use terms from your lesson. Let's say you are teaching about inlets and fjords. Write those two words on the sections of the Venn. Have students decide if they would rather be an inlet or a fjord and write in their journals why. This kicks up the exercise to the metaphorical level. This opening ritual sparks conversation centered on literacy and focuses the class, as well as gives feedback to the teacher about how each student perceives himself or herself. If your class is particularly large, you might designate a row of students for each day of the week who might participate in the activity.

Check-In Questions

Begin class with a check-in question. Ask the same question of each student in the class and give students an option to say "pass." The question can be related to the lesson or it can be personal, such as "Where would you most want to travel?" or "What is your favorite food?" Once again, the teacher receives feedback on the preferences of the students; the students learn something about each other; the students' focus changes to the classroom; each student's voice is valued; there isn't a right or wrong answer; and each student fulfills the teacher request, even if he or she declines to answer. As students answer the question, note whether each student looks relaxed and ready to learn. If students are not ready to learn, then you need to do something to get them ready. This may be energizing movements or even an individual check with students who appear unfocused or unhappy. Offering a personal comment tells the student you are aware of his or her current state and are ready to give the support needed.

An elementary teacher shared that she uses this questioning strategy each Monday in her fifth-grade class. One morning she was absent for a workshop, so before she left, she asked the substitute to perform the opening class ritual. The substitute did, yet when the teacher returned after lunch, her students asked to do the activity again because, they said, "We didn't get to do it with you!"

High Five

Another teacher gives her students a high five when they enter her room. In her absence, her students complained that the substitute did not do the high five. So the teacher made a picture of her hand on the school copy machine and taped it to her door. She told her students that if they wanted to, in her absence, they could high-five the copy of her hand on the door as they left the room. Many did.

You can use a simple signal that tells the students it is time to learn. For example, you might say, "Turn your brains on," as you forward snap your hand at brain level. Even though high school students may laugh when you do this, it is a cognitive reminder to focus on what is to come.

Music

Use music to affect mood. One teacher shared she used the theme from the *Cops* television program in her middle school classroom. Learners knew they had to be in their seats when the theme stopped. She then used Bach piano concertos in the background as students wrote in their journals and calmed down, getting their brains ready to learn. She followed this with a check-in, and then a choral reading of classroom procedures posted on a poster at the head of the room.

Student–Teacher Relationships

Relationships profoundly affect student readiness to learn (Sousa, 2001; Sylwester, 2000; Tomlinson, 2003). Whether they are ELs, students from different cultures, students living in poverty, or students with learning disabilities, students need to know that teachers care about them (Haycock & Hanushek, 2010; Tomlinson, 2003). Below are several brain-friendly strategies to show your students you care and build relationships in your classroom.

Level: Elementary/Middle/High
Subject: Cross-curricular

- Select a difficult student and find a way to connect with her or him about something unrelated to school. Do this daily, outside of instructional time, until you see a change in the student's attitude toward you. This works! Try it over the next two weeks with one of your students. You may be amazed at his or her reaction to your caring conversation.

(Continued)

(Continued)

- Student as expert: Learn what your students know and incorporate it into your lessons. For example, students at the high school level who live in the inner city could explain to students who live in the outer suburbs directions to many cultural and sporting centers. The suburban students will be impressed with the urban students' knowledge of and ability to navigate the city.
- Try a "Friday Final Five" strategy: choose topics such as sports, music, hobbies, and special interests. Students who are experts on a topic sign up to do a Friday Final Five. They share their expertise with the class during the final five minutes of class on Fridays. They are allowed to bring preapproved props and demonstrate their expertise to their classmates.
- Snaps and taps: During class time, allow students to write positive comments about other students on slips of paper and drop them into a bowl. During the last minute of class, one student pulls out a slip of paper and reads the positive comment aloud to the class. The class gets five seconds to tap or snap. *Snap* consists of snapping the middle finger and the thumb, modeling the beatnik applause. *Tap* consists of drumming on the table or desks as loudly as they want—five seconds of controlled motor activity. Since one teacher began doing snaps and taps in her special education classroom, she reports that students are reserving their tapping for the end of class rather than tapping pencils or feet or hands throughout the class.

(Middle/High)

- Take students to an event that reflects their culture. Just accompanying students to a restaurant that serves food that reflects their culture builds relationships.
- Start a support group. See Chapter 17 for a model for a 4 As group, or start a chess club, a writing group, a book club, and so on.
- Give your challenging students a responsible position in your class. One seventh-grade girl challenged classroom management procedures, so the teacher talked with her privately, complimenting her on her leadership skills, and put her in charge of seeing that the other students followed the procedures. She became a role model. When others began to talk during teacher instruction, she used peer pressure to positively coerce them to reengage with the lesson.
- Take some bananas and muffins and meet with a group of challenging students once a week for breakfast. Within six weeks, you should see a significant change in their behavior.

(Elementary/Middle/High)

- Use authentic projects to drive your curriculum and improve achievement (Sousa, 2001; Tate, 2003). You will build relationships with students if you conference with them during their work on authentic projects. For example, if they are interviewing veterans and creating a book, you will build a classroom community of learners as well as improve your relationship with each individual learner.

- Attend extracurricular events in which your students participate.
- Create a library in your classroom by shopping at flea markets, book sales, and so on. Invite your students to take books they want to enjoy. Consider it a success, not a failure, if one doesn't come back.
- Do a "walk and talk." One staff member volunteered to take a small group of boys with behavior issues on a daily walk during an extra class designated for alternative instruction. The boys enjoyed the outside, the walk, and the talk, and their behavior issues diminished in not only her class but in the classes of the entire team.
- Use students' names in your examples when you teach. Personalize your lessons in as many ways as possible.
- Send postcards to students when you vacation. Bring back free mementos for your students.
- Create a classroom newsletter. Ask your district to provide professional development in PageMaker or some other software that allows you to easily produce a class newsletter. Include each student's voice. Send it home to parents to foster parent-teacher relationships.
- Create a buzz book and include student and parent interests.
- Have students fill out information sheets at the beginning of the year so that you can have their interests on file. Try to include their interests in your instructional planning when relevant.
- Talk about your interests with your students. By sharing yourself with your students, you build relationships. My fifth-grade teacher taught each student to knit. We made scarves and mittens. What do I recall from fifth grade? I remember it as my favorite year in elementary school because of this teacher. Teachers are interesting people, and you have much to share. Some teachers have shared with their students the following interests: elephants, motorcycles, sports, knitting, the books they read, travel, exotic flowers, hiking, and many, many more.
- Videotape yourself. Analyze your body language. Are you consistently friendly with all children? Do you try to build relationships with all children? Do you move away from some children and lean in to others as you communicate about your interests to your students?
- Investigate Teacher Expectations: Student Achievement (TESA) training. It looks at fifteen teacher behaviors and how they inhibit or promote academic achievement.
- Do some reflection. If 20 percent of your students are into hip-hop and you can't stand it, how might that play out in your class? If you find some students' cultural norms, behaviors, or hidden rules repugnant,

(Continued)

(Continued)

how might that be reflected in your body language as you interact with them? Note: Recently, in a workshop, a young teacher asked what he should do if he despised hip-hop. When asked what he thought he should do, he said respect the students and do his best. He answered his own question. We can't always bond with student interests, but we can respect that they might have different interests than we do.

- Establish journal buddies with your students.
- Get to know your students through their journal responses. Honestly respond to them. You will see a marked improvement in their behavior and academics using this strategy.
- Smile at your students and smile with them.
- Listen to your students.

Write down your strategies for building relationships with your students and families.

_____

_____

_____

_____

_____

_____

I hope you found several strategies in this chapter to build relationships with your students and their families. Once the relationship is in place, learning can flow. Chapter 11 offers strategies to build a school culture that honors all staff, students, and families.

❖ ❖ ❖

SUGGESTED READINGS

Bailey, Becky. _Unconscious Discipline: 7 Basic Skills for Brain Smart Classroom Management_ (Oviedo, FL: Loving Guidance, 2000).

Schreck, Mary Kim. _You've Got to Reach Them to Teach Them_ (Bloomington, IN: Solution Tree, 2011).

Sylwester, Robert. _A Biological Brain in a Cultural Classroom: Applying Biological Research to Classroom Management_ (Thousand Oaks, CA: Corwin, 2000).

11

Creating a School Culture That Welcomes Students, Staff, and Families

How do we build a school culture that welcomes culturally diverse learners and their families? How do you create a climate of collegiality among staff? These are challenges for every school. We learned from Brenda's narrative in Chapters 3 and 7 that culturally different families may feel isolated and become disengaged from their children's schools. Teachers, too, may feel isolated and disengage. So what are strategies administrators and staff can use to ensure every child's family feels a sense of belonging to the school, and each staff member feels a part of the school family? Fortunately, every school has one or more isolated classrooms that welcome culturally diverse learners and their families with teachers who know how to connect with families, students, and colleagues. However, small pockets of excellence do not create an excellent school. To create a school of excellence, a positive, academic culture must flourish with staff members collaborating together to design instruction, assess student learning, and support learners in a myriad of ways all the while connecting with their families. This chapter examines school culture and its impact on culturally diverse learners and their families and the staff that works with them.

School culture is extremely important. It shapes the norms of the environment. It says what is cool and what is in. If that culture is one of academic rigor, then that's cool; that is the goal. By achieving, students are buying into the culture, into their environment of acceptance. By failing, they are failures of that culture. A student's perceived acceptance into the school culture directly affects his or her motivation to achieve.

Both teachers and students can be caught in a perceived reality that keeps each individual from attaining his or her potential (Lindsey, Roberts, & CampbellJones, 2005). Garcia (quoted in Artiles & Ortiz, 2002) suggests that in order for culturally diverse learners to feel included in the academic school culture, teachers must see their cultural differences as assets to their achievement, rather than as deficits to be modified by the dominant culture.

Describe the current culture of your school.

_____

_____

_____

How does that culture influence you?

_____

_____

_____

Read the following scenarios and reflect on how the culture in each of these school districts affects student achievement.

SCHOOL DISTRICT A

In School District A, students are taught and supported and expected to attend the local community college, the state universities, or no college at all. Fewer than half attend college. There seldom is a National Merit Scholar finalist. District scores usually fall just above the median score on state tests. The students are respectful, follow middle-class rules, and mostly do what they are told. Sports are important in the schools, and morning announcements in the secondary schools often center on school sports events. The schools are kept clean and have adequate technology and support help. There is a general mistrust of the administration by the teachers, and an us-versus-them attitude exists. Yet teachers usually have the resources they need and are generally satisfied and do an adequate job. Professional development is viewed with suspicion, with a minority of staff enthusiastically taking part in any professional development not mandated by the district. Others grin and bear it, or don't grin at all. Teachers seldom leave; in fact, several teachers attended as children the very schools in which they now teach. The community surrounding the school is comprised of several generations of families with similar religious and ethnic backgrounds. Diversity usually is not welcomed in the schools, and newcomers are expected to assimilate and acculturate quickly in order to be successful in their new surroundings. Families usually do not participate or intervene in school affairs, except for sports, and are generally satisfied with their child's education.

SCHOOL DISTRICT B

In School District B, students often enter from the impoverished neighborhoods in a large urban area. The student population primarily consists of Students of Color; however, the majority of the teaching staff is White. Students are expected to drop out, attend local technical schools or a community college, or pursue no advanced schooling. District scores on state tests fall far below the median scores, except at the district college prep school. Schools are kept clean, yet facilities vary from severely lacking to adequate. In some schools, one finds challenges such as nonworking bathrooms, ceilings that leak when it rains, lack of breakfast for every hungry child, young students forced to stand outside in the bitter cold waiting in lines to go through metal detectors, broken desks, inadequate or lack of necessary supplies, and a lack of access to technology. Teacher mistrust is high because teachers are often treated as children, as in a "parent-child" relationship, being told what to do and how to do it as though they lack efficacy. The teachers union is strong, and the administration and the union are often at odds. Teachers often are moved from school to school, and often they teach next door to uncertified staff or substitute teachers. It's not unusual to find teachers teaching core subjects without a college major in the area. Students in the schools are orderly or disruptive, depending on the administration at each building and the teacher in the classroom. Yet even in the most orderly of buildings, students seldom reach high levels of academic rigor. Teacher expectations and student expectations often wane with each passing year, and seniors find themselves unprepared for college and unable to compete with students from districts that lie within five miles of their schools. Families come to the schools to complain; teachers contact families to complain. There is little collaboration or connection among the families, administration, and staff.

SCHOOL DISTRICT C

In School District C, the schools are reputed to be among the best in the state. District scores rank at top levels, and 99 percent of the high school graduates attend college. From kindergarten on, there is an expectation that students will attend an Ivy League school or a private liberal arts college in another state, preferably on the East Coast. Students are challenged from the day they enter school, and the evidence of academic success permeates the entire district. Academic rituals abound in this district. Juniors are involved in a lengthy awards ceremony where alumni of Ivy League schools give book awards to the most promising students. Students usually are involved in several extracurricular academic activities outside of school. Kumon math, music study with symphony performers, Sylvan Learning Centers, weekly tutors, and additional foreign language classes are common evening activities for the district's resident children. Sports are important, but all-inclusive, so a student can be a member of any sports team, regardless of ability. Schools are clean but not necessarily more modern or better equipped than in School District A. The priority obviously is not on the facilities but on the learning that takes place inside. Teachers usually have master's degrees in their content area and often consider it a failing of theirs if a child does not succeed. There is a high degree of efficacy on the part of the teachers and most students. There is a sense that "we're all in this together." Morning announcements focus on academic successes, and a day seldom goes by when one does not hear of a student or an entire student group winning a prestigious award. Administrators generally treat teachers as equals and as adults capable of making important classroom decisions. Teachers work in collaboration and continuously refine their practice through professional development and self-study, putting in many hours outside the school day to improve. From the moment a student enters the halls of this district's schools, he or she knows that college means another step toward personal and economic success. Students learn how to play the stock market, do out-of-state college visits during their junior year, and are carefully directed by a college counselor. Diversity usually is valued. Students mix in social groups, and many have traveled to other countries and even lived there. African American students who attend this school system through a voluntary, court-regulated desegregation program enter this world of academic expectations. The result? The achievement gap is more narrow in this district than in most other districts involved in the desegregation program. Why? For a variety of reasons, although one is climate, the school culture of academic excellence. Buying into this culture brings acceptance, not alienation. Teachers call families before each school year begins and establish a positive connection. There are several family functions held throughout the school year. Teachers make positive phone calls home, send student work home weekly, and e-mail a weekly newsletter. Families are visible in the schools, volunteering in classrooms and staying connected to their child's education.

Reflect on the three scenarios. List why you think School District C has higher achievement.

_____

_____

_____

What can you do to establish a school culture of academic excellence?

_____

_____

_____

HOW-TO STRATEGIES

> **Level: Elementary/Middle/High School**
> **Subject: Cross-curricular**
>
> - Use professional mentors from the community. (elementary/middle/high)
> - For role models, post pictures of People of Color in various professions. (elementary/middlc/high)
> - Ask retired teachers to volunteer in schools to provide time for teacher collaboration. (elementary/middle/high)
> - Post visuals of universities in the halls and public places. (elementary/middle/high)
> - Organize orientations for students and parents that revolve around college placement and financial aid. (middle/high)
> - Encourage staff to share their stories of how, when, and why they attended college. (elementary/middle/high)
> - Have staff mentor students. (elementary/middle/high)
> - Have college recruiters visit and meet with students during their sophomore year. (high)
> - Administer the PSAT to students in English classes during their sophomore year and go over the test with all students, teaching them test-taking strategies. (high)
> - Require English teachers to teach the SAT/ACT vocabulary lists as a regular part of their classes. (high)
> - Have English teachers assign the college essay as one of their regular assignments during Grades 10, 11, and 12. Have contests celebrating the best. Consider having the students read their essays over the public address system on occasion. (high)
> - Have English teachers mentor students through the college application process. Use the English research paper to investigate college choices. (high)

BUILDING A COLLEGIAL CULTURE AMONG STAFF

Just as teachers need to hold high expectations for their students, administrators need to hold high expectations for staff and treat them accordingly, offering them the same respect they expect in return. Professional attitudes of high expectation can develop from being treated professionally by supervisors and peers. For example, consider Nancy's experience. Nancy experienced a big "a-ha" moment when she was "just" a teacher in a district where she thought she was respected. She had worked very hard to bring a Tibetan dance group to the high school as part of the international education project. After the performance, the central office personnel, dance group, and university people were invited to a luncheon in the school's library. As she stood in line talking with the university folks, the assistant superintendent came over and said, "Nancy, you need to go to the back of the line and wait to see if there is enough food for you to eat with us." After just having introduced the group to the students and faculty in a large assembly, she was now being treated as someone invisible. This made a lasting impression. The hierarchical attitude of this administrator clearly showed her that in the scheme of things, she was not valued as highly as others.

How many times have you attended meetings for teachers in your building where the food served was inferior to the food served to the administrators in the same district at their meetings? Do administrators have access to free coffee in central office buildings while teachers much pay for theirs? Some may say that cost is a factor, but the way we treat people shows our real attitudes toward them. Teachers have to be treated as equals to administrators, not as inferiors.

What do educators in your building do to encourage professional attitudes among teachers? Below are suggestions you, as an administrator or teacher, may implement to improve professional attitudes among all staff.

HOW-TO STRATEGIES

- Greet each colleague daily with a warm smile.
- Keep each colleague's interests in mind and share professional development opportunities with him or her. (Once a department head said he threw away the professional development notices because he knew we, his department, would not want to do anything in our free time—we had to tell him to let us make that decision.)
- Learn about your colleagues, share interesting news articles with them, and other things of interest.
- Consider starting a group that your colleagues could take part in and share, such as Zumba, yoga, a knitting group, hiking group, or volleyball.
- Consider a newsletter about staff interests. This could include school want ads with things the staff wants to sell, find, do, communicate about, work at, and so on.
- Have a weeklong staff presentation to faculty and students alike. Sign up staff to present on an area of interest; then book the library, have teachers bring their classes, and display books related to the interests. Everything is free. When one school did this, several staff members said it was the most positive experience of their years at the school.
- Institute incentive programs throughout the year. This can include meal passes, movie tickets, and other donations from the community.
- Post a bulletin board with staff recognitions, new babies, achievements, and the like.
- Have a potluck luncheon once a month revolving around a different theme. One school did this and said it improved staff morale more than

anything they had tried over the years. Leave the food out for all lunch periods and ask staff to gather and enjoy.

- Have an ice cream social during lunch hour for staff. A student multicultural club did this for a school's staff, and several teachers said it was the first time they had talked with the students in a casual atmosphere. It was a win-win situation.

Most of these kinds of activities can be implemented without additional costs and can be divided among interested staff and open to all. Consider one of these activities at your school over the course of at least a couple of weeks. Report to your group or team how it influenced morale.

Sometimes, the simplest things can build morale in a school and bring educators together so that they can begin to focus on professional attitudes. When teachers feel undervalued and invisible, they tend to hinder change rather than embrace it. Just as students need to feel valued and visible, teachers need this, too.

HOW-TO STRATEGIES

Suggestions for administrators to build a positive school culture include the following:

- Honor the history of the school. Every school has a "historian" who knows the history. Value that person and ask for her or his input throughout the year. Value and acknowledge the contributions of the past.
- Use humor at staff gatherings. Begin with jokes, play, or movement that causes staff to laugh with each other.
- Celebrate staff members when they have birthdays, babies, grandbabies, weddings, and so on.
- Conversely, offer sympathy when appropriate. Talk privately to staff members who are going through hard times; put cards in their mailboxes, and so on.
- Involve the staff in decision making. Don't "lay" things on them.
- Hold high expectations for staff, and forget the past.
- Ask advice from staff, targeting the strengths of each, making each staff member feel special in some way.
- Create spaces and times where staff can be collaborative.
- Don't be afraid to take risks.
- Openly share your mistakes and demonstrate you are equal to, not better than, the staff. Make it okay to struggle and make mistakes as part of the journey to excellence.
- Allow staff to have input into their own professional development, understanding that some staff members will want to take more control of their professional development and career than others.

COLLABORATIVE RELATIONSHIPS

When we show *respeto* to others, we honor others. When we honor and value others, we listen to them, and this mutual respect builds a strong platform for collaboration. Collaboration works when everybody appreciates the role they play in student achievement and modifies what they do to serve the mission of the school. Strong relationships build successful collaborations, and successful schools begin their collaboration with relationships. Schools succeed based on the collaborative relationships they foster, both academically and personally. Learning occurs when the teacher-student relationship is established and strengthened every day. Teachers realize they can't do it alone, and once the trust and relationships are established, they find ways to do it together. Time is always an issue; however, creative teachers find ways to plan throughout their school day. Even though teachers need formal collaboration time, they also learn to use their time more judiciously, talking in the halls, sharing lunch and talk, and meeting during planning time. Soon the routine of sharing becomes the norm, and teachers accomplish more teaming and planning within the school structures.

HOW-TO STRATEGIES

Suggestions for building collaborative relationships among staff include the following:

- Celebrate staff member birthdays.
- Create school rituals.
- Drop positive notes into staff mailboxes.
- Have staff share positive things about their colleagues at staff meetings.
- Surprise staff with a chair massage on staff work days.
- Have parents bring family dishes for a special staff luncheon.
- Set up a cadre of volunteers to help staff with menial tasks.
- Set up a cadre of volunteers to help staff work with students in small groups.
- Say hello each time you see a staff member. Too many teachers tell me their administrators walk right by them in the halls without acknowledging them.
- Get local businesses to donate services, gifts, and coupons for staff.
- Set up a one-on-one discussion with staff members and meet with each one once a month.
- If you are an administrator, do a "walkthrough" each day. At midmorning, walk through each staff member's room and acknowledge the teacher and the students. Make this a daily routine, and you will reap amazing benefits from it.
- Add humor to your staff meetings, your faculty room, your classrooms, and your hallways.
- Approach the most unapproachable staff member and ask her or him for advice on creating a more pleasant school culture.

- Create a pleasant room where staff can share ideas, relax, and regenerate. Too often, schools have unattractive, windowless staff rooms that are cluttered with old papers and machines that no longer work. Or there may be an ancient refrigerator that is too dirty to hold food. As a teacher, I believe that what the administration creates for its staff says a lot about how they value staff. A fresh coat of paint, a clean refrigerator—with a system for keeping it clean and fresh—attractive furniture, and no clutter tells staff they are appreciated and valued. Add a free hot beverage machine, a book lending library, healthy available snacks, and art on the walls, and you will make your staff feel special. Consider using students and the PTO or other parent groups to create the room for staff, thus building community among all the stakeholders in the school.

CONNECTING TO FAMILIES

In a school that values collaborative relationships, the staff knows that collaboration goes beyond working with other staff members. It also means the collaborative efforts between the staff and the community, the families, the parents, and the caretakers. Mutual respect for families is shown in numerous ways: when parents are included on school committees and councils; when educators speak the first language of the parents; when staff do home visits; and when schools provide parent and guardian centers.

Family Centers

One way to connect with families is to have a family center at the school, where families can congregate and share their joys, concerns, and ideas. Often these centers are staffed by volunteer parents who offer other family members refreshments and opportunities for volunteering in their child's school. There is often a library of books of interest to families, as well as other items of interest. There may be, as observed in a school in a high poverty area, a closet of clothes to give away to children who need them.

These centers need to be warm and welcoming, and when they are, you find parents congregating and collaborating with the schools. The room can be decorated like a coffee shop or a garden room, something to appeal to adults. The money to create these parent centers may come from various sources: vending machines, local or state grants, business donations, community donations, and families themselves. At one school, a local furniture store donated furniture for one center. At another, a food supplier gave free coffee and tea for the year. With a little imagination and creativity (and you can bet some of your parents can provide this), you can equip a center for your parents and guardians that will welcome them into your school and build collaboration with the entire community.

Some parents and guardians are not comfortable coming to school. If this is the case, it is best first to meet where families are most comfortable. This might mean having the meeting in a church hall or tribal center near their home, in a community center or library in their community, or in a coffee shop.

Whatever it takes to form that collaborative relationship with the parent will pay off later in the child's achievement. When parents unite with us, the child has a much better chance of excelling in our class.

REACHING OUT TO THE COMMUNITY

Ray Chavez, principal of Apollo Middle School in Tucson, set up a community school where community members can learn about computers, take English classes and classes in other areas, and exercise. His College Academy for Parents, which lasts for nine weeks, is a place where parents learn how to save for tuition, how to apply to colleges, and other things needed to support their children. Parents also visit local universities. These initiatives go beyond the school walls and are changing the community. In the Webster Groves School District, Webster Groves, Missouri, a new male principal in a largely African American community went to the Black churches to build collaboration between the school and the church communities. When he had his first open house (which had few participants in previous years), he found a room full of community members. He had reached out, changed his behavior, and gone to the community, rather than expecting the community to reach out first to him.

How did these educators reach families and the community using culturally considerate strategies?

_____

_____

_____

HOW-TO STRATEGIES

- Respect all voices and bridge language barriers.
- Send school paperwork home in English and in the families' home languages.
- Develop and sustain a welcoming and supportive community for families.
- Provide opportunities for parents and caregivers to develop skills.
- Ask parents to volunteer to be part of the actual school day, for example by serving meals, tutoring students, or monitoring physical breaks.
- Establish a parent center.
- Offer English as a second language classes for adults.
- Have a family treasures night and invite families to bring and share a special dish from their culture.
- Have an oral history night and ask parents and grandparents to come and share their stories.
- Hold a school rummage sale, car wash, bake sale, picnic, or the like.

- Hold a schoolwide book club for families. Offer it in more than one language. For example, *The House on Mango Street* (Cisneros, 1989, 1994) is available in Spanish and in English.
- Create a school families album. Invite families to share a family picture for the album, which can be displayed in the school library or the family center.
- Create a school garden and have families tend the garden. Celebrate with a dinner with food from the garden.

Choose one or more strategies from this chapter you will commit to implementing and write them below.

_____

_____

_____

This chapter focuses on creating a positive school culture for students, their families, and the staff who teach them. Hopefully, you feel empowered with what you have already completed: you have looked inside yourself, you have learned about and from others, and now it is time to integrate that awareness and new knowledge. Part III jumps into instruction with lessons aligned to the CCSS and being taught with success in today's classrooms.

❖   ❖   ❖

SUGGESTED READINGS

Hutchins, Darcy J., Marsha D. Greenfeld, Joyce L. Epstein, Mavis G. Sanders, and Claudia L. Galindo. *Multicultural Partnerships: Involve All Families* (Larchmont, NY: Eye On Education, 2012).

Muhammad, Anthony. *Transforming School Culture: How to Overcome Staff Division* (Bloomington, IN: Solution Tree, 2009).

Reeves, Douglas B. *The Learning Leader: How to Focus School Improvement for Better Results* (Alexandria, VA: ASCD, 2006).

Sylwester, Robert. *A Biological Brain in a Cultural Classroom* (Thousand Oaks, CA: Corwin, 2000).

PART III

Integrating New Knowledge

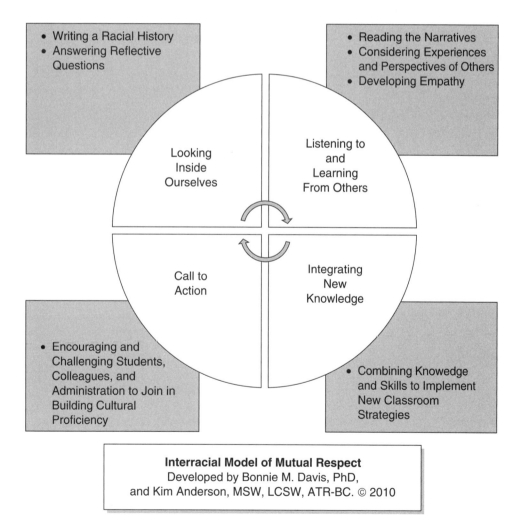

- Writing a Racial History
- Answering Reflective Questions

- Reading the Narratives
- Considering Experiences and Perspectives of Others
- Developing Empathy

Looking Inside Ourselves

Listening to and Learning From Others

Call to Action

Integrating New Knowledge

- Encouraging and Challenging Students, Colleagues, and Administration to Join in Building Cultural Proficiency

- Combining Knowedge and Skills to Implement New Classroom Strategies

Interracial Model of Mutual Respect
Developed by Bonnie M. Davis, PhD,
and Kim Anderson, MSW, LCSW, ATR-BC. © 2010

12

Strategies to Teach and Engage Culturally Diverse Learners and ELs

How do you maintain good classroom management, teach to the standards, infuse culturally responsive instruction, do formative and summative assessment, and maintain your sanity? I didn't really mean that last one, but today teachers are being asked to do more and more and hearing fewer and fewer good things about what is done—at least it often seems that way. The teachers with whom I work are tired: they are tired of being criticized, and they are tired of classrooms with more than forty students. They are tired of new "programs" being implemented each year. They are tired of a revolving door of administrators. They are tired of hearing all the great things they should be doing but not being given the time to plan how to do them. They want good, concrete strategies that work with all, or at least most, students, and they want something simple enough they can learn quickly and implement correctly. In this chapter, you find some simple things that work. These strategies are based on what real teachers are doing, and they also are standards-based and culturally responsive.

The integration of culturally responsive instruction and standards-based instruction is "critical to the goal of high achievement for all students. Culturally responsive teaching addresses the needs of students by improving motivation and engagement (Ginsberg & Wlodkowski, 2000), and standards-based teaching provides all students with the opportunity for rigorous, high-level learning. CRSB (culturally responsive standards-based) teaching means doing both, together" (Saifer et al., 2011, p. 8). The marriage of these two provides us with a framework for good instruction.

When I began teaching more than forty years ago, we thought good instruction was all about the content—what we knew and imparted to the students. Most educators entering the field today know better. While knowledge of content is critical, it is not everything. When students who don't look like us walk into our classes, they expect more from us than a lecture on *The Great Gatsby*. They expect us to establish a safe place for them to learn, to connect with them through passion for our subject matter, and to engage them in the learning by connecting the lesson to their personal lives all the while maintaining a lively instructional pace, incorporating technology, and using a variety of research-based strategies. As we do this, we must assess their learning, and monitor and adjust to ensure they understand the content and learn the skills we are teaching. No small order!

Students may not be able to articulate the how-to strategies they wish their teachers would use, but they will articulate when they feel their teachers do not hold high expectations for them. Jerome says his teacher walks right past his desk when she collects homework, sending him a signal she does not expect him to do it. Jeremy adds that his teacher asks him the easy questions, saving the more difficult ones for the same three students in the class. Of course, most teachers do not do these things, but when our children who don't look like us share what they perceive as low expectations from their teachers, their engagement wanes and their achievement plummets. As a result, we face the challenge of how to maintain high expectations when students don't do their homework or study for tests. If we allow students to think that we don't expect them to turn in their homework, even though that may have been their pattern, they may feel we hold low expectations for them. Rather than assigning homework and assuming some students will not do the work, we must operate from the premise of shaping instruction to challenge students and set them up for success. What does that look like?

What does good teaching look like? How do you teach students who don't look like you?

_____

_____

_____

What do you expect to see and hear in a classroom when good teaching occurs?

_____

_____

_____

Think about your students who do not look like you. What is school like for them? What do they find when they walk into your classroom?

If they are with quality teachers, they may experience a class such as the one described below. This is not on an exciting topic—it is on phrases, with an emphasis on prepositional phrases. It is boring to most, but this teacher manages to connect to the learners by using strategies available to anyone.

Imagine you are a freshman at Central High School and your name is Rhonda. Read the following vignette, and as you read, reflect on how you feel.

It's Monday, and Rhonda can't wait to go to Mrs. Smith's English class. Every day Mrs. Smith stands at her door and welcomes Rhonda, saying her name and often offering a positive comment specific to something she is wearing or has recently accomplished. On Mondays, she often asks if Rhonda had a good weekend. Rhonda feels and believes that Mrs. Smith wants her in class. Music with an upbeat tempo is playing as Rhonda enters the room, and Rhonda's mood improves as she sways to the music.

Since Mrs. Smith drilled procedures into the students' minds the first few weeks of class, Rhonda knows exactly what to do as she enters: she takes her writing folder from the plastic crate, sits down, takes out her daily assessment and feedback chart and marks the effort she plans to expend and her level of background knowledge about today's topic in the appropriate space, as well as writing down the Common Core State Standard, the Language Standard, and the objective for the day, which is clearly posted on the board in the same place every day. She also adds the SWBAT (Students Will Be Able To DO) into the graphic organizer provided weekly. She puts this back into her folder until the end of class, when she will then mark her effort for the day and the degree to which she understands the material taught. Next she takes out her class notebook and dates the page, then begins to write the prompt for the "Do Now" in her notebook. For the first few minutes of class (there is a digital timer clearly displayed on the front white board), she writes her response to the Do Now. The Do Now is a prompt based on today's lesson that connects the learning to Rhonda's life.

Students are learning how to use prepositions today, and the Do Now asks Rhonda to write for five minutes about all the ways she relates to a phone, using as many prepositions as she can from the word wall posted in the room. A sample sentence is also posted on the board that states, "When the phone rings, I look for it, pick it up, and talk into it by putting the phone next to my ear." When the timer goes off, she puts down her pen, and waits for Mrs. Smith to begin the daily sharing time.

Because Rhonda has been welcomed, knows exactly what will be taught in class that day and what she is expected to learn as a result of that teaching—and she has completed the Do Now prompt that ties into the lesson that will be taught—Rhonda is relaxed and ready to share her answer to the prompt. She knows in Mrs. Smith's class she does not have to worry about being made fun of or ridiculed by either students or the teacher. Mrs. Smith asks for three students to share, but the students are so excited about sharing their sentences that she allows several more students to share. The class laughs several times as they listen

(Continued)

(Continued)

to students' sentences packed with prepositions. Even with all the sharing, this exercise takes just a few minutes and the class is soon ready to begin the lesson.

Rhonda knows they will laugh during Mrs. Smith's class more than once every day. Rhonda is relaxed. Her brain is ready to learn. She feels good, and she is interested in what is to come because she likes and trusts Mrs. Smith and believes that Mrs. Smith is teaching them things she needs to learn. After the Do Now sharing, Mrs. Smith teaches the new lesson on phrases, specifically prepositions and prepositional phrases. She shares with the students why they need to learn about prepositions and connects it to their lives, stating they need to learn how to use prepositions correctly because they are the glue of standard English, which she calls "money English" and "green English." She emphasizes that for students to be successful in the careers or colleges they choose, they must be able to read, write, and speak green English.

Mrs. Smith has several students come to the front of the room, where they choose a part of speech, including the prepositions, and create sentences by standing in different formations. The students laugh and learn at the same time. Mrs. Smith continually checks for understanding throughout the lesson by using an assortment of formative assessments. She has students call out phrases, and when it is a prepositional phrase, students stand up. They are raising the energy in the room as well as energizing themselves. Next, students go to the class computers and find the news of the current day. They choose an article that interests them and read it, noting the prepositions. They copy one sentence into their notebook, underlining the prepositions. They return to their preassigned cooperative groups and share their work, while Mrs. Smith walks around the room and checks on each student's progress. Music plays softly in the background during the cooperative group work and the writing time. During the final minutes of class, the students use the prepositions to create a persuasive paragraph about whether cell phones should be allowed to be used by students during class time. Rhonda is interested in this topic since it relates to her life.

At the end of the hour, Mrs. Smith asks students to take out their assessment sheet and mark their level of effort and understanding for the day's lesson. Rhonda completes her sheet, picks up her books and writing folder, and places the folder in the crate on her way out of the room. Rhonda knows her homework is to continue reading in her self-selected novel in preparation for the long-term project she is doing. She hands Mrs. Smith her assessment sheet and the paragraph she has written as she walks out the door. Mrs. Smith smiles at each student and thanks them for working hard in class that day.

A feedback and assessment chart like the one mentioned above can be found in Jane Pollock's (2012, p. 23) book, *Feedback: The Hinge That Joins Teaching and Learning.*

❖ ❖ ❖

Granted, that lesson was mostly lower level thinking, yet Mrs. Smith found a way to make even that fun and enjoyable. If we can engage students around learning something as mundane as prepositions, then we certainly can engage them in lessons involving higher level evaluation, synthesis, and creativity.

What strategies did Mrs. Smith use to engage her students?

_____

_____

_____

Mrs. Smith uses a myriad of instructional strategies, as well as relationship strategies. She builds relationships with her students and supports learning through the following:

- Offering warm welcomes
- Connecting the Do Now activity to the lesson
- Having students record the objective and write the SWBAT for the day
- Connecting the lesson to students' lives
- Using humor
- Using clear and explicit procedures and guidelines
- Teaching to the CCSS for language arts
- Posting the language standard and incorporating it into her instruction
- Expecting students will meet the objective
- Giving clear and explicit direct instruction
- Using guided practice
- Using a visual timer for discussion, reflection, and other work
- Using graphic organizers
- Using nonverbal commands
- Using direct verbal commands
- Incorporating formative assessment throughout the lesson in the forms of the "white boards," "thumbs-up, thumbs-down," students standing up, and other nonverbal responses
- Incorporating formative assessment by asking questions of the class
- Incorporating formative assessment by the use of the formal self-assessment chart
- Using movement by having students stand at desks when they know the answer
- Using movement by having students create sentences at the front of the room
- Using visual and kinesthetic cues when students tie the parts of speech to certain students
- Having students talking with each other
- Having students using higher level thinking when they begin creating their own paragraphs
- Holding high expectations
- Using good classroom management strategies
- Having students work with others
- Ending with a creative activity to embed the learning and collecting it at the end of class

- Collecting student paragraphs as a "check-out" activity to assess what the students have learned to support her planning for the following day
- Telling the students goodbye by standing at the door, smiling, and making comments

To view videos of exemplary teachers demonstrating the strategies that Mrs. Smith uses in her lesson, go to School Improvement Network's *PD 360 Bonnie Davis Group* (http://www.schoolimprovement.com/experts/bonnie-davis) and check out the following videos.

Formative Assessment

- Learning 360 Framework E & S—Segment 5, Formative Assessment

Cooperative Groups, Pair/Share (Any Kinds of Student Groups or Collaborative Work)

- Achievement for Students With Special Needs E & S—Segment 11, The Value of Grouping and Working in Teams

Note Taking and Summarizing During Direct Instruction

- Classroom Instruction That Works E & S—Segment 4, Summarizing and Note-Taking

Setting Objectives, Setting Goals, Teaching to the Standards

- Learning 360 Framework E & S—Segment 5, Formative Assessment (Teaching to the Standards)
- Learning 360 Framework E & S—Segment 9, Cue Sets (Objectives, Goals)

Brain-Based Strategies Such as Physical Movement, Music, Repetition

- Achievement for Students With Special Needs E—Segment 10, Classroom Practices That Work (Repetition)
- Growing Dendrites: 20 Instructional Strategies That Engage the Brain—Segment 4, Music, Rhythm, Rhyme, and Rap

Making Students Visible and Acknowledging Students (Culturally Responsive Instruction—Your Best Examples of CRI)

- Effective Professional Development—Segment 4, Study Elementary: At the Brink
- Courageous Conversations About Race—Segment 8, Equity in a School Community
- How to Increase Minority Student Achievement—Segment 1, Closing the Gaps

Differentiated Instruction

- Differentiated Instruction Applied E—Segment 8, The Applied Differentiation Map: What?

Questioning Strategies, Higher Level Questioning, Equitable Calling on Students

- Learning 360 Framework E & S—Segment 4, The Guiding/Essential Questions
- Learning 360 Framework E & S—Segment 7, Summative Assessment and Backward Design

Individualized Project-Based Learning

- Equity and Innovation: Kihei Charter School—Segment 3, Project-Based Learning
- Teaching Strategies, Secondary, Differentiating Projects in a Science Class

Vocabulary, Writing, and Reading Instruction

- Differentiated Instruction Applied E & S—Segment 7, The Applied Differentiation Map
- Achievement for Students With Special Needs E & S—Segment 4, Strategies—CLC Level 3

In addition to these listed videos, do a general search on the PD 360 Web site and check out videos that demonstrate teachers using the following strategies: Teaching Literacy (all levels); Assessment; Note Taking and Summarizing During DI; Questioning Strategies; Higher Level Questioning; Equitable Calling on Students; and any others that interest you.

Mrs. Smith demonstrates how to teach a "boring" content piece in an interesting way. In no way is this an example of a higher-level instructional class; rather, it is intended to show how even teaching prepositions can be designed to engage and motivate students. In the next chapter are several lesson ideas that depend upon higher level thinking, rigorous investigation, creativity, and individualized project based learning.

USING TWENTY-FIRST CENTURY TECHNOLOGY

If Mrs. Smith is fortunate to teach in a district that honors the use of technology and provides it for staff and students, we would add the use of the iPad or iPod Touch or iPhone to the description above. In *Apps for Learning: 40 Best iPad, iPod Touch/iPhone Apps for High School Classrooms*, Harry Dickens and Andrew Churches (2012) suggest using technology to extend learning and embed content and skills into long-term memory. Dickens believes "we must embrace mobile technologies as a teaching tool, as well as a delivery mechanism for relevant content for classrooms" (p. i). In fact, "it is no longer enough that we educate only to the standards of the traditional literacies. To be competent and capable in the 21st century requires a completely different set of skills—the 21st-century fluencies" (p. vi). With the lesson described above, Mrs. Smith might have learners use the following Apps: iThoughtsHD; Skype (for interviewing authors); and StoryKit (for creating stories). In the book are scores of others to use with lessons across the disciplines. This is an area where students love to be involved and suggest uses for the apps they find.

In her book *Transformers: Creative Teachers for the 21st Century*, Mary Kim Schreck (2009) tells us that "in the past decade, educators have shifted from emphasizing learning *about* technologies to learning *with* technologies" (p. 157). She suggests that if you don't already have the standards for teaching technology, you can obtain copies of the National Educational Technology Standards (NETS) for students and for teachers from the International Society for Technology in Education (ISTE) at www.iste.org. Schreck's suggestions for using technology in the classroom include the following:

- Increase engagement with the curriculum by incorporating complex, real-world problems and investigate them learning with technology.
- Provide access to information and tools that professionals use to create high-quality work. Third graders can create professional looking PowerPoint presentations. Students can use the same search engines, such as Google or Yahoo!, as professionals. Students can compose their own music using sequencers and notation software and perform it using Musical Instrument Digital Interface (MIDI) software.
- Scaffold learning using technologies such as calculators, spreadsheets, databases, data visualization tools—such as InspireData from Inspiration Software, Geometer's Sketchpad, Google's free SketchUP solftware—and the role-playing Decisions, Decision software.
- Provide opportunities to reflect on student understanding and identify changes in student learning using concept maps and graphic organizers, and digital journals or portfolios.
- Collaborate and communicate with others using e-mail and the range of online pen pal programs, such as ePals, Skype, Weblog, iChat, MySpace, and Facebook. Be sure to follow your district guidelines for social media! (pp. 161–170)

Granted, this book does not focus on technology, yet we acknowledge the importance of infusing technology into instruction, and we cite Web sites and examples of lessons that infuse technology in Chapters 15 and 16. In addition, for your own professional development, there are Web sites listed throughout the book pertaining to the material presented in the chapters, and we suggest you go to School Improvement Network's site (http://www.schoolimprove ment.com/experts/bonnie-davis) and watch the PD 360 videos provided that align with many of the strategies described in this book.

CLASSROOM MANAGEMENT: USE OF RITUALS AND ROUTINES

One of the strongest teachers I recently observed is Jessica Jones, a high school English teacher in California. With classrooms of more than forty students, she is like a conductor of a symphony: always in control and leading the way. She says she does it through her use of daily rituals and routines. She shares below:

RITUALS AND ROUTINES

Jessica Jones

I have the same basic routine every day, regardless of the class or grade level.

The first one to three minutes after the bell rings I stand in the middle of the room, with my clipboard in hand, thanking students (individually and by name) who have already started the Do Now. For example: "I see one, two, three, wait... four students working already. Thank you James, thank you Melissa, thank you Melanie, thank you Thomas." Once I begin thanking students, the room usually quiets immediately because everyone wants to be acknowledged in front of the class.

The next four or five minutes, I circulate the room as students silently complete the Do Now. This is probably my favorite time of day; everyone is quiet and on task! After I have circulated the entire room, I write down the names of two students as the "positive role models" for the day.

The next five or six minutes, we read the objective for the day's work, the class rules, go over the Do Now together, do a vocabulary/grammar sentence on the board, and complete the infamous check-in.

By this point, everyone is engaged and "checked in," so I proceed with the day's agenda. I spend a moment to remind students of upcoming assignments and quizzes, and then we review whatever was discussed the previous day. I ask students to look back at the notes from the day before as I ask general questions; they receive points on the clipboard for participating. This generally takes three to four minutes.

Next we read whatever selection we're currently discussing. We read for no more than twelve to fifteen minutes (with reading check questions and discussion as we go). After reading as a group, I let students pair off to complete whatever partner assignment I have prepared. It may be under-the-surface questions or some type of graphic organizer based on the selection. They usually have seven to ten minutes to complete the task. I circulate the room, frequently announcing how many minutes are left to help students stay on task. At the end of the allotted time, I walk around and stamp their work (most work is completed in their notebooks).

At this time, we review the reading and partner tasks together. This usually takes about five minutes.

Depending on the depth of the discussions, we may have about five to seven minutes left of class. I use this time for "one-minute speeches." I pull four student names from a stack of index cards, while another student chooses four topic cards at random. Each student chosen has one minute to stand to talk about whatever comes to mind with that particular topic (such as food, sports, movies). I love this activity because not only do we utilize every minute of class, it's a fun way for students to practice public speaking skills and also to learn more about each other. Even my name is in the stack of cards, so occasionally I'm chosen to speak as well.

OK, there it is—a day in the life of H622!

The check-in mentioned above is a community-building exercise in which the teacher asks a question and each student has the opportunity to give a one-word answer or say "pass."

❖ ❖ ❖

Jessica uses the same basic class framework every day with every level, ninth grade through twelfth grade. Students come in knowing they will

- Be respected and treated fairly
- Be involved in several different activities within the class period, which makes the time go faster and maintains a lively pace
- Be working with peers
- Have a chance to hear from peers during the check-in and other activities
- Receive proximity and be noticed by Ms. Jones
- Receive help when they need it
- Be expected to work, participate, and follow the class rules

Jessica is successful with all learners. She uses a framework of rituals and routines that reduce stress and threat, build community among all class members, and set the stage for learning. Her consistency, calm demeanor, and clear expectations support all students. In her classes, African American males have their hands raised and can't wait to participate. Over the three years I observed her classes, I have yet to see a student who was not participating. In addition, her daily vocabulary and grammar exercises and repetition of expectations support ELs as she includes language goals in her daily practice.

ENGLISH LANGUAGE LEARNERS

After the publication of *How to Teach Students Who Don't Look Like You* in 2006, an educator who worked with teachers of ELs contacted me. She complimented me on the strategies to teach ELs in the book. I was happy to hear this, but I had no training in this field and was surprised to hear her comment. Yet now after reading about and working with ELs in a large urban district on the West Coast for the past several years, I understand better what she meant. The strategies we need to use with ELs consist of good teaching practices we learned in brain-based workshops, cooperative learning, culturally responsive workshops, and other professional development work. These strategies work, yet there are also additional strategies we need to use when we are working with ELs. Determined to learn what these are, I read several books on the topic and worked with EL teachers. I learned that we all need to be teachers of English and reading. This can be daunting to teachers in other content areas, but we can employ concrete strategies, such as teaching vocabulary before one begins the lesson (sometimes called *frontloading*). You can find other strategies throughout this chapter. In addition to these strategies, we need to keep in mind the diversity of our ELs.

Because students with limited English proficiency come from 400 different language backgrounds and number more than 5 million, there is an immense diversity among ELs. However, nearly 80 percent of these are Spanish speakers (Kindler, cited in Goldenberg & Coleman, 2010, p. 11). Surprisingly, "recent statistical trends in U.S. secondary schools indicate that 80% to 90% of ELs in middle and high school are actually born in the United States" (Calderón & Minaya-Rowe, 2011, p. 1). The challenge then is in understanding how ELs learn best. What works and what doesn't? Fortunately, Claude Goldenberg and

Rhoda Coleman have done much of the work in the field to find the answers for us, and they published them in their book, *Promoting Academic Achievement Among English Learners*, in 2010. In their book, they list many recommendations for working with ELs, including the following:

- Use reading and other instructional materials students recognize.
- Use interactional styles students recognize and are familiar to them.
- Involve parents and families in students' education.
- Make home visits to get to know families and the community. (pp. 132–133)

They conclude their studies by offering a final set of recommendation, ones that speak to teachers in the classroom:

- Remember that the foundation of effective practice for ELs is the same as effective practice *in general*.
- ELs receiving instruction in English will need additional supports.
- Choose strategies based on an understanding of research-based practices.
- Focus on academic language.
- Take advantage of professional development.
- Provide instruction for ELs throughout the school day.
- Administer uniform and consistent assessments of student outcomes in literacy, content areas, and English language development.
- Work with colleagues to identify important academic goals for ELs.
- Use peer coaching. (pp. 168–170)

Their list is comforting because so many of their suggestions are what good teachers already do. Understanding that EL students will need extra support, we can take advantage of professional development, work in collaboration with our colleagues, and choose research-based strategies for ELs such as those found in *Classroom Instruction That Works With English Language Learners* (Hill & Flynn, 2006). The strategies identified in this book are the result of a meta-analysis, a combination of "the results of many studies to determine the average effect of a technique or strategy" (p. 6). The researchers at McREL identified, as a result of the meta-analysis, nine categories of instructional strategies that proved to be exceptionally effective in increasing student performance:

1. Setting objectives and providing feedback

2. Nonlinguistic representations

3. Cues, questions, and advance organizers

4. Cooperative learning

5. Summarizing and note taking

6. Homework and practice

7. Reinforcing effort and providing recognition

8. Generating and testing hypotheses

9. Identifying similarities and differences (p. 6)

This list of research-based strategies is one place to begin with your professional learning community to study what can best support your ELs. You might choose one strategy, all practice implementing it for three weeks, and then share results. In this way, you will keep the focus on your EL students, and that can improve your relationships with them.

Many other strategies and suggestions can be found in books for teachers with ELs in their classes. In their book, *Preventing Long-Term ELs*, Calderón and Minaya-Rowe (2011) have the following recommendations for teachers. These recommendations come from the Carnegie Panel on Adolescent EL Literacy (Short & Fitzsimmons, 2007). The panel of thirteen recommended the following for teachers:

- Integrate listening, speaking, reading, and writing skills into instruction from the start.
- Teach the components and processes of reading and writing.
- Teach reading comprehension strategies.
- Focus on vocabulary development.
- Build and activate background knowledge.
- Teach language through content and themes.
- Use native language strategically.
- Pair technology with existing interventions.
- Motivate adolescent ELs through choice. (Calderón & Minaya-Rowe, p. 8)

Looking over this list, the only ones that are not part of a strong teacher's repertoire are teaching language through content and themes and using native language strategically. The others are integral to good teaching that uses a strong literacy focus of writing and reading across the content areas, as well as the brain-based strategies such as choice and activating background knowledge.

When classroom teachers express that they don't know how to teach ELs, you can remind them that if they are using good instructional strategies, they are already part way there. Learning additional strategies to specifically meet the needs of ELs is the next step. In *Implementing RTI With English Learners*, professors and practitioners Fisher, Frey, and Rothenberg (2011) suggest that to effectively teach ELs, teachers need to view themselves as language teachers and know the proficiency levels of their students. (I sometimes find teachers who cannot tell me the country a particular student is from—"Oh, he's Asian"—and they don't know the learner's proficiency level.) After examining the available models for instruction, Fisher, Frey, and Rothenberg find the following standards of teaching practice embedded within all of them.

- Teachers and students producing together
- Developing language and literacy across the curriculum
- Making lessons meaningful
- Teaching complex thinking
- Teaching through conversation (p. 25)

They emphasize that these standards can all be taught in Tier I of Response to Intervention (RTI), or taught in the general classroom by the teacher.

After reviewing the research and reading several books on teaching ELs, I learned the following:

- Use research-based teaching strategies with ELs.
- Go over vocabulary deliberately before the lesson and use it repeatedly throughout the lesson.
- Use culturally responsive relationship building strategies.
- Explicitly teach the "mental models" of your discipline. For example, for English teachers, this means we teach the model of a plot line explicitly.
- Assess often in order to remain aware of the learner's needs.
- Know the country of origin of each EL, something about that country and culture, and what level of English the student has mastered.
- Care about your ELs and express that to them by calling on them in class, keeping your expectations high, building a community that welcomes all learners, and smiling and enjoying what you teach.

Returning to the example of Mrs. Smith, we find that she meets the needs of her ELs by also embedding language standards into her lessons. She addresses each of the standards of teaching practice for ELs suggested by Fisher et al. (2011) in the example at the beginning of this chapter.

In Mrs. Smith's lesson, she works with her students throughout the class to develop language and literacy skills that will be used across the curriculum. She makes her lessons meaningful by connecting them to students' lives and by stressing their importance. She frontloads the vocabulary for her ELs and checks for comprehension, making sure they understand the work. She teaches complex thinking by having students practice using the new information to create their own paragraphs, and she has the students work together in groups, thus practicing their learning during conversation. She also understands the importance of connecting with each learner and makes sure she greets each student at the door.

❖ ❖ ❖

RELATIONSHIPS AND RELATIONSHIPS

These practices show Mrs. Smith's students she cares about them and expects them to succeed. Some educators find it a stretch to connect relationship building to actual instruction and student achievement. Yet as learners we usually perform better when we feel safe and comfortable, and that occurs when we are surrounded by people we enjoy and we believe care about us. Think about a time when you were asked to do something with a person you didn't like, versus a time when you were asked to do something with someone you cared about and liked. Didn't you find yourself dreading doing the first task but not as hesitant to work on the second? The environment, both physical and emotional, affects the engagement of students, and when students feel they are liked (or loved), they respond in kind.

Also, when students believe they are being held to high expectations of material that is neither too difficult nor too easy, they respond in kind. Mrs. Smith, who does not look like her students, relates to them in ways that demonstrate she holds high expectations for them, and she engages students with connections to their experiences showing she respects them. She knows she must learn about her students' cultures, and she devotes time and effort to study the cultures of her students. She has participated in professional development focusing on building relationships with students and learning the cultural homogeneities (norms of a culture reinforced by the culture) of her students' cultures. Putting into practice what she has learned has given Mrs. Smith a knowledge base from which she draws as she confidently interacts with students who don't look like her. Her body language is relaxed and respectful, and her students sense her respect for them. Throughout this book, you will find how-to strategies to build relationships with students that connect to their ethnic and racial cultures within the context of standards-based instruction.

FEEDBACK

In Jane E. Pollock's 2012 book, *Feedback: The Hinge That Joins Teaching and Learning*, we find an answer to engaging students and improving student achievement. Pollock writes: "The hinge factor to improving student learning in schools is feedback. . . . When we address feedback as a strategy that teachers can teach students to use, student engagement increases and so does student achievement" (p. xi). This was a new idea to me, and even though I have had students do reflections, I have never embedded it as a strategy within instruction. I am so excited about the possibilities for doing this that I've spread the word about this book, with its simple charts, to use to teach students to self-assess their engagement and their learning. Several teachers are using Pollock's work to do just that and are beginning to see results. From AP classes to struggling readers, this feedback strategy works.

It only makes sense. We know most engaged learners achieve more, and when we engage, we want feedback. Pollock writes that high-achieving students have learned to seek feedback, thus staying more engaged with the work. Therefore, if we can teach our disengaged learners techniques for seeking feedback, this will also keep them more engaged.

Pollock coauthored *Classroom Instruction That Works* with Robert Marzano and Debra Pickering (2001), a seminal text in the area of classroom instructional strategies. In that work, the authors

> posited that teachers at any grade level in any subject area could significantly improve learning if they deliberately taught students to use high-yield strategies in order to retain knowledge better, or learn better. One of the strategies, setting goals and providing feedback, showed a strong effect on learning ($d = 0.61$, or a 23 percentile point gain, considered to be very high). (quoted in J. E. Pollock, 2012, p. 3)

Pollock continues to research the effectiveness of feedback as an instructional strategy, and her findings were published in the 2012 book *Feedback: The*

Hinge That Joins Teaching and Learning. In this book, she expands on the role of feedback in instruction, stating that feedback "tied to a criterion or goal also clarifies relevant prospects for learning more information or for acting" on that goal. This action, whether learning or acting, "intends to improve outcomes and as a result, provides the opportunity for a newly advanced goal." As a result, feedback "can be the hinge factor for improving student learning" (J. E. Pollock, 2012, p. 3).

Why have we not recognized student self-assessment and feedback as an answer for engaging students and improving achievement? Pollock points to two reasons. First, most feedback has been from the teacher to the student, mostly as an assessment of student progress, and asking teachers to do more feedback elicits negative comments from those already feeling overworked. Second, most teachers

> provide a curriculum goal (and objectives) to students, but not deliberately for explicit interaction (setting objectives and providing feedback), so students have not typically learned to self-evaluate or self-regulate their progress using curriculum objectives, thereby reducing the gaps between what they know and can do and the desired goals for their grade level and subject area. (J. E. Pollock, 2012, pp. 3–4)

Therefore, if we can teach learners the tools they need to self-assess, we mediate the first concern; and for the second concern, if the teacher provides "curriculum goals and objectives daily, with a strategy and time for students to interact with them," they teach learners how to engage and achieve (p. 4).

Consider using Pollock's (2012) book *Feedback: The Hinge That Joins Teaching and Learning* with your professional learning groups. You and your colleagues can use the charts found in the book to do your own action research. For example, use the charts with one of your classes, or if you teach in elementary school, use it for part of the day, and then notice if you see improved student engagement and learning after a month. Pollock's research states that in just weeks, teachers see a marked difference in effort and achievement. Marzano writes: "Having students track their [own] progress using [a] rubric is a hidden gem. This strategy involves multiple types of assessments, increases interactions between teachers and students, and provides students with clear guidance on how to enhance their learning" (quoted in J. E. Pollock, 2012, p. 87).

The feedback strategy may well be the most important instructional strategy you can use, for you are having learners attend to the standard and what is to be taught that day, assess their effort and build self-efficacy through the practice, and stay focused on the lesson, thus engaging student brains. When learners do this, they are goal setting, and that is research-based practice.

Feedback strategies for formative and summative assessment are also available in Kay Burke's 2010 book, *Balanced Assessment.* In this book you will find dozens of tools to use for assessment that support you in creating assessments leading from formative to summative. These are excellent tools to share with your professional learning groups.

FOUR QUESTIONS TO ASSESS ENGAGEMENT

Secondary teachers often voice their concerns about the lack of student engagement in their middle and high school classrooms. Fortunately, Robert J. Marzano and Debra J. Pickering (2011), in their book *The Highly Engaged Classroom,* offer a perspective with a strategy to mediate this concern. They "articulate an internally consistent perspective on engagement that K–12 classroom teachers can use to plan and execute specific strategies that enhance student engagement" (p. 3) and offer teachers four questions to use when planning instruction: "How do I feel? . . . Am I interested? . . . Is it important? . . . Can I do it?" (pp. 1–2). We presented these questions in a professional development session at an urban high school. Teachers were intrigued, and a week later during their next collaboration, several teachers said using these four questions supported them in understanding which parts of their instruction they needed to focus on and improve. Most acknowledged they need to begin class with a positive-feeling tone, such as Mrs. Smith did in the earlier vignette. Next, a department of math teachers said they get caught with "Am I interested?" because their students are not interested in math. Therefore, they need to work on strategies to interest learners. The science department at the same high school said they can usually interest students with demonstrations and labs, but they get hung up on "Is it important?" and need to find ways to connect the learning to students' future lives. Finally, the question "Can I do it?" was a wake-up call for the entire staff as they realized that in their school many students believe they can't do the work, and the staff needs to work in collaboration to find ways to support student success and empower the belief systems of their students and staff. To address this, one professional learning group elected to do a bookstudy on Carol Dweck's (2006) book, *Mindset: The New Psychology of Success,* and report back to the staff. This book addresses the challenge of working with learners who possess a fixed mind-set and gives ways to support changing mind-sets or belief systems.

In the past decade, we have been blessed with a body of research and thoughtful practices that have made teaching more of a science, while our understanding of its art continues to expand. Sometimes we teachers complain that teaching is hard work. It is! It is a profession that demands long hours, emotional give and take, and just about everything else one has to give on a job.

When good teaching occurs, you usually will find the following:

- Good relationships between students and the teacher
- High expectations for students
- The classroom bonding as a community of learners
- Good classroom management
- Lesson plan design based on research; the use of a model
- Standards-based instruction
- Goal setting for instruction
- Explicit instruction
- Graphic organizers; nonlinguistic representation
- Rubrics before instruction or completion of assignment
- Assessment and accountability
- Goal setting for future achievement

- Support from professional personnel such as counselors, special education instructors, nurses, administrators, and so on
- Good relationships with colleagues
- Valuable feedback from evaluators
- The belief that teaching is a profession, not just a job
- Professional development opportunities
- Opportunities to practice the discipline you teach—if you teach English, the opportunity to write for publication, and so on

When there is engagement between the teacher and the content, and students believe the teacher cares for them, the students will engage with the content and with the caring teacher.

Think about your teaching. What are your instructional strengths and challenges?

_____

_____

_____

How does the research inform your instructional practice?

_____

_____

_____

How would you like to improve your instructional practice?

_____

_____

_____

Set three goals to improve your instructional practice.

_____

_____

_____

This chapter examined powerful instruction and offered practical strategies for you to include in your practice. Once again, to see these strategies in action, go to PD 360 (http://www.schoolimprovement.com/experts/bonnie-davis) and check out their videos.

Do you like to read and write? Hopefully, you said "Yes!" Far too often, we find students, particularly secondary students, who have lost their love of reading and writing. How do you get that back? The next chapter tells you how and focuses on moving learners from apathy to passion and supporting them in learning to love reading and writing.

❖　❖　❖

SUGGESTED READINGS

English Language Learners

Calderón, Margarita E., and Liliana Minaya-Rowe. *Preventing Long-Term ELs: Transforming Schools to Meet Core Standards* (Thousand Oaks, CA: Corwin, 2011).

Fisher, Douglas, Nancy Frey, and Carol Rothenberg. *Implementing RTI With English Learners* (Bloomington, IN: Solution Tree, 2011).

Goldenberg, Claude, and Rhoda Coleman. *Promoting Academic Achievement Among English Learners: A Guide to the Research* (Thousand Oaks, CA: Corwin, 2010).

Hill, Jane, and Kathleen Flynn. *Classroom Instruction That Works With English Language Learners* (Alexandria, VA: ASCD, 2006).

Saifer, Steffen, Keisha Edwards, Debbie Ellis, Lena Ko, and Amy Stuczynski. *Culturally Responsive Standards Based Teaching: Classroom to Community and Back,* second edition (Thousand Oaks, CA: Corwin, 2011).

Soto-Hinman, Ivannia, and June Hetzel. *The Literacy Gaps: Bridge-Building Strategies for English Language Learners and Standard English Learners* (Thousand Oaks, CA: Corwin, 2009).

Engagement

Dweck, Carol S. *Mindset: The New Psychology of Success* (New York: Ballantine Books, 2006).

Pollock, Jane E. *Feedback: The Hinge That Joins Teaching and Learning* (Thousand Oaks, CA: Corwin, 2012).

Marzano, Robert J., and Debra J. Pickering. *The Highly Engaged Classroom* (Bloomington, IN: Marzano Research Laboratory, 2001).

Schreck, Mary Kim. *You've Got to Reach Them to Teach Them* (Bloomington, IN: Solution Tree, 2011).

SUGGESTED WEB SITES

English Language Learners Resources (www.ascd.org/research-a-topic/english-language-learners-resources.aspx

Focus on Effectiveness: Current Education Challenges (www.netc.org/focus/challenges/ell.php)

Teachers of English to Speakers of Other Languages (www.tesol.org)

Teaching Long-Term English Language Learners (http://teacher.scholastic.com/products/teach-english-language-learners/english3d.html)

Teach-nology.com (www.teach-nology.com)

13

Moving Students From Apathy to Passion

Learning to Love Reading and Writing

How do we teach diverse learners to love to read and write? Students should love to read and write. Reading takes us to other worlds, offering us excitement, solace, understanding, and companionship. Writing gives us power—the power to influence and change our world, the means to ameliorate friendships through written communication, the tool to understand our inner selves. Yet, all too often, our students resist reading and writing. This chapter discusses ways to encourage students to fall in love with reading and writing.

Do your students resist falling in love with reading and writing? Why? There are several reasons.

- They may have had teachers who were not readers and writers themselves.
- They may be in schools where a culture of reading and writing is not valued.
- They may not see themselves in their assigned texts in schools.
- They may never be offered the opportunities to write about themselves and tell the most important story—their own.
- They may not know how to read or to write.

What can you do to motivate all of your students to love reading and writing? Reading is a complex, recursive thinking process (Fielding & Pearson,

1994; Ogle, cited in Tovani, 2000), and successful readers use the following strategies to navigate the process (Pearson et al., cited in Tovani, 2000):

- They use existing knowledge to make sense of new information.
- They ask questions about the text before, during, and after reading.
- They draw inferences from the text.
- They monitor their comprehension.
- They use strategies when they don't comprehend.
- They decide what is important.
- They synthesize information to create new thinking. (p. 17)

Knowing that students need these strategies, what do you do to encourage your students to develop these skills and learn to love reading? For too many students, reading is just "eating" words with no time to savor them, thinking about the text, and connecting it to their world (Keene & Zimmermann, 1997). And for diverse learners, who may not find themselves represented in the required texts, this can be an even more formidable task.

COMMON CORE STATE STANDARDS

The CCSS for Reading Literature are K–12.RL.1 to K–12.RL.10. And the ones for Reading Informational Text are K–12.RIT.1 to K–12.RIT.10.

TEXTS THAT REFLECT CULTURES

It is important for students to read texts that reflect their cultures and reflect them accurately. Students need to recognize stereotypes, either by omission or by caricature (Fountas & Pinnell, 2001). Finding ways for students to make connections to their own lives and to other texts can build motivation in the most stubborn of readers. For example, finding the "right" text for the unmotivated reader can open him or her to the world of reading. Hispanic students can perhaps find themselves reflected in books such as *Mother Goose on the Rio Grande* by Frances Alexander (1997) or *My Name Is Jorge on Both Sides of the River* by Jane Medina (1999). The Bluford Series has hooked scores of readers in our metropolitan area. These books are short, with compelling covers illustrated with African American adolescents, and the stories relate to young lives. You can buy them online at www.townsendpress.com, and they are offered in a kit with a teacher's guide.

You can find additional books that teens enjoy in *I Hear America Reading* by Jim Burke (1999b). Burke lists books that teenage boys enjoy, such as *Always Running* by Luis Rodriguez (1993), *Ender's Game* by Orson Scott Card (1985), *The Things They Carried* by Tim O'Brien (1990), and *Way Past Cool* by Jess Mowry (1992). He includes lists of books such as *Books for a Small Planet: A Multicultural-Intercultural Bibliography for Young English Language Learners* by Dorothy Brown (1994) and *Great Books for Girls: More Than 600 Books to Inspire Today's Girls and Tomorrow's Women* by Kathy Odean (2002).

A school that reflects a powerful reading and writing culture invariably has a powerful librarian who builds, influences, and nourishes that culture. This librarian is a gatekeeper; he or she can impede students in their reading journeys or open worlds of possibilities for them. I was fortunate to work with Marti Gribbins, a librarian who opened these worlds of possibilities for middle school students at Wydown Middle School, one of the highest achieving middle schools in the state of Missouri. Marti knew the reading interests of each student, and she always had a book to hand them as they searched for their next reads. The seventh graders read a book a week, or 36 books a year, and we posted our book list on the walls of the school for everyone to see. However, this reading culture did not begin at the middle school; it existed in the elementary schools in this district, and most probably in the homes of the students.

Another powerful librarian is Nancy McCormac, librarian at North Glendale Elementary School in the Kirkwood School District. Nancy builds a reading culture, along with reading specialist Roberta McWoods, by individualizing learning and knowing each student as an individual. Students see themselves reflected in the book covers that line the shelves of the library and are posted in the hallways. Librarian Nancy suggests the following books for elementary students:

Whoever You Are by Mem Fox (2006). Illustrated with Leslie Straub's folk art style painting, the book celebrates the similarities and differences of the world's many diverse cultures.

All the Colors of the Earth by Sheila Hamanaka (1999). Colorful paintings and text describe children's skin and hair colors, referencing such phenomena as nature, animals, and flavors.

Being Wendy by Fran Dreschler (2011). Wendy learns to follow her dreams and not be limited by what others think she should be.

The Sandwich Swap by Queen Rania Al Abdullah and Kelly DiPucchio (2010). Lily and Salma always eat lunch together, Lily having her peanut butter sandwich, and Salma, hummus. In this story, they and their classmates learn that friendship is more powerful than their differences.

One of Us by Peggy Moss (2010). Roberta struggles to find her place in a new school until she discovers a group of kids who accept her because they, like her, are all different and "perfect" that way.

The Colors of Us by Karen Katz (2002). Lena learns that brown comes in many shades and begins to see and appreciate them as colors of her favorite foods.

Drita, My Homegirl by Jenny Lombard (2006). The story of two girls, one a refugee from war-torn Kosovo, who become friends in a very unlikely way.

The Skin You Live In by Michael Tyler (2005). Rhyming verses and colorful illustrations look at diversity and focus on skins, differences, and similarities.

Yo! Yes? by Chris Raschka (1998). In just thirty-four words and with vibrant illustrations, this book tells of a beginning friendship between two very different boys who meet on the street.

Shades of People by Shelley Rotner and Sheila Kelly (2009). Minimal text and wonderful photos of children with different hair colors, facial features, and skin tones, emphasizing that you can't tell from their features what someone is like.

Skin Again by Bell Hooks (2004). A powerful reminder that helps children understand that we are more than the color of our skin.

Chamelia by Ethan Long (2011). A little girl chameleon learns that she can be different in her own ways and still fit in.

Amazing Grace by Mary Hoffman (1991). Grace loves stories and has a vivid imagination. She's determined to win the role of Peter Pan in her classroom production even though she's a girl, and black.

It's Okay to Be Different by Todd Parr (2009). This book inspires kids to celebrate their individuality with important messages of understanding and acceptance.

Young Adult Library Services Association (YALSA: www.yalsa.ala.org) recommends the following books published in 2010 and 2011 for readers ages twelve to eighteen:

Where the Streets Had a Name by Randa Abel-Fattah (2010). Hayaat wants to get soil from her ancestral homeland to save her dying grandmother, but to get it, she must illegally cross the wall dividing Jerusalem's West Bank.

I am J by Chris Beam (2011). The story of J., a genetically assigned female, who struggles to become the man he is.

Bronxwood by Coe Booth (2011). Tyrell confronts his dad, searches for equipment for his DJing gig, and pursues his love interests.

Hush by Eishes Chayil (2010). A girl's ultraconservative Jewish community will not listen to a young girl who tries to share another's secrets.

Where I Belong by Gillian Cross (2011). A Somalian girl goes to England in search of work for money to send to her family.

My Name Is Not Easy by Debby Dahl Edwardson (2011). Alaskan Inupiaq young people are forced into boarding schools away from their families.

Under the Mesquite by Guadalupe Garcia McCall (2011). Lupita's mother has cancer, and this tightly knit Mexican American family faces many changes.

Akata Witch by Nnedi Okorafor (2011). American-born Sunny, an albino, lives in Nigeria and discovers juju and magical powers to survive being a misfit.

Guantanamo Boy by Anna Perera (2011). Fifteen-year-old Khalid Ahmed visits family in Pakistan and ends up being arrested and sent to Guantanamo accused of being a terrorist.

YOUR READING LIFE AND HISTORY

Finding that right book for each reader is an art and a skill that we continue to refine as we share our own love of reading with our students. Who we are as readers is important. Take the following survey to check your love of reading.

❑   Are you a reader?

❑   Do you love to read?

❑   Do you always carry a book with you?

❑   Do you read a daily newspaper?

❑   Do you know what books are on the bestseller lists?

❑   Do your students see you reading?

❑   Do your students hear you talk about what you are reading?

❑   Is your voice passionate when you talk about reading?

❐ Are you expecting your students to do and love something for which you show no passion?

❐ Can we really ask another human being to do what we are unwilling to do?

Write a short reflection about what these questions say personally to you.

_____

_____

_____

_____

_____

_____

Think about reading in your life. Did your parents read to you? Was your childhood home filled with books? Did you observe your parents reading? What is the first book you read? What was your _favorite_ childhood book?

Answering these questions can reveal just how important reading is to you. Do you think your students will think reading is more important than you think it is? Unless you are a voracious reader who speaks passionately about reading to your students, you may find that your students are less than passionate about reading.

Write your reading history in the space provided below.

_____

_____

_____

_____

_____

_____

Let me share my story.

I grew up in a home where my mother read a story to my sisters and me each night at bedtime. I kept lots of children's books in my bedroom. I don't recall ever seeing my parents read a book, but both of my parents read the daily newspaper. On Sundays, my dad would read the funnies to me from the Sunday newspaper.

I remember learning to read in first grade. I remember practicing the letter sounds. I loved reading from the start. I checked out library books whenever I could, and I read every spare moment. During the summer, I would pride myself on reading a book a day. By fifth grade I was reading mysteries and historical fiction. I read the Nancy Drew series and remember them as my favorites for those middle years. By junior high I was reading biographies, and I remember my mother begging me to go "outside and play" instead of sitting inside on summer days reading a book.

In high school I began to read serious literature, and I was blessed to have an outstanding English teacher, Sister Francesca, for my last three years of high school English. She laughed often and loved literature. When I commented to her that I liked Robert Frost, she handed me a paperback copy of his poems. I still have it today. It has the price clearly marked on the front cover—35 cents. I continued to read for hours each day.

Needless to say, I became a good reader, and when I didn't know what major to declare when I began college, I chose the subject in which I had made an A—freshman honors English. I didn't grow up wanting to be an English teacher. Loving to read led me to that vocation.

My love of reading continues today. I am always reading several books. Usually I am reading a couple of nonfiction texts, one text of fiction, several magazines, a newspaper, and several periodicals. I tear articles out of newspapers, magazines, and periodicals weekly and store them in my categories of interest. Several of my friendships revolve around reading; we discuss and love books.

Books are my friends. You can show your students who search for companionship how books can be their friends too.

When you have a reading life that you passionately share with your students, you build the foundation for a classroom of readers. How does that work? Try these strategies.

Level: Elementary/Middle/High School/Adult
Subject: Cross-curricular

- Share daily with your students the book you are currently reading. You can do this during those empty final three minutes of class or as an opening positive ritual to begin each class day. Read a short passage to them. Do a think-aloud activity for your students. During the mid-1980s, researchers studied the merits of thinking out loud or "mental modeling" (Pearson, Rohler, Dole, & Duffy, 1992). When you model for students your invisible reading process, you empower them with reading strategies. Students who can think aloud about what is happening in their minds are better able to summarize information (Silven & Vauras, 1992). When you model aloud your thinking and the act of summarizing, you actively show students how to do it. As you read aloud, tell your students to ask questions about the book. Ask them to predict or infer about the plot based on what you share with them. Ask them to compare this book with others. (elementary/middle/high)

- Post your book list in the room along with theirs so that students can see what you are reading. Post yours near the door entrance or light switch. (elementary/middle/high)

- Take students to bookstores. If your school is close to a bookstore, you might do this during the school day. One teacher walks her high school students to the book store (ten minutes), lets them peruse (twenty minutes), and walks back (ten minutes), all during their assigned English hour. Walking to and from the store gives the teacher an opportunity to interact informally with students and builds classroom community. (elementary/middle/high—though the lower levels may require an aide or parents to accompany you.)

- Check out books from the local library. One middle school teacher checks out 100 books at a time. He keeps them on a cart in his classroom, and students use them for sustained silent reading (SSR). The local librarians now know him, and they suggest books and help him load them into his car each trip. (elementary/middle/high)

- Arrange for a storyteller to come to your class. Survey your parents. You probably have at least one parent who tells stories. Check your local cultural institutions for information on local storytellers. (elementary/middle)

- Ask an author to come to your class. Once again, check with your cultural institutions for local authors. Publishers usually have a list of authors who present. Check with your PTO or district to find a funding source to support author appearances. (elementary/middle/high)

- Make reading, writing, and thinking, not lecturing, the focal point of your classroom. Begin units with literally piles of books that cover your topic. Give students one class hour to peruse and find something that interests them to share at the end of class or the following day. This works especially well with poetry. Students read poems during the class hour, and then find a poem they are willing to read to the class the following day. Students have an opportunity to hear twenty or more poems read by peers. This builds an interest in and acceptance for the study of poetry. This works with topics as diverse as dinosaurs (in elementary school), historical periods (in middle school), and universities (in high school). Try it with your discipline. (elementary/middle/high)

- Give books to students. Occasionally surprise a student with a book after he or she expresses an interest in the book or related topic. (elementary/middle/high)

- Have students order their own books from student book clubs. (elementary/middle/high)

- Allow students to choose some of the books you order for your class library. (elementary/middle/high)

(Continued)

(Continued)

- Be sure that your classroom books reflect all the students in your classroom. (elementary/middle/high)
- Make SSR an integral part of your instruction. (elementary/middle/high)

Imagine a classroom where all of your students love to read. What would it look like? What sounds would you hear or not hear? How might you create that classroom?

_____

_____

_____

COMMON CORE STATE STANDARDS

The CCSS for writing are K.W.1 through K.W.8, beginning with kindergarten to grades twelve, 12.W.1 to 12.W.10.

ENGAGING STUDENTS IN WRITING

Many of us are readers, but we may not think of ourselves as writers. Yet we are called upon to teach students to write. Do you eagerly anticipate teaching your students to write, and do they enjoy writing in your classroom, no matter what the subject or grade level?

If our students are to be effective writers, they need certain conditions. Donald Graves (cited in J. Burke, 2003) identifies seven conditions for effective writing: time, choice, response, demonstration, expectation, room structure, and evaluation. In addition, students need to feel comfortable in the classroom community in order to write and share, and possibly even to feel motivated enough to try to write and share. Writing teachers also must feel passion about their own writing in order to instill the passion to write in their students (Tsujimoto, 2001).

Take this survey to check your love of writing.

- ❏ Are you a writer? Do you write letters, notes, or grocery lists?

- ❏ Do you have regular e-mail correspondence with others?

- ❏ Do you keep a journal?

- ❏ Are you a secret poet?

- ❏ Do you keep scrapbooks with annotations for yourself or your children?

- ❏ Do you carry a notebook with you or in your car?

❏ Do your students see your writing?

❏ Do you write on the overhead or computer to demonstrate for your students?

❏ Do you give written feedback to students beyond correcting their errors?

❏ Do you communicate with your students through classroom journals?

❏ Do you contribute to a school newsletter?

❏ Do you send a classroom newsletter to parents?

❏ Is your voice passionate when you talk about writing?

❏ Have you submitted any written work for publication? This may be for a school publication, a newspaper, a journal, or other forms of publication.

❏ Are you expecting your students to love writing if you show no passion for the task?

Write a short reflection about what these questions say personally to you.

_____

_____

_____

YOUR WRITING LIFE AND HISTORY

Think about writing in your life and recall your earliest memories. Did you write stories in elementary school? Did you receive positive feedback for your writing when you were young? Did your parents support your writing? Did your teachers provide multiple opportunities for you to write and share with others? Did you enter writing contests or perform your writing for others? Did you do well on college papers? What writing are you working on now?

Unless you are a teacher who writes and risks sharing your writing with your students, you may find your students less than enthusiastic about writing for you.

Trace your writing history.

_____

_____

_____

_____

_____

Let me share my story.

I learned to write in early elementary school. My father was an accountant, and my mother, a homemaker, wrote copious lists of things to do in addition to weekly letters to relatives.

I remember writing no stories or creative pieces in elementary school, but by high school I was writing long letters to friends and keeping a diary. English classes in the early 1960s were mostly grammar and essay tests, and I don't remember writing a paper to be graded until freshman year in college. As an English major, I wrote numerous papers leading up to a thesis and dissertation. However, I never recall thinking of myself as a writer but rather as a teacher who wrote to learn. It wasn't until I was forty years old that someone suggested I write an article based on my experience. At forty-six, I participated in a writers workshop based on the Iowa Writing Project, and for the first time wrote creative pieces to share with others. Sharing personal stories with others altered the way I saw myself. For the first time, I valued my writing and felt I might have something to share. Even now, believing that I am a writer is a scary thought. For me, writing is so much more personal and difficult than reading.

SELF-STRATEGY

One of the best ways to explore your writing life is to join a writing group. Find a small group of friends who want to meet regularly to write and share. You may decide to meet weekly or monthly. You may rotate locations, using each other's homes, or meet at a local coffee shop. You may include food or simply write and share. Another way to explore your writing life is to keep a morning journal. Save those first precious waking moments for you. Putting your writing life on your calendar is one method of ensuring that you write regularly and flex your writing muscle.

When you write regularly and you passionately share your writing in your classroom, you build the foundation for a classroom of writers. How does that work? Try the following strategies.

Level: Elementary/Middle/High

- Use a journal prompt to begin each class period. Students write in their journals. Choose different students to share each day.
- Write daily with your students. Share your journal entries on a regular basis. Note: In disciplines other than English, you can use journal prompts that refer to your subject matter and current class topics.
- Let the students create 20 journal prompts to be used for one month.
- Enter student work into contests. This can build a groundswell of excitement and pride in your classroom.

- Model your writing using the overhead. Let students see you make errors, correct, and revise. Help students understand that writing is messy.
- Create classroom slogans for student writing. For example, the slogan "When in doubt, take it out" allows students to delete wordiness.
- Spotlight a weekly student author. Allow the student author to share his or her favorite writings.
- Keep student books of writing in the classroom. Allow students to read from these during SSR.
- Invite writers from local newspapers to share with your students.
- Invite staff members who write to share with your students.
- Allow student writers to read their writing over the school's public address system.
- Schedule a writers' showcase monthly. The following is a model we developed in a high school that worked beautifully and continued to grow in numbers. Use student lunch hours so as not to disrupt class time. During lunch, students who want to participate gather in a room where they are allowed to eat. Students sign up the week before the showcase with the teacher in charge. The teacher schedules the students, and students read their poems, stories, or pieces. The audience listens and gives positive feedback. Often, staff members join in and also share their writing. This is a *no-cost* method of building a writing culture in your school. Create your own model.
- Start a writers club. Meet with students before or after school one day per week and let students write and share. Provide snacks, if appropriate.
- Pair your class with pen pals at a different school or even in a different country via satellite. You can build bridges through writing when students communicate with each other and discover their similarities, no matter where they live.
- Do a round-robin story. Have one student write a paragraph and then hand it to another student to write the next paragraph. Continue for as long as you want. Students usually like to write stories with their peers.
- Visit a school where students write often, display their writing, and win contests. Interview students and ask them what occurs in their school that supports their writing successes.
- Post written student work (but not work with errors or inflated grades). Lisa Delpit (1995) points out in *Other People's Children* that we do our students a disservice when we imply that the "product" is not important. In our society, students will be judged on the product. We must teach our students the hidden codes or rules of the product at hand; otherwise, our students from other cultures may believe that there are secrets being withheld from them and that the teacher is not teaching them what is necessary for them to succeed. As Lisa Delpit states: "Pretending that gatekeeping points don't exist is to ensure that many students will not pass through them" (p. 39).

Imagine a classroom where all your students love to write. What would it look like? What conversations would you hear? What would you see posted on the walls? Describe that classroom.

_____

_____

_____

Decide which strategies you are willing to implement to create a classroom of readers and writers. List them below.

_____

_____

_____

Teaching students to love to read and write creates an abundant classroom—one alive with literacy. Students rush in for SSR, anxious to delve into their books. They rush to the computers, anxious to continue writing their stories. Once again, when the writing and reading connects to the students' lives, literacy is alive with meaning.

In the next chapter, we find literacy lessons that engage students and are aligned with CCSS. Give me feedback on how your students engage with these lessons. You can e-mail me at a4achievement@earthlink.net or join the conversations online at School Improvement Network's PD 360. Check out the following PD 360 videos on literacy instruction:

- Legacy Videos on Instructional Strategies
- Reading in the Early Years
- Read, Write, Speak, and Listen
- Reading in the Content Areas
- Helping Students Read Beyond Grade One

SUGGESTED READINGS

Dr. Betty Porter Walls, assistant professor at Harris-Stowe State University and member of the board of directors (and former president) of Missouri State Council International Reading Association (MSC-IRA), recommends the following books for us:

Brough, Judy, Sherrel Bergman, and Larry Holt. _Teach Me, I Dare You!_ (Larchmont, NY: Eye On Education, 2006).

Hicks, Troy. _The Digital Writing Workshop_ (Portsmouth, NH: Heinemann, 2009).

McIntyre, Ellen, Nancy Hulan, and Vicky Layne. _Reading Instruction for Diverse Classrooms_ (New York: Guildford Press, 2011).

Morrow, Lesley Mandel, Robert Rueda, and Diane Lapp. *Handbook on Literacy and Diversity* (New York: Guildford Press, 2010).

The following are books I have used recently in literacy work at the elementary and secondary levels:

Middle and High School Levels

Atwell, Nancie. *In the Middle,* second edition (Portsmouth, NH: Boynton/Cook, 1998).
Fisher, Douglas, and Nancy Frey. *Teaching Students to Read Like Detectives: Comprehending, Analyzing, and Discussing Text* (Bloomington, IN: Solution Tree, 2012).
Schreck, Mary Kim. *Engaging Literacy: What It Looks Like in the Classroom* (Bloomington, IN: Solution Tree, 2012).

Elementary Level

Fountas, Irene C., and Gay Su Pinnell. *Guiding Readers and Writers, Grades 3–6: Teaching Comprehension, Genre, and Content Literacy* (Portsmouth, NH: Heinemann, 2001).
Fountas, Irene C., and Gay Su Pinnell. *Teaching for Comprehending and Fluency: Thinking, Talking, and Writing About Reading, K–8* (Portsmouth, NH: Heinemann, 2006).
Graves, Donald H. *Experiment With Fiction* (Portsmouth, NH: Heinemann, 1989).
McEwan-Adkins, Elaine K. *40 Reading Intervention Strategies for K–6 Students: Research-Based Support for RTI* (Bloomington, IN: Solution Tree, 2010).

14

Standards-Based, Culturally Responsive Lessons That Engage Learners

Sometimes educators say, "It's the relationship that matters when we teach students who don't look like us." And it is. It is wonderful when we build relationships across cultures. But the relationship is not all. We must teach students content in lessons filled with rigor that prepare them for college and career. It is not enough for students to like us; they must learn from us. We need both relationship strategies and research-based instructional strategies. When we teach lessons that honor cultures, we motivate and engage students who don't look like us. Remember, we learned in Chapter 12 that what is needed is the integration of culturally responsive instruction and standards-based instruction. In fact, it is critical if we want to meet the goal of high achievement for all students. Using culturally responsive teaching and aligning the curriculum to the CCSS is our starting place as we plan relevant lessons to engage learners. In *Aligning Your Curriculum to the Common Core State Standards*, author Joe Crawford (2012) states that the new curriculum that addresses the standards should fit the following criteria:

- Based on and aligned to the CCSS
- Standards based, not content based

- A learnable, not a teachable, curriculum
- Nonprescriptive
- Addresses the *what* and the *when* of student learning
- Encourages creativity and use of alternative learning sources
- Results in common, formative assessments (p. 80)

In addition, there are noteworthy characteristics that describe a standards-based curriculum, such as these:

- Content is not addressed.
- The standard defines the skill(s) that are expected to be mastered.
- The verbs define the level of Bloom's Taxonomy at which students are expected to perform.
- There is no attempt to prescribe an instructional strategy. (p. 8)

The literacy lessons found in this chapter fit these criteria and possess these characteristics. In addition, they include many differentiated instructional (DI) practices, and Response to Intervention (RTI). RTI is an educational model that promotes early identification of students who may be at risk for learning difficulties (Tileston, 2011). These lessons are used by a classroom teacher using Tier I of RTI instruction (in the classroom without additional support from a special education teacher in the room) and give her or him the opportunity to work closely with students to identify possible learning challenges. The lessons also naturally lend themselves to DI due to the fact that they are student constructed and filled with choices.

These literacy lessons were used in heterogeneous classrooms with diverse learners, taught by English teachers in Grades 7 to 12. None of the activities was used in an honors class, although they could be—this is important to mention, since some educators are quick to point out that suggested activities might work with honors students but not with "regular" or "at-risk" students. Just the opposite is true: the more authentic and exciting the project, the more it might engage all students (Dornan, Rosen, & Wilson, 1997).

The interesting thing about these assignments, specifically the guidebook, the oral history, and the Cliffs Notes, is that they incorporate far more class work aligned to CCSS than the usual kinds of assignments we often give in an English class. In other words, these are authentic assignments that cause students to develop and sharpen life skills. In *Educating Everybody's Children: Diverse Teaching Strategies for Diverse Learners* (Cole, 1995), Strategy 4.15 suggests practicing English by solving problems and doing work in cooperative groups. For when teachers organize work into heterogeneous, cooperative groups composed of native and nonnative speakers of English in order to give EL children opportunities to practice their English in problem-solving situations, they learn more (p. 65). In addition, students were engaged, on task, and working cooperatively. With the guidebook and Cliffs Notes projects, you can choose the groups or perhaps ask each student to choose one other student for a group, and then you fill in with the others. The groups for these projects were teacher chosen to ensure a mix of ethnic diversity, gender, ability levels, and diagnosed learning disorders.

EXAMPLE 1: GUIDEBOOK PROJECT

Common Core State Standards

Writing: 9.W.4; 9.W.5; 9.W.7; 9.W.8
Speaking and Listening: 9.SL.1; 9.SL.2; 9.SL.3; 9.SL.4; 9.SL.5
Language: 9.L.1; 9.L.2; 9.L.3; 9.L.4; 9.L.6
TESOL's pre-K–12 English proficiency standards addressed in this lesson: Standards 1 and 2

Culturally Responsive Teaching Strategies

- Connecting to the lives of the students
- Goal setting
- Proximity
- Higher level thinking: creating
- Interaction with others through interviewing, peer editing, and sharing writing
- Connecting to families (they were invited to Publication Day)
- Movement both inside and outside of the classroom

DI and RTI, Tier I

- Choice of topic
- Work alone or with partners
- Work at own pace
- Work in general classroom at own pace
- One-on-one interactions with teacher during project
- Peer Support

Technology

Students use the Web to investigate their topic. The guidebook is published on the Web in addition to one hard copy per student, but if cost is a factor in the printing, it could be launched on the Web, forgoing the hard copy.

Armed with a new teaching assignment in an unfamiliar high school and assigned to teach ninth-grade nonhonors students, I realized that my students were also new to this building and perhaps as frightened as I was. How could we quickly learn about the staff, the hidden rules, and the physical places in this school setting? We decided to write a guidebook to the high school.

The students thoroughly enjoyed this, and it relieved stress for both them and me. Following is a brief outline of one way to do this.

Guidebook Outline

- Discuss with your students the need to create a guidebook to interest and motivate and engage them.
- Ask them to select something or someone they want to interview, investigate, and write a chapter about for the guidebook, someone they will be interacting with or want to interact with during their high school career.

- Make a list of the student choices and post it. Each student or pair of students must write about a different person or topic. For example, one student, interested in basketball, interviewed the basketball coach. One student, interested in becoming a nurse, interviewed the school nurse.
- A student interested in art could draw a map of the campus and design the cover.
- Set up interview schedules.
- Students interview staff.
- Begin the writing process.
- Have students write drafts, read aloud to peers, peer edit, revise, proofread, and so on.
- Continue and complete the writing process.
- Do a final proofreading.
- Print and bind at a printing office or have your district print and bind the guidebook. Each student receives one book. In order to find money to pay for the printing and binding of the guidebooks, ask your department head, administrators, district literacy coordinator or curriculum director, PTO, local chamber of commerce, and so on. There is always money out there to support school projects. Finding it is the key.
- Have a Publication Day and invite parents.
- Do something especially nice for yourself the following weekend.

Students loved this assignment because it gave them something tangible they could use in their new life at the high school; they got to work with others; the classroom was active with talking and movement; their families were involved and grateful; they really got to know the other students in the class and built relationships with them, thus reinforcing a positive classroom climate; and they ended up with a souvenir of their freshman year at the school. It definitely was a win-win for me. Our first project was a grand success, and they were primed to go on to more rigorous literary explorations.

EXAMPLE 2: ORAL HISTORY PROJECT

Common Core State Standards

Reading: 7.RIT.3; 7.RIT.4; 7.RIT.5; 7.RIT.6; 7RIT.9; 7.RIT.10
Writing: 7.W.3; 7.W.4; 7.W.5; 7.W.6; 7.W.10
Speaking and Listening: 7.SL.1; 7.SL.4; 7.SL.5
Language: 7.L.1; 7.L.2; 7.L.3; 7.L.6
TESOL's standards: Standards 1 and 2

Culturally Responsive Teaching Strategies

- Connecting to the students' personal family and family members
- Goal setting
- Preserving and honoring cultural history
- Student talk, working together and individually
- Movement, proximity, respect for space and learning modalities

DI and RTI, Tier I

- Student choice
- One-on-one interaction with teacher
- Peer review and sharing
- Working at one's own pace

Technology

Students research the professions of the people they interview. They film the subjects of the oral histories and post them on the Web. See the following Web sites:

- Best of History Websites (www.besthistorysites.net/index.php/oral-history)
- EMP/SFM Oral History Resources (www.empmuseum.org/education/index.asp?articleID=884)
- Exploring Family Heritage (www.scholastic.com/teachers/collection/exploring-family-heritage)
- The New Americans Lesson Plan Index: Immigration Oral History (http://www.pbs.org/independentlens/newamericans/foreducators_lesson_plan_09.html)

Oral History Outline

The oral history project was a favorite of the heterogeneous, seventh-grade middle school students, and it built a new sense of community in the classroom. This was a major six-week project that used a balanced literacy and brain-compatible instructional approach to create a literacy product of which the students could be proud. There were *no* honors English classes at this middle school, so all levels were in these classes.

The following is a condensed version of what occurred in the classroom:

- Experts from a local museum came to the classes to explain the oral history.
- Students read several oral histories.
- Students chose a person for their oral history and completed a letter and contract with that person.
- Students interviewed their chosen subjects.
- Students transcribed their interviews.
- Students shared their interviews in groups.
- Students made decisions about the use of the interview. They were to use the information from the interview to create an oral history. The oral history would not be a word-by-word transcription of the interview.
- Students began the creative revision process. They engaged in the entire writing process: peer editing, revising, editing, proofreading, and writing a final draft.
- The teacher did a final proof and edit. Students typed the final oral history.
- Students created a cover for their oral history.
- Students bound their oral history with a spiral bind on the school machine.

- Students created a class invitation for Oral History Day and gave it to their parents and the people they interviewed.
- Students planned the Oral History Day celebration, including typing the agenda for the celebration and student order for sharing.
- Everyone participated in the Oral History Day celebration. Once again, students participated as *real* writers in an authentic literacy assignment.

Students' oral histories brought tears to the eyes of the audience. One young man wrote about the elderly crossing guard who helped them across the busy avenue on the way home from school. It turned out that in the 1940s, this man was a railroad porter. He shared stories of historical segregation. He attended the celebration.

Another student shared her grandmother's story. She had to interview her grandmother by phone because she was ill and in Burma and under house arrest, for she was the wife of the former ruler of the country. The grandmother died the night before the celebration, and as the young girl read her poem and her story about her grandmother, we were in tears.

Students wrote about their grandfathers, veterans of World War II. Students wrote about their fathers, veterans of Vietnam. Students wrote about their mothers, aunts, uncles, and others. Parents related how the oral history had caused their family to communicate in ways they had not previously done. The Celebration Day found a library filled with families from all the cultures of the learners. We shared food, oral histories, tears, laughs, and love.

This is a powerful, authentic writing experience that allows students to enter the stories of real, living people as they share their stories in their own authentic voices. It's a win-win assignment.

Fortunately, there are several books available that detail how to do an oral history project in the classroom. Find one and use it for this project.

EXAMPLE 3: CLIFFS NOTES PROJECT

Common Core State Standards

Reading Literature: 10.RL.1 to 10.RL.10
Writing: 10.W.2; 10.W.4; 10.W.5; 10.W.7; 10.W.8; 10.W.9
Speaking and Listening: 10.SL.1; 10.SL.2; 10.SL.3; 10.SL.4; 10.SL.5
Language: 10.L.1; 10.L.2; 10.L.3; 10.L.4; 10.L.5; 10.L.6
TESOL's pre-K–12 English proficiency standards addressed in this lesson: Standards 1 and 2

Culturally Responsive Teaching Strategies

- Connecting to the lives of the students because they had to read the book
- Goal setting
- Proximity; cooperative learning groups
- Higher level thinking: creating
- Interaction with others through interviewing, peer editing, and sharing writing
- Movement

DI and RTI, Tier I

- Choice of topic
- Choice of specific task in the group work
- One-on-one interaction with teacher during project
- Peer support
- Graded both individually and as a group project

Technology

This project was done back in the 1990s, so today it would be *so* much simpler with the technology to format the book and post it on the Web. See the following Web sites:

- English Homework Tips (homeworktips.about.com/od/englishhomework/a/acliffsnotes.htm)
- Free Essays Links (www.wowessays.com/links.shtml)
- Math and Literature Idea Bank (www.mathcats.com/grownupcats/ideabankmathandliterature.html)

Cliffs Notes Outline

When students could not find Cliffs Notes for Barbara Kingsolver's (1988) *The Bean Trees* back in the 1990s, they gave me an idea for a writing assignment to accompany our study of this required text for high school sophomores in a nonhonors English class.

We formed cooperative learning groups and asked that each group create a Cliffs Notes for *The Bean Trees.* We used a similar process to the ones outlined in Examples 1 and 2.

This project required that each student read thoroughly the entire novel, digest it, and re-create it. Each student in the group selected a task. One student selected to format the book; one student wrote the introduction, consisting of the author information, list of characters, and brief overview; one student wrote the summaries and commentaries; one student wrote the analyses; and one student wrote the bibliography and selected reviews and critical articles. Students used a standard writing process to complete this project with a rubric provided throughout the assignment.

When the students concluded their Cliffs Notes, the class selected the best example. They then composed a class letter and mailed it to Cliffs Notes. In only weeks, the students received a wonderful letter congratulating them and telling them that their Cliffs Notes was selected to be displayed at national conferences. The people at Cliffs Notes also said that other teachers had already done what we thought was an original idea and had sent their students' work to them. But, they added, our students' work was the most authentic that they had received. Even though we had done a final edit and proofread and required the students to do a final revision in order to have a perfectly correct final version, I did not insert my voice or alter the writing of my students. The publisher said that prior models they had received showed obvious teacher intervention. A good writing teacher must not co-opt her students' writing and turn it into her own teacher prose.

This project received acclaim and criticism. One community member wrote a letter saying that I was corrupting students with this assignment. He even appeared before the school board to complain. His children were not in the class.

On the other hand, Cliffs Notes liked the results so much that they displayed the students' work at national conferences, and the city newspaper did a nice story with a picture of the students.

These first three class assignments included the following:

- Standards-based instruction
- Higher level thinking
- Hard work for the students
- Hard work for the teacher
- Authentic writing: writing that students did in response to real-world issues or real tasks, such as writing an oral history or creating a Cliffs Notes
- Balanced literacy: literacy activities that balance talking, listening, reading, and writing in the instruction
- Long-term goal planning
- Backward planning for student and teacher
- Cooperation among students
- Community building in the classroom, school, and community
- Positive interaction with parents
- Student work for display
- Student work for publication
- Working like a real author
- Computer literacy
- National recognition
- Media recognition
- School board recognition (OK, that was negative. But later in the year, several of these same students were recognized for their award-winning writings.)
- Fun and humor
- Intrinsic and extrinsic rewards

Write about a time when a favorite assignment, project, or lesson caused controversy. How did you handle it? What was the outcome?

_____

_____

_____

_____

_____

EXAMPLE 4: POETRY ASSIGNMENT PROJECT

Common Core State Standards

Reading Literature: Upper elementary to high school
5–12 Reading Literature Standards
Writing: 5–12 Writing Standards focusing on creative writing
Speaking and Listening: 5–12 Speaking and Listening Standards
Language: 5–12 Language Standards
TESOL's pre-K–12 English proficiency standards addressed in this lesson: Standards 1 and 2

Culturally Responsive Teaching Strategies

- Connecting to the lives of the students because they choose the poems they like and want to share
- Connecting to families by inviting them to share with learners
- Goal setting
- Proximity
- Higher level thinking when analyzing poetry
- Interaction with others through interviewing, peer editing, and sharing poetry they write
- Movement

DI and RTI, Tier I

- Choice of poetry to read and write
- Choice of length and format
- One-on-one interaction with teacher during project
- Peer support through peer editing, sharing, and publication

Technology

See the following poetry Web sites:

- CreateSpace (www.createspace.com)
- Education World: Poetry Lessons (https://www.educationworld.com/a_special/poetrymonth.shtml)
- Kids Poems (www.mywordwizard.com/kids-poems.html)
- Poem Websites for Teens (www.ask.com/questions-about/poems-for-teens)
- Teaching Channel (www.teachingchannel.org)

Poetry Outline

This poetry format works for any class. You can use it at the middle school and high school level in English classes. It works at the elementary level too.

Students love poetry. And why not? Poetry is fun and begs for participation.

- Begin your poetry unit with choice, reading, and relaxation.

- Pile as many poetry books as you can gather from the school library, other classrooms, and your own library into the middle of the room.
- Move the desks to the outer edges of the room and invite the students to spend the hour looking through the poetry books, reading the poems that attracted them, and then choosing one to share with the entire class. This ensures that each student becomes involved and invested in the poetry experience.
- Invite poets into your classroom. Place an invitation into the mailboxes of all your staff members and invite them to drop by on their planning periods to read a favorite poem to your class. You may find that there are poets among your staff. Some staff members may choose to read their own writing. When students see the football coach read a favorite poem, they understand that poetry is something to be shared by everyone.
- Bring music into the mix. Have students bring in lyrics of their favorite songs that are classroom appropriate. Ask them to find poetic devices in the song lyrics.
- Immerse your students and yourself in poetry for several days or weeks. Begin the writing process. My favorite writing prompt for poetry is William Carlos Williams's poem "This Is Just to Say."
- Place that poem on an overhead and have students read it several times and discuss it.
- Model writing a poem for each class. Don't use one you have already written, because you don't want this to be a polished piece. You want to model for students how rough the initial jottings are so that they will model the same process as they write poetry.
- Laugh at your attempts. Invite students to suggest words. Play!
- Then ask students to write a poem that begins "This is just to say . . ."
- Have students write, share, revise, edit, proof, and then type a final draft.
- Have a poetry party and invite teachers to read their poetry to the class. Invite another class. Invite parents or grandparents.
- Read the poems over the public address system. Display students' work.
- The poetry unit (of which this is just the beginning) will continue to build the reading and writing culture of the school. As more and more teachers (even some from outside the English department) share their poetry, writing poetry becomes normalized instead of being seen as outside the norm. Use poetry to build school culture!

EXAMPLE 5: YOU CAN BE IN A BOOK PROJECT

Common Core State Standards

Reading Literature: 10.RL.1 to 10.RL.10
Reading Informational Text: 10.RIT.1 to 10.RIT.10
Writing: 10.W.2; 10.W.3; 10.W.4; 10.W.5; 10.W.7; 10.W.8; 10.W.9
Speaking and Listening: 10.SL.1; 10.SL.2; 10.SL.3; 10.SL.4; 10.SL.5
Language: 10.L.1; 10.L.2; 10.L.3; 10.L.4; 10.L.5; 10.L.6
TESOL's pre-K–12 English proficiency standards addressed in this lesson: Standards 1 and 2

Culturally Responsive Teaching Strategies

- Connecting to the lives of the students because they put themselves into the book or the nonfiction piece
- Goal setting
- Proximity
- Higher level thinking: creating
- Interaction with others through interviewing, peer editing, and sharing writing
- Movement; music (played in background as students work)

DI and RTI, Tier I

- Choice of character in fiction and nonfiction
- Choice of nonfiction articles based on reading level
- One-on-one interaction with teacher during project
- Peer support through peer editing, sharing, and publication
- Working with the same novel but writing a different character (themselves) into the book, so differentiated naturally by person

In addition to language arts, you can ask students to imagine what it would be like to live in different periods of history and then to write about it and share with the class.

Students become characters in the texts, both fiction and nonfiction. This works for all ages, kindergarten to college. Ask students to choose a fictional text that they enjoy, or assign one you are studying in class. Tell them to write themselves into the action! Or if they are reading nonfiction texts, have them place themselves into history or current-day events!

A group of sophomores used this strategy while reading *Lord of the Flies* by William Golding (1959). It was one of their favorite assignments. They keyboarded pages from the text and inserted themselves into the story. They made up dialogue for themselves, and it had to fit the overall style of the author.

This accomplished several things:

- Students who normally don't know how to begin a writing assignment had only to choose some pages and begin typing.
- Students programmed their brains with the style and syntax of a famous writer.
- Students were forced to pay attention to quotation marks and to use them correctly. This kind of exercise worked and was less painful to students than worksheets of exercises on quotation marks.
- Students had to extend the plot through their character yet match the intent of the author. This involved higher level thinking skills.
- Students vicariously lived the adventures of the characters in famous books.
- Students enjoyed this assignment and enjoyed sharing it with their peers.

How can you grade this so you don't go crazy looking for the students' writing within the text of the novel?

- Students highlighted their prose.
- Students were required to write a stated number of words.
- Students were required to use quotation marks and other punctuation correctly.
- Students were required to match the syntax and the writing style of the author.
- Students were graded on completion of the assignment, creativity, and correctness.

These papers were students' favorites. They loved sharing them with peers, "showing off" as they faced danger along with famous literary characters or were actively involved in a historical or current event. This lesson engaged students. When it is about us, it's hard to disengage. Like the art teacher who says he engages his students when they walk in the door by having them draw a self-portrait, this lesson has learners "draw" a self-portrait in writing about themselves.

EXAMPLE 6: THEME BOOKS PROJECT

This literacy activity is appropriate for elementary and middle school students. You can try it with high school students in a creative writing class. Once again, students created a class book as in the first lesson idea in this chapter. But this time, they wrote genre fictional stories. One group of students wrote detective stories, another group wrote mystery stories, and another group wrote romance stories. Also, students who enjoyed art drew the covers, and the writing process followed those previously discussed. Students were expected to write fictional stories in their genre of choice that were a minimum of three typed pages.

Since we did not make copies of these for each student, we simply bound their final typed stories into books with a cover on a machine that the school owned, and these books became part of the library in our classrooms. This library consisted of hundreds of books scoured from garage sales, used bookstores, book order clubs, and student writing. Students *always* want to read their own writing, so when they participated in sustained silent reading (SSR), they often chose a theme book to read. This settled them into reading, since students are interested in what their peers have written.

EXAMPLE 7: WRITING CONTESTS

Submitting students' writing to essay contests is an incredible motivator and way to engage students in writing. It is culturally responsive because students feel special when their work is submitted, and they work harder to improve their writing. If you have not done this before, consider it. You don't have to be a terribly organized person; you just need a system.

Look for contests in student magazines or writing magazines, such as *Poets and Writers*, at your local bookstore. One win will hook your students! You can always begin with an in-house contest to ensure a win.

Consider starting a writing club that meets weekly. Even a twenty-minute block of time in your classroom before school works. Invite at-risk diverse learners. All they can say is no, and most likely, they will be pleased by your invitation, which signals to them that you believe they can write well enough to win contests.

The weekly meetings give you and the students time to share their writing, which is the best motivator for other students. It also gives you time to complete the logistics of submission. Find a student who is really organized who will handle much of this work.

When students win, make sure their names are read over the public address system to the entire school. You will find that success breeds success and winning is contagious. More and more students will want to join your group.

One national contest a local high school writing club entered focused on inner-city students' lives. They submitted six personal stories from males who lived in the inner city of St. Louis and were bused to this school as part of the desegregation program. A woman in charge of the contest called from Houston to tell me that they had the winning stories. She then asked, "Do all of your students write this well?" "Yes, they do," was my reply. When children are invited to use their authentic voices and given the support that they need, they do achieve.

In another incident, there was a notice of a book to be published about African American adolescent girls' stories. I remembered a girl's story I had heard in a class I had recently observed. I called the teacher and told her about it. The girl had to get her mother's permission to submit her story. That was not an easy task, but it was finally accomplished. Doing these things is not always a snap. It takes hard work and extra effort, but this teacher was willing to do it. They sent in the story. The girl was notified that it would be published as a story in this book. Recently, she was invited to read her story at a public book signing when the author was in St. Louis. Will that experience make that girl believe that she is a writer? Yes!

And this is why you might choose to do the messy work to submit your students' stories. Students begin to see themselves as real authors of their lives. Other teachers see them as winners. And they are.

Once you enter the contest circuit, you will receive all kinds of contest information. But one place where your students can submit is *Teen Ink*, a publication written by teens. You can contact them at www.teenink.com. There are contests and competitions in all disciplines, and getting students involved in them increases student interest and creates authentic work.

If you create ways to make your assignments authentic (meaning they write for real audiences and real situations, such as a contest or a newspaper editorial) using authentic student voices, you will find students engaged and academically achieving. Students want to achieve, and it is up to us to offer them opportunities for academic achievement.

Web sites for student writing contests include the following:

- 40 of the Best Websites for Young Writers (http://education-portal.com/articles/40_of_the_Best_Websites_for_Young_Writers.html)
- Creative Communication (www.poeticpower.com)
- Creative Writing Contests (writingcontests.wordpress.com)

- firstwriter.com Writing Competitions (www.firstwriter.com/competitions/)
- Young Writer Contests (www.kimn.net/student.htm)

The lesson ideas offered in this chapter give opportunities for culturally diverse learners to interact with their classmates while they engage in rigorous, higher level academic work. These projects are aligned with multiple standards and can be adjusted to meet your students' needs. They also produce work that you can keep for years to use as models for future students, and in addition, the projects can become part of your in-class library and provide highly motivating reading materials for SSR.

In her book *Active Literacy Across the Curriculum*, Heidi Hayes Jacobs (2006) suggests using speaking rubrics such as those available at www.nald.ca/CLR /Btg/ed/evaluation/speaking.htm#speaking. Using these rubrics offers learners an opportunity to self-assess and self-monitor their pace and volume in the same way that writing rubrics offer learners the opportunity to self-assess their writing.

What lesson ideas might you adapt to your grade level and try in your class?

_____

_____

_____

This chapter offered a variety of CRSB lessons. To view PD 360 videos that demonstrate teacher strategies found in these lessons, go to http://www.school improvement.com/experts/bonnie-davis. Check out the following videos:

- Formative Assessment: Learning 360 Framework E & S—Segment 5
- Achievement for Students With Special Needs E & S—Segments 11; 4; 10
- Classroom Instruction That Works E & S—Segment 4
- Growing Dendrites: 20 Instructional Strategies—Segment 4
- Differentiated Instruction Applied E—Segment 8
- Equity and Innovation: Kihei Charter School—Segment 3
- Differentiated Instruction for All
- All Means All: What Is It About Me You Can't Teach?

How do we increase rigor in reading and writing instruction? Consider implementing a readers and writers workshop. The next chapter focuses on a workshop format aligned to standards and filled with opportunities for implementing culturally responsive strategies.

15

Readers and Writers Workshop

A Model for Standards-Based, Culturally Responsive Instruction

In the districts where I have worked during the past several years, I have failed to find working reading and writing workshops except at the elementary level. I find this sad. However, I understand the culture of testing sucked most of the life out of the readers and writers workshop structure, which allows for, and includes with proper implementation, differentiation, Response to Intervention, personal mastery, engagement, and higher level thinking. In its place, we find pacing guides with little flexibility for teachers and learners. With the implementation of the CCSS, this can change. Teachers once again will have more flexibility and freedom to design lessons that challenge students and prepare them for career readiness and college.

With that in mind, I believe there is still a place for this structure that supports working at high levels of engagement with reading and writing. Thus, this chapter offers you a snapshot of how reading and writing instruction in such a structure might unfold in culturally diverse educational settings such as a middle school, a high school, a college class, or a prison. You may be surprised by the commonalities. I was. Teaching in these four settings allowed me to see the research in action. We do know what creates good literacy classrooms, and this chapter spells out what good writers and readers need to be successful. To support the focus of the CCSS, consider having students read more nonfiction during reading workshops and write in genres other than the personal narrative and literary analysis, without abandoning them, during writing workshops.

Several years ago, I took a job teaching seventh-grade English in a diverse classroom. I had never taught seventh-grade students, and in fact, for the previous fourteen years, I had only taught seniors in high school and adults. I naively thought it would be easy. I knew English, and I thought that was all it would take to be a successful English teacher of seventh-grade children.

How wrong I was! The first day was a disaster. I soon found that these seventh graders were not impressed at all with having a new teacher who held a PhD in English. I had always believed that I had good classroom management, but within minutes, these adolescents convinced me otherwise.

I was desperate! I needed to find some pedagogy that would engage these children while maintaining the classroom atmosphere that I found acceptable. I found it in a reading and writing workshop.

A colleague introduced me to Nancie Atwell (1987), and I found my survival guide for the year in her book *In the Middle: Writing, Reading, and Learning With Adolescents.* In a foreword to Atwell's second edition (1998), Donald Graves writes that *In the Middle* is for the teacher with a "strong desire to help students make sense of their world through reading, writing, and sound thinking" (p. ix).

He adds that it also is for the teacher who commits to "grow in her own ability to write and read with students" (p. ix). One cannot occur without the other. This book changed the way I taught English, and it supported my students as they learned to love reading and writing. Actually, many of my students came to me already loving to read and to write because of their previous experiences, but Atwell's book allowed me to create a framework for a literacy-rich environment in my classroom.

Impressed by the results of using Atwell's workshop format, I extended the reading and writing workshop to three additional teaching assignments—the community college and the prison, where I taught Composition 101 and 102 one night a week, and then, two years later, to the high school classroom.

What follows is what it might look like in the classroom when you use a reading and writing workshop approach. For middle school and high school, consider arming yourself with Nancie Atwell's books. For elementary school classrooms, try *Guiding Readers and Writers, Grades 3–6: Teaching Comprehension, Genre, and Content Literacy.* This book, by Irene C. Fountas and Gay Su Pinnell (2001), is so comprehensive that it actually spells out day by day (for the first twenty days) what you do to include balanced literacy in your elementary school day. In addition, the differentiated instruction books by Gayle Gregory and Carolyn Chapman (2002) and others offer you a firm base for your planning. Check out these Web sites for additional support:

- A Curricular Plan for the Writing Workshop, Grade K (www.heinemann.com/products/E04301.aspx)
- Teachers College Reading and Writing Project (tc.readingandwriting project.com)
- Welcome to Reader's Workshop (www.ourclassweb.com/sites_for_teachers_readers_workshop.htm)
- Writers Workshop (mywritersworkshop.com/writers-workshop/)

INSIDE THE READING AND WRITING CLASSROOM

Imagine a group of individuals writing, some rather feverishly, some more relaxed, yet all intense, writing their stories, writing their lives. Imagine four very different settings: a seventh-grade class in an affluent county suburb, an English class for juniors and seniors at a suburban high school, a community college class in a middle-class neighborhood, and a prison class housed behind razor wire.

What do these four classes have in common?

These four classes share a writing and reading class environment that is almost identically structured, and they share the things that good writing classrooms provide: time, choice (Marzano, 2004), and positive response from teacher and peers (Caine & Caine, 1997).

Josh, a seventh-grade boy, can't wait to share his fourth story with the class. It's about a giant killer peanut.

Jenna, a senior girl, can't wait to share her story about the summer camp where she assisted a terminally ill adolescent in a wheelchair.

Janet, a nineteen-year-old student in my community college class, can't wait to share her first story with the class. It's about an event on her sixteenth birthday that changed her life forever—a rape.

Luke, a lifer for murder in this maximum security prison, can't wait to share his current story with the class. It's about the day his mother came to visit him in prison and died three hours later. (His story won first prize in a national fiction contest and was published in a magazine.) Donald Graves (1989) states that everything we tell is a fiction and a version of our own reality. This student turned his reality into fiction.

Each class sits in a circle as members share their stories. The seventh graders sit in a brightly lit, plant-filled, and colorful room, meticulously maintained.

The juniors and seniors sit in a classroom with bare walls on the lower level of an old four-story brick school building.

The college class chooses to sit in the park next to the class building, sharing coffee and rolls as they share their stories during their Saturday morning class.

The prison class sits in a stark concrete block room with no window, far too little ventilation, and barely enough room between the desks to move.

The four groups work in similar ways. Each student shares a story. Members give positive, specific feedback—and all receive peer response. The writings are rich, revealing, and rewarding.

Common Core State Standards

The CCSS and corresponding college and career readiness (CCR) anchor standards align beautifully with writers and readers workshops. In reading the standards for Grades 7 through 12, there are none that cannot be embedded in a writers and readers workshop format. Readers and writers workshop formats cover reading literature and the CCSS relating to that, as well as those for reading information text, writing, speaking and listening, and language. Consider discussing with your professional learning group or department how and when you will address each standard. As you read through this chapter, note how the standards are a natural fit for so much of what occurs when students read and write together.

Because good writers learn from reading (Marzano, 2004), these four groups of students are required to read, read, read! The seventh graders read a book a week (or the equivalent of 150 pages), the juniors and seniors read four novels per semester class, the college class reads five classics a semester, and the prison class reads a classic a week. Each student is given a book list of authors from which to choose books. The list includes Toni Morrison, Alice Walker, and Barbara Kingsolver, as well as William Faulkner, Ernest Hemingway, and F. Scott Fitzgerald, and many young adolescent (YA) novels for the younger students.

Common Core State Standards

Reading Literature: 7.RL.1; 7.RL.3; 7.RL.4; 7.RL.5; 7.RL.6; 7.RL.7; 7.RL.9; and 7.RL.10 can be incorporated in the reading described here.

Each week, time is spent discussing the students' reading. One student is responsible for leading the discussion or conducting a "book talk." Then all students join in to discuss what they are reading. Shifting from personal narrative and literary fiction involves some adjustment. Consider forming a professional learning group of history or social studies teachers and English teachers. Discuss the standards you plan to teach and then search for the best nonfiction pieces you can use with students. Consider having the social studies teachers or history teachers guide the content, with the English teachers supporting their instruction.

CCSS addressed when students switch from literature to informational text.

Common Core State Standards

7–12.RIT.1; 7–12.RIT.2; 7–12.RIT.3; 7–12.RIT.4; 7–12.RIT.5; 7–12.RIT.6; 7–12.RIT.7; 7–12.RIT.8; 7–12.RIT.9; 7–12.RIT.10.

The Prison Class

In the prison class, a discussion about John Steinbeck so inspired the men that the following classes became a Steinbeck seminar. Steinbeck especially appeals to these men, who share a common denominator: poverty. The past experiences of these men caused them to connect to the lives of literary characters living in poverty, and this commonality inspired rich classroom conversation and writing.

Steinbeck's portrayal of those who suffer from hardships and poverty causes talk to erupt, and the men can't wait to search for copies of *The Grapes of Wrath, Tortilla Flat, Of Mice and Men,* and others. The book talks become a powerful force that causes the group to bond men of different races and gangs who would not speak to each other outside this prison classroom. Both African American and White men talk and share ideas, not a common occurrence in an institution often rife with racial tensions.

Another popular book for these prison book talks is *The Autobiography of Malcolm X* (1973). Men who came into the class complaining that they did not like to read devoured this book. It is one of those books that motivates students to read above their grade level or reading ability. Try it with challenging middle school and high school students; it is a high-interest book that motivates students.

Mostly, I stay out of the book talks. Once the men were hooked on books (and Steinbeck and *The Autobiography of Malcolm X* hooked them), they controlled the talk. One man, imprisoned in his teens, commented after reading *The Great Gatsby*, "I don't know what I think about it. I think I'll read it again." What more could a teacher ask?

The Seventh-Grade Class

Choice is a must for seventh graders who believe that they must choose their own readings (at least some of the time) in order to prove their independence. Marzano's (2004) research on SSR programs stresses the need for students to have choice in their reading materials. When assigned *Across Five Aprils* (Hunt & Pucci, 1964) to accompany their study of the Civil War, student responses varied tremendously.

Students reacted positively and negatively as they interacted with the literature, bringing to the work their own personal experiences and interpretations. One student said, "I have tried so hard to come up with something good to say about this book, but nothing comes to mind." Then she went on to write several paragraphs in her journal about her interpretation of the novel, proving that she had indeed interacted with the text and had learned from it. (Rosenblatt [1995] stresses that students must interact with the texts they read, bringing something to the text as well as taking something from it, resulting in a transactional interaction. Students who are aware of this two-way relationship with the text both are better readers and comprehend more than those students who do not understand this powerful relationship.) Her journal proved to be so cogent that it was accepted for publication in a national journal. Publication is a powerful motivator to the entire class, so consider any opportunity to publish your students' works both in the classroom and to a wider audience.

Students could honestly respond to the literature, and this created an open atmosphere that motivated students to read beyond their assigned texts. Both the students and I posted our book lists on the classroom walls and added a new book each week. Students eagerly checked to see what their peers and I had read and if the latest book had been recommended. The room was full of lists of recommendations. No student ever wondered what he or she could read; it was simply a matter of which book to read next.

On many Fridays, I came dressed as "Book Woman," surprising the students with a crazy costume and a new book recommendation. (Note: I did *not* do this in the other classes.) After Book Woman disappeared, the rest of the class period was devoted to SSR. It was a wonderful, peaceful way to end the week with a room filled with high-energy seventh-grade students. This SSR also gave me time to keep up with my reading and to model reading for my students.

Common Core State Standards

Reading Literature: 7.RL.1; 7.RL.2; 7.RL.3; 7.RL.4; 7.RL.9; 7.RL.10
Writing: 7.W.1; 7.W.2; 7.W.3; 7.W.4; 7.W.5; 7.W.6; 7.W.7; 7.W.8; 7.W.9; 7.W.10
Speaking and Listening: 7.SL.1; 7.SL.2; 7.SL.3; 7.SL.4; 7.SL.5; 7.SL.6
Language: 7.L.1; 7.L.2; 7.L.3; 7.L.4; 7.L.5; 7.L.6

The High School Class

The high school class had to cover the curriculum, consisting of many familiar classics: *The Great Gatsby, Death of a Salesman, The Scarlet Letter,* and others. Their writing assignments often revolved around their interactions with these texts, yet I offered options as often as possible. For example, after reading *Death of a Salesman,* students were allowed to write plays in cooperative groups and then perform them for the class. This was, by far, the most enjoyable writing assignment of the semester. Other options included the literary analysis (the most dreaded), students writing a first-person journal as one of the characters in the story, creating a curriculum guide for the text, and students inserting themselves into the text as characters and expanding the action to include themselves.

After completing early drafts of their writing, the high school students enjoyed taking part in the "Friday Buffet." This consisted of laying their anonymous papers out on a table on Fridays and using part of the class hour to read the papers of classmates. Stapled to each student paper was a colored sheet of paper on which the author asked a question of his or her readers. For example, a question might read, "Are there any parts of this that you think I should expand or explain better?" The student readers would read papers from the buffet and answer the question on the attached sheet of paper. At the end of the buffet time, students retrieved their papers and read the feedback from their peers. This feedback was then incorporated into next drafts, and the process continued until final drafts and publication, when students shared their papers from the "author's chair." I also participated in this Friday Buffet, sharing my drafts of stories I was writing for a local university writing class, and as in the seventh-grade Friday SSR, this offered a calming and pleasant way to complete the academic week.

Common Core State Standards

Grades 11 and 12 Literature: 11–12.RL.1; 11–12.RL.2; 11–12.RL.3; 11–12.RL.4; 11–12.RL.5; 11–12.RL.6; 11–12.RL.7; 11–12.RL.9; 11–12.RL.10.

Creative Writing: 11–12.W.1; 11–12.W.2; 11–12.W.3; 11–12.W.4; 11–12.W.5; 11–12.W.6; 11–12.W.7; 11–12.W.8; 11–12.W.9; 11–12.W.10.

The College Class

The Saturday morning college class at a local community college was comprised mostly of working women earning minimum wage who wished to better their lives. (Consider reading *Nickel and Dimed* by Barbara Ehrenreich, 2001, for a comprehensive look at the working poor in the United States.) Their reading history also had a common denominator—few had read any of the traditional or new classics or canon, and few were aware of the concerns of women from around the world.

As they read such novels as Mary Crow Dog's *Lakota Woman* and Alice Walker's *The Color Purple* and *Possessing the Secret of Joy*, these women were shocked to find what women suffered throughout global societies.

They kept weekly journals to describe their reading journeys (Atwell, 1998; Calkins, 1986; Macrorie, 1984). One student, after reading *Lakota Woman* (Crow Dog, 1990), wrote that the book changed the way she looked at others. She said she was determined not to become one of those Americans who thinks his or her way is the best way. Instead, she resolved to open her heart and mind to learn the ways of others.

The content of the novels that these students read opened their minds to worlds they would never have known had they not been required to pick up these books. We teachers have a responsibility to give our students provocative works of literature that expose them to many worlds. Our diverse learners need to see themselves reflected in the literature they read, yet today only 5 percent of the books being published are culturally diverse. Culturally diverse texts accurately and respectfully portray people of different cultures and perspectives. This literature offers all students the opportunity to read and discuss issues of freedom, bias, justice, and equality and has the "power to humanize us and increase our sensitivity, tolerance, and compassion for people and other cultures" (Routman, 2000, p. 75b).

According to Galda (quoted in Routman, 2000, pp. 74–75b), the culturally diverse literature about African Americans continues to increase, and there are some powerful Asian characters in the current literature; however, there are few accessible texts about Latino/a culture and a dearth of literature depicting our indigenous population. This continues to be a challenge for educators as we reach out to diverse learners.

WRITING IN THE FOUR CLASSES

Common Core State Standards

Writing: 7–12.W.1; 7–12.W.2; 7–12.W.3; 7–12.W.4; 7–12.W.5; 7–12.W.6; 7–12.W.7; 7–12.W.8; 7–12.W.9; 7–12.W. 10.

Writing in the four classes was just as important as reading. Using Atwell's (1987) guidelines for writing proved successful for students at all levels. To these I would now add rubrics and an assessment component.

The guidelines for writing in the four classes are the following:

- Student choice of topics using nonfiction and fiction
- Personal conferences
- Teacher writes with students
- Peer response
- Specific, positive feedback
- Publication of student writing
- Student choice of reading
- Shared discussions about reading and writing
- Journal writing and sharing

Journal Response

The journal was an integral part of all three writing classes (Atwell, 1998, 1998; Calkins, 1986; Macrorie, 1984). At the seventh-grade level, it functioned as a procedure to mark the beginning of each class, as well as student writing. Students were asked to respond to questions or prompts written on the board. They then shared responses before they began their daily writing or reading tasks.

At the high school level, it functioned as a resource for future reading and writing ideas, as well as the place where students interacted transactionally on paper about their books.

At the college level, students used their journals for reflection and processing. During the first classes of the semester, students would share their fears and doubts, and that sharing, and the ensuing discussion, would help build the class reading and writing community.

In all of the class discussions, one thing is paramount: the interaction that results from students confronting texts and each other. When students could construct their own meanings through their discussions, a community of readers and writers arose to support the discovery and learning of its members (Atwell, 1998).

THE TEACHER'S ROLE

So what is your role in a literacy classroom? The final component of this learning in a rich reading and writing environment is the teacher. Teachers, like musicians, are artists as well as practitioners (Palmer, 1998). The teacher who creates writing and reading magic in her or his classroom has a distinct voice, a timbre that resonates throughout the classroom. That teacher is not afraid of his or her own voice or the distinct voices of students, whether those students are young or old, Black or White, rich or poor, innocent or guilty. Those teachers allow their students to take risks, and they also take risks.

Teachers must write in front of and with their students and share their failures and successes. Students also must be allowed to fail, but the teacher must offer the scaffolding and needed support that bolsters them to success. Consider allowing students to write and rewrite their papers over and over as often as they want in order to improve their grades. Think of sports. When basketball players begin to play the game, they do not perform perfect free throws over and over. It takes years of practice. When students begin writing, they must practice. Grading the practice shuts down the process. Instead, assess and give specific feedback, yet allow students to revise and rewrite until they believe it is the best they can do (J. Burke, 1999b). You can give points for completing the earlier drafts, but assign a letter grade only to the finished product. This creates a writing and reading environment that supports discovery and change, growth and development.

So what is the challenge for the teacher who wants to create a rich, balanced literacy program that supports reading and writing? Is it to impart a body of knowledge? Is it to get students to regurgitate "important" facts? Or is it to teach students to be reflective writers and readers who know how to gather information, process information, and synthesize information? The balanced literacy teacher must include all of the above. But if that teacher wants to get the very best from students, the teacher must create a climate of mutual trust and understanding where human beings can come together, no matter what their ages, to share their stories and writings of their lives within a common community (Gregory & Chapman, 2002).

Reflect upon the classrooms described above. How do they match what you already do? What aspects of the reading and writing workshops described above could you use in your instruction?

_____

_____

_____

_____

_____

_____

Following are some tools for your classroom.

Quick Self-Edit Ideas

- Use a good word processing program that includes a grammar and spell check. It will catch most of your errors.
- Read to the sky: Go outside and read your piece aloud to the sky. (OK, you can read inside and call it "read to the wall." Have students line up, facing the wall, and read their papers aloud, simultaneously). Listen for the parts you like and listen for the parts that sound awkward. Revise accordingly.
- Find the real beginning of your piece. If your piece contains more than twenty pages, consider cutting the first page and a half; if your piece contains fewer than twenty pages, consider cutting the first paragraph and a half. Read your piece aloud to a reader and ask what he or she remembers. What is remembered may be the real beginning of your piece.
- Make people, not things, the subjects of your sentences.

(Continued)

(Continued)

- Eliminate passive voice and use active voice. Following the above often takes care of that. Example of passive voice: "The ball was thrown by Mike." Example of active voice: "Mike threw the ball."
- Eliminate linking verbs. Example with linking verb: "She was tired and fell asleep." Example without linking verb: "Tired, she fell asleep."
- Use active verbs to show the action. Do not put the action into adjectives or adverbs. Example with adverb: "John awkwardly walked across the room." Example without adverb: "John shuffled across the room."
- Cross out your prepositional phrases; then decide which ones you really need. Often they contain wordiness.

Other suggestions? Brainstorm.

REVISION

Donald Murray (1990) tells us that revision is "re-seeing" that allows us to see what we are writing and what it means. Consider these strategies for your students.

Suggestions for Revision

- Read your piece aloud several times.
- Put it away for several days.
- Have others read your piece and give you feedback.
- Change the point of view. If you used a third-person point of view, change it to first person and see what happens. Or try the opposite.
- Begin at a different place in your writing.
- End before you think it is finished.
- Write past the present ending.
- Reorder time in your piece.
- Change the number of words. Take a 3,000-word story and rewrite it in 1,000 words.
- Tighten your language.

In this chapter, you have examined a reading and writing workshop model in practice. What were the successes? When using the workshop model, I found that behavior issues disappeared, except in rare cases, as students found their "flow" in the texts they wrote and read. Another outcome was the creation of a community of learners at all levels. Students listened and respected each other's writings, and our caring community grew. Academic achievement improved overall as students improved their reading and writing skills. Students became readers and writers, and the school culture of academic literacy flourished. We built on the academic literate environment by using project-oriented instruction throughout much of the year at the middle and high school levels. Finally, this format is a natural fit for the CCSS.

In the next chapter, you will find lessons being taught today in an elementary school, middle school, and high school. These are real teachers' lessons that they designed and want to share with you.

❖   ❖   ❖

SUGGESTED READINGS

Atwell, Nancie. *In the Middle: Writing, Reading, and Learning With Adolescents* (Portsmouth, NH: Boynton/Cook, 1998).

Atwell, Nancie. *In the Middle: New Understandings About Writing, Reading, and Learning,* second edition (Portsmouth, NH: Boynton/Cook, 1998).

Fountas, Irene C., and Gay Su Pinnell. *Guiding Readers and Writers, Grades 3–6: Teaching Comprehension, Genre, and Content Literacy* (Portsmouth, NH: Heinemann, 2001).

Gregory, Gayle, and Carolyn Chapman. *Differentiated Instructional Strategies: One Size Doesn't Fit All* (Thousand Oaks, CA: Corwin, 2002).

SUGGESTED WEB SITES

ClassTools.net (classtools.net)

Common Core State Standards App for iPad by MasteryConnect (itunes.apple.com/us/app/common-core-standards/id439424555?mt=8)

Google Drive (drive.google.com)

Piratepad (piratepad.net)

Wordle (www.wordle.net)

16

Teachers in Today's Classrooms Share Their Lessons

Over the past decade, I have been fortunate to work with many wonderful educators. In this chapter, teachers share lessons their students learned from and loved. These lessons embody culturally responsive practices and are aligned to standards, some to the CCSS and others to state or district ones. The teachers practice culturally responsive teaching in their classroom instruction and in their interactions with colleagues. They do this through powerful collaboration and a strong belief in equity. To them, equity means believing all children can learn and doing what it takes to afford all learners the opportunities to do so. In these lessons, you will find many culturally responsive practices. As you read over them, consider the ways in which they support equity for all learners.

Perhaps ironically, I did not think about ethnicity, racial identity, or gender when I asked the staffs at several schools if anyone wanted to share successful lessons for this book. These are the teachers who shared, and they are all women. One is Latina, three are African American, one is Filipino, and the rest are White. They range from new teachers in their first three years to veteran teachers, and some are tiny framed ladies with others being of a more average size (I state this because sometimes a teacher will tell me someone can maintain classroom management because they are physically large, and that's just not true, in my experience). These women engage students, and these women are lifelong learners who continue to learn and grow.

MATH, SCIENCE, AND LANGUAGE ARTS AT THE ELEMENTARY LEVEL

Dr. Todd Benben is the principal of North Glendale Elementary School in Kirkwood, Missouri. He is a White male who is deeply invested in equity. He not only believes in equitable opportunities for all; he makes them happen. Todd begins each school day by standing outside and welcoming each family to school. Families often walk to school with their dogs, and Todd stops to pet the dogs while remembering names of parents, children, and dogs! He is also there at the end of school, but he does something additional during the day that sets him apart as an effective administrator. During workshops, I often share this powerful strategy with administrators: Todd's *daily walkthrough.* Each day Todd walks through the school and lightly touches each person on the shoulder, including all staff and all children. He has done this for years. This simple procedure takes about thirty minutes a day and offers tremendous payback. Each day Todd grasps the big picture of his school as he walks through each room and acknowledges each human being in the building. He can assess the emotional tone of the classrooms and note if any teacher or learner is having a bad day. There is no invisibility at Todd's school, for he sees his staff and students, and they see him. It took his staff a few weeks to get used to Todd being in their rooms every day, never knowing when it would be walkthrough time, but after the first month of the first year, staff is comfortable and simply continue teaching and students continue learning. Read Todd's words below about the progress at his school, and then examine some of the lessons from his staff.

Dr. Todd Benben

Principal, North Glendale Elementary School

At North Glendale, we believe all students will learn and grow each and every day. Our daily pledge states that as learners we will be cooperative, respectful, responsible, honest, and we will persevere. We take our pledge seriously and every member or our learning community strives to live our pledge on a daily basis. We have made major strides to build our capacity to be culturally responsive teachers and use what we have learned from each other and from our resources. We are forever indebted to Bonnie for her time and energy encouraging and teaching our learning community members to become effective and compassionate teachers for all students and not just most students.

Purposeful and engaging work has allowed our learning community to make real progress with our student achievement. Currently 85% of our students were proficient or advanced on the MAP in Communication Arts, which is a 10% improvement over the last three years. Eighty-three percent of all our students were proficient or advanced on MAP in math, which is a twelve percent improvement over the last three years. Eighty percent of our fifth grade students scored proficient or advanced on MAP in Science. A site called SchoolDigger.com currently ranks our school as the #4 elementary school in the state of Missouri.

❖   ❖   ❖

While I am grateful for Todd's acknowledgment, I must acknowledge his work with his staff. He has an open door policy and continually shares with his staff the importance of being honest and open with him. Todd listens; Todd adjusts; Todd learns, just as he expects all the adults and children in his building to do. He is deliberate in his planning to support the staff journey as they continue to become increasingly culturally responsive in their instruction and interactions with each other and the children in the building.

At North Glendale Elementary, we began several years ago by examining White women's hidden rules that play out among female teachers in an elementary school. All of the classroom teachers are White females. The only African American females are the reading specialist and the social worker. Because the school culture reflects a White female culture, we began studying the socialization of White females in the United States to better understand how we White women might become more effective with students who don't look like us. We began by learning about ourselves. We used the work of Carol Gilligan (1982), Deborah Tannen (1990), and Becky Bailey (2000) to learn about and begin to understand how our language shapes our cultural lens. For the past three years, the staff at North Glendale has been participating in book studies before and after school, using *Courageous Conversations About Race* by Glenn Singleton and Curtis Linton (2006), *Conscious Discipline* by Becky Bailey (2000), and *The Biracial and Multiracial Student Experience* (2009), one of my books. As a result of examining *race*, the staff has moved from "not seeing color" to acknowledging their own biases and prejudices and learning what "they don't know they don't know" about the cultures of the students in the schools. Test scores continue to rise as teachers change their practice and refuse to give in to the notion that Students of Color will do less well than White students.

❖ ❖ ❖

The lessons that follow are from teachers at North Glendale. First is a fifth-grade math lesson by teacher Laura Sammon. Laura is a dedicated veteran teacher who holds the highest expectations for all students. Laura connects the learning to students' background knowledge and lives, and she uses group work to do many activities in her class.

Fifth Grade Math Lesson

Laura Sammon

Lesson Plan for Fifth Grade Mathematics by Laura Sammon, North Glendale Elementary School
Based on the Three Stages of Understanding by Design

Stage 1. Desired Results

Established Goals	Transfer
1. Relate volume to the operations of multiplication and addition and solve real-world and mathematical problems involving volume. 2. Apply the formulas V = l × w × h and V = b × h for rectangular prisms to find volumes of right rectangular prisms with whole-number edge lengths in the context of solving real-world and mathematical problems. From Common Core State Standards for Mathematics.	Students will be able to independently use their learning to apply the formula V = l × w × h for rectangular prisms in the context of solving real-world mathematical problems.

	Meaning

Understandings	**Essential Questions**
1. Students will understand volume is an attribute of solid figures and understand concepts of volume measurement.	1. How are area and volume related? 2. Why do we need an understanding of volume in the real world?

Acquisition

Knowledge	**Skills**
Students will know that a unit cube, a cube measuring one cubic unit, can be used to measure volume.	Students will be able to measure volume by counting unit cubes, using cubic centimeters, cubic inches, cubic feet, and improvised units.

Stage 2. Evidence of Learning

- Students are using factors and multiples of numbers to 24.
- Students are using the area of the cupcake containers to determine the area of the shopping bag.
- Students are combining and breaking numbers apart in various combinations.
- Students are using the formula for area (l × w) and the formula for volume (l × w × h).
- Students are using graph paper to represent the units.

Stage 3. Learning Plan

Learning Events

This lesson comes at the end of a unit on measurement, specifically the study of perimeter, area, and volume. Students are presented with the following scenario:

A cupcake designer is opening her own small business. Previously, she made cupcakes in her basement kitchen, but now she is opening a retail space on a busy downtown street. She has cupcake containers in the following sizes: 1 × 1, 1 × 2, 1 × 3, 2 × 2, and 3 × 3. The 3 × 3 size holds either five cupcakes or nine cupcakes. (See diagram.)

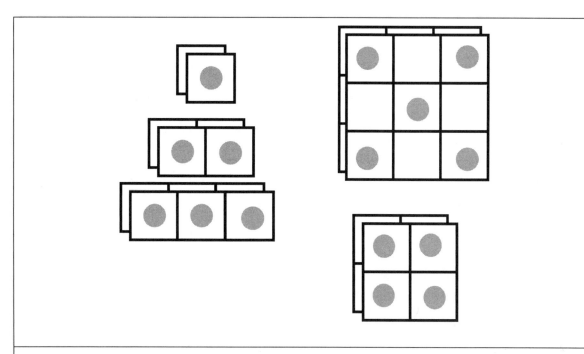

The designer is meeting with the vendor of a shopping bag company. From looking at the catalog from the bag company, she knows that as the size of the bag increases, so does the price. Before the vendor talks her into buying bags she cannot use, or a more expensive size for all her cupcakes, she asks her sister's fifth-grade students to (a) Figure out the minimum number of bags needed to fit all her cupcake containers up to twelve cupcakes. (No one buys more than twelve, as the cupcakes are $6.00 each.) (b) Make a chart that shows her high-school-aged employees what bag to use for what number of cupcakes.

Students work in small groups in order to help the teacher's sister know which size shopping bags to buy. Students will need graph paper and pencils, but no other special tools are necessary.

The teacher circulates among the groups and records her observations of students' thinking. Students work in groups until they reach consensus about the answer to the first problem.

Bring the whole group back together in order to share their thinking and reach whole group consensus. Once the bag issue is decided, students work on the chart that shows how to bag the cupcakes up to twelve cupcakes.

After much rich discussion, my class chose three bag sizes with the following bases: 1×2, 2×3, and 3×4. We decided that the bags should have a height of four units, and that the top unit should remain unfilled so that the cupcakes would not fall out of the bag and would allow the handles to come together with ease.

The students in my class came up with the following chart.

Number of Cupcakes	Container	Bag	Layers
1	1×1	1×2	1
2	1×2	1×2	1
3	1×3	2×3	1
4	2×2	2×3	1
5	3×3	3×4	1

(Continued)

(Continued)

Number of Cupcakes	Container	Bag	Layers
6 (4 + 2)	2 × 2 and 1 × 2	2 × 3	2
7 (4 + 3)	2 × 2 and 1 × 3	2 × 3	2
8 (4 + 4)	2 × 2 and 2 × 2	2 × 3	2
9 (5 + 4)	3 × 3	3 × 4	1
10 (5 + 5)	3 × 3 and 3 × 3	3 × 4	2
11 (9 + 2)	3 × 3 and 1 × 2	3 × 4	2
12 (9 + 3)	3 × 3 and 1 × 3	3 × 4	2

While the price of the containers is not discussed in this lesson, the same idea holds true for the cupcake containers. The larger the container, the more expensive.

The lesson ends with a debriefing session on the math skills the students used to complete the investigation. The students' list might include their knowledge of factors and multiples and their understanding of multiplication, composing and decomposing numbers, calculating volume, calculating area, and problem-solving skills.

What instructional strategies does Laura use during this lesson? What culturally responsive strategies?

_____

_____

_____

❖   ❖   ❖

Deb Preuss is also a fifth-grade teacher at North Glendale Elementary School and a colleague of Laura's. In this science lesson, she uses pendulums as an introduction to science inquiry. Once again, students are engaged, doing higher level thinking, and sharing with others—Deb makes sure of that!

Pendulums: An Introduction to Science Inquiry

Deb Preuss

Objectives/Standards Using National Academy of Sciences Framework (Three Dimensions)

Dimension 1—Scientific and Engineering Practices

3. Planning and Carrying Out Investigations—students will plan an investigation of how to change the number of swings on a pendulum.

Dimension 2—Crosscutting Concepts

2. Cause and Effect—students will decide what changes to the pendulum affect the number of swings.

Dimension 3—Core Ideas

Physical Sciences 2—Motion and Stability: Forces and interactions—students will generalize the relationship between the length of the pendulum and the number of swings.

Vocabulary/Previous Knowledge

Testable question, hypothesis, manipulated variable, responding variable, controlled variable, data, conclusion

Materials Needed per Student

- Ten large paperclips
- One unsharpened pencil
- Eraser tips
- Three washers
- Masking tape
- Paper and pencil for notes and data recording

Hook

Build it and they will come! Have a pendulum ready for display (five paper clips linked together with a washer attached to the bottom). Slide the top paperclip onto the pencil and make sure it swings freely. Attach the eraser tip to the end. Have the students build their own from the display—it's very simple and takes just a few minutes. Be sure to give a little time for them to play! After a few minutes, have them attach the pendulums to the side of their desks or table. Six inches of the pencil should be on the desk with the eraser tip pointing out and fastened with masking tape. This will be considered the standard pendulum system.

Discussion

Yesterday we discussed some of the parts and processes of science investigations and today we are going to apply that learning to a real investigation. Ask students about the terms and ideas that were discussed and record them for the class to see. Ask them to be thinking of those ideas and terms as we go through the first activity.

Activity 1

As a class you will see how many times the pendulum swings in ten seconds. Using your standard pendulum system, you will all do trials simultaneously to establish some base data.

Demonstrate the following: Hold the washer at the end of the pendulum even with the table surface—the paperclips should be taut, not sagging. This will be called a zero degree release point. Set a timer for ten seconds. As you release the pendulum start the timer and count the number of times the pendulum swings back toward you for ten seconds. This is the counting system everyone will use. As a class do three to five trials. The number of swings should be fairly consistent among the group. If the pendulum hits something or is interfered with, that trial is not valid. Calculate the average number of swings from all of the valid trials.

Discussion

Students share their data and discuss why it is similar. What pieces of the standard pendulum system caused the results to be so similar? List ideas on the board. Answers should be weight (washer), release point, number of paperclips (length), amount of pencil sticking out from the desk, and so on. These are the possible manipulative variables.

Activity 2

Structure a class investigation. Choose one of the possible manipulative variables mentioned above (I usually choose weight). Model how to compose a testable question. Does changing the weight on a pendulum affect the number of swings it makes? Remind the students that testable questions must include the manipulative (weight) and responding variables (swings). Have students discuss their predictions about this question. Then compose a hypothesis: If I increase the weight on a pendulum, the number of swings will decrease. A hypothesis must be more specific and make a prediction about the outcome.

Now add the two other washers on the pendulum. Conduct three to five trials, record the data, and find the average.

Discussion

Ask the class how those trials were the same as the standard pendulum system and record:

- Same number of paper clips
- Same release point
- Same pencil
- Same length hanging off the desk
- Same amount of time
- Same way of counting

- Ask the students what kind of variables those are? (Controlled)
- Ask what changed in the experiment? (Weight—the number of washers)
- What kind of variable is that? (Manipulative)
- Ask what they are measuring? (Swings)
- What kind of variable is that? (Responding)

Now discuss the results of the trials. The number of swings should have remained the same. What can you conclude from this trial? (Weight does not change the number of swings.) In other words, is there a cause and effect relationship? No, weight does not cause any change.

Activity 3

Students choose and design their investigation. It is important that they only make one change from the standard pendulum system in order to conduct a fair test. They need to record their testable question, hypothesis, and variables on a sheet of paper, along with their data and conclusion based on the results. Have timers on hand for the trials, as students will need them at different times.

Assessment

Observe the students as they discuss and plan their investigations, making sure that the testable question mentions a manipulative and responding variable and the hypothesis makes a prediction.

Do students conduct trials accurately? Are the controlled variables evident? Is the data accurate? Does the data support the conclusion? Does the conclusion mention a cause and effect relationship or lack thereof?

Collect the notes from the investigation to help identify the need for ongoing instruction and practice.

Extensions

If you could do your investigation again, what would you do differently? Why?

Do you think your results would hold true for any pendulum, even if it were made with different materials?

Look into the history of pendulums. Who invented the pendulum and what are its uses? Can you think of a new use for a pendulum?

What instructional strategies does Deb use to engage? Which culturally responsive strategies does she use throughout the lesson?

_____

_____

_____

❖   ❖   ❖

Barb Swalina, a first-grade teacher at North Glendale Elementary, is a warm, loving teacher who makes each first-grade student feel at home. She uses writing throughout her curriculum and shares this writing lesson with us. She asks, "How do we get first graders to learn to love writing?" Barb does it through this lesson and others like it. Students work at the highest levels of thinking: they are creating, and their creations are published for the families, so she is connecting to the community.

Publishing Student Poetry Books

Barb Swalina

Common Core State Standards, Language Arts

1.W.5; 1.W.6; 1.SL.4; 1.SL.5; 1.SL.6; 1.L.2; 1.L.5; 1.L.6

Common Core Standards–Crosswalk to Missouri GLEs/CLEs for English Language Arts			
Writing Standards Grade 1			
CCR Anchor Standards	*Grade-Specific Standard*	*Missouri GLE Alignment*	*Explanation*
Production and Distribution of Writing			
5.	**W.1.5** With guidance and support from adults, focus on a topic, respond to questions and suggestions from peers, and add details to strengthen writing as needed.	**W.1A.1.a, d, e** Follow a writing process to (a) brainstorm and record ideas in written form, (d) revise writing to clarify meaning and enhance descriptions (such as describing words, relevant details), (e) edit for conventions with assistance.	**W.1A.1.a, d, e** Direct alignment
6.	**W.1.6** With guidance and support from adults, use a variety of digital tools to produce and publish writing, including collaboration with peers.	**ICTL5A.1** Record relevant information, with assistance, in at least one format (e.g., writing, pictures, audio recordings, photos).	**ICTL5A.1/ ICTL1B.1/ W.1A.1** Aligns to multiple GLEs
		ICTL1B.1 Contribute to the construction and exchange of ideas through independent, cooperative, and/or collaborative work.	
		W.1A.1.a–e Follow a writing process to (a) brainstorm and record ideas in written form, (b) generate a draft in written form on student-selected topic, (c) reread writing, (d) revise writing to clarify meaning and enhance descriptions (such as, describing words, relevant details), (e) edit for conventions with assistance.	

First Grade Report Card Scoring Guide Rubrics for Poetry Writing			
Communicates Ideas: All Units			
Beginning	*Approaching*	*Meeting*	*Surpassing*
I need reminders to communicate relevant ideas.	I occasionally communicate some relevant ideas in a meaningful way but may misinterpret various styles and genres.	I can communicate relevant ideas in a meaningful way using various styles and genres (e.g., nonfiction, poetry, letters, and stories).	I consistently communicate ideas in a meaningful way by using writing craft and mentor authors in various styles and genres.
Develops Personal Voice: All Units			
Beginning	*Approaching*	*Meeting*	*Surpassing*
I need reminders to show creativity or personal engagement with my topic. I am unaware of my audience.	I occasionally show creativity or personal engagement with my topic. My style may be awkward and audience may or may not be considered.	I can show creativity or personal engagement with my topic. I am aware of my audience.	I consistently show creativity or personal engagement with my topic. I am aware of my audience and adapt my writing style accordingly.
Explores Elements of Poetry: Unit 6			
Beginning	*Approaching*	*Meeting*	*Surpassing*
I need reminders to explore word choice to visualize and act out poems. I contribute to shared poems.	I occasionally explore word choice to visualize and act out poems. I contribute to shared poems.	I can explore word choice to visualize and act out poems. I contribute to shared poems.	I consistently explore word choice to visualize and act out poems. I consistently contribute to shared poems and I can independently write my poems.

In our school district, each grade level has curriculum-based reading and writing programs. In first grade, we teach and assess our students on various genres of writing, including poetry units of study.

In Unit 6 of *Being a Writer: Exploring Words Through Poetry*

- Students hear, visualize and act out poems.
- Students write shared and individual poems.
- Students get ideas by listening to one another.

One of my favorite things about teaching writing is publishing my students' stories, regardless of which genre I teach. (I have accomplished this with my second, third, fourth, and, most recently, first graders.)

Writing is a process, and so is this lesson from start to finish. It is a project that takes a village! On the evening of our open house (at the beginning of the school year) I solicit parent participation in many classroom activities. For writing I ask parent volunteers to

- Construct book covers using the discontinued wallpaper samples from local paint stores, colorful duct tape, and recycled cardboard.
- Assist the students with editing and using word processing to type the second draft of their writing during writer's workshop on Fridays.
- Publish the students' stories I e-mail to them.
- And sew the books.

Book Cover Instructions

1. Cut cardboard into two 5½-inch × 8-inch pieces.

2. Cut wallpaper into two 8-inch × 10-inch pieces.

3. Rubber-cement cardboard to the center of each wallpaper piece.

4. Cut off corners of wallpaper just at edge of cardboard.

5. Fold paper edges over cardboard and tape with transparent book tape.

6. Use duct tape (comes in many colors and patterns) to tape the two cardboard pieces together, leaving ¼ inch between the two pieces.

Sewing Instructions

Use an 8½-inch piece of construction paper as the base and place the pages of the story in order. On a sewing machine, sew the story to the center (space) of the cardboard cover. Once the story is sewn to the piece of construction paper, the construction paper can now be rubber-cemented into the constructed cardboard booklet.

Publishing Instructions

1. Open file in Microsoft Word or WordPerfect.

2. Save file as another name (or add *edit* to the end of the original file).

3. Format the story to two columns.

4. Do File, Page, Setup and change the layout to Landscape.

5. Print the story.

6. Mark the story up into section numbers.

7. Choose an appropriate template per number of sections.

8. Cut and paste sections per the template.

9. Save the file and print.

Printing Instructions

Short Book (Ten Sections or Less)

1. Print Pages 1 to 3 first.

2. Put the pages in order with Page 1 on top, Page 2 second, and so on.

3. Put pages back in the printer tray.

4. Print Pages 4 to 6. (If using WordPerfect, select the box to "Print in Reverse Order" if the option is available.)

5. Put pages in order and fold like a book.

Long Book (Eleven to Eighteen Sections)

1. Print Pages 1 to 5 first.

2. Put pages in order with Page 1 on top, Page 2 second, and so on.

3. Put pages back in the printer tray.

4. Print Pages 6 to 10. (If using WordPerfect, select the box to "Print in Reverse Order" if the option is available.)

5. Put the pages in order and fold like a book.

It is truly a rewarding process when a child can create a piece of writing, get it edited, use word processing to type it, choose from a plethora of book covers, illustrate the pages, and then share the published piccc with his or her peers!

Sample of a First Grader's Pattern Poetry

I Am BIG!

by Zoe Silkwood

My dog Yaz is big, but not as big as his brother Orr.

Orr is big, but I am bigger.

I am big, but not as big as my dad.

My dad is big, but not as big as a hippo.

A hippo is big, but not as big as an elephant.

An elephant is big, but not as big as a bus.

A bus is big, but not as big as a whale.

A whale is big, but not as big as the ocean.

The ocean is big, but not as big as the earth.

The earth is big, but not as big as the sun.

The sun is big, but not as big as the solar system.

What is bigger than the solar system?

Space!

After Zoe shared her published book with the class, many of her peers were inspired to write their own patterned poetry book!

I am big, but not as big as my dad. My dad is big, but not as big as a hippo.

A hippo is big, but not as big as an elephant. An elephant is big, but not as big as a bus.

Drawn and written by Zoe.

What instructional strategies does Barb use throughout the lesson? What culturally responsive, standards-based strategies does Barb use?

_____

_____

_____

❖   ❖   ❖

LESSONS FROM MIDDLE SCHOOL TEACHERS

I met Tracey during a workshop, and she ran with the ideas presented. In this chapter, she shares a lesson plan she uses in Business Information Management and Concepts of Engineering and Technology in the Career and Technical Education department at Maurine Cain Middle School. She is the chair of the department. She begins by describing her principal, Jason L. Johnston, and follows with her lesson.

> *Jason L. Johnston, my principal, is an administrator who cares about educating every child and ensuring his staff has the required support and materials. Our campus is a place where he guides us to ensure all students are mastering objectives. He models challenges to his staff's thought process to create effective facilitators of education for our students. He has established nets of educational safety around each student at our school, as we have an effective response to intervention system and professional learning community. Lessons must be designed so that students receive work that is both engaging and challenging.*

International Business Project

Tracey M. Black

Envision a classroom where students are authentically engaged in the learning process. They ask each other questions and perform effective research to investigate the answers. This international business project is designed for my students to perform at higher levels of learning in a fun and safe environment. This project empowers and inspires my students to get involved in making the economic world around them a better place. They just love this project as they take ownership of becoming successful entrepreneurs. I enjoy watching them use twenty-first century learning skills such as effective problem solving, listening skills, teamwork, critical thinking, collaboration, creativity, innovation, and communication as they prepare for the global economy. This project helps set the stage for students as they are, in reality, preparing to compete in the global economy. This project creates a win-win for all students and facilitators of learning.

Summary of Lesson

As our economists, politicians, and business persons engage in discussions of the U.S. economy, our students can become knowledgeable on options of helping to enhance our economy. The international business project provides students with a real-world opportunity to implement personal and interpersonal skills, as well as apply business letter-writing skills, calculating costs, and multimedia presentation skills as they engage in business internationally. They collaborate in teams of two or three students and choose from a list of countries to form partnerships for international business that will enhance the economy of the United States. A foreign country can only be chosen once in all classes. Many students are unaware of how international business influences the U.S. economy. After a country is chosen, each group begins the research process. They receive rubrics to keep them informed of requirements and deadlines. This project allows the students to learn marketing and business strategies of different countries. They prepare professional business presentations, and about 95 percent of students tend to be authentically engaged in this project and create well-planned businesses. Some examples of the companies they have created are bakeries in France, technology centers in Japan, a telecommunications company in Finland, and travel agencies in China. The students are required to dress in business attire when they make their presentations.

Project Planning Form					
Name of Project	*International Business Project*		*Duration: 4 weeks*		
Class(es)	*BIM*		*Semester: 2*		
Content/Curriculum Areas to partner with	social studies, English, accounting, career portals, marketing				
Project Idea (investigation, scenario, problem, challenge, issue, and so on)	Students will create a business in the United States and form a foreign partnership to enhance their business.				
Entry Event (grabber) to launch inquiry and spark curiosity	(*Goonies* scene: teaches taking risks) Movie that grabs attention relating to project: Teacher created.				
The Driving Question, problem or challenge statement or issue	What are the benefits of international business for the U.S. economy in the twenty-first century?				
Content and Skills Standards addressed	130.114 10 (A,B,C); 11 (A) i, ii; (B); 12 (A,B,C)				
		T	**P**		**T**	**P**
Partnership for P21 Skills to be taught (T) and practiced (P): Check all that apply.	Critical Thinking/ Problem Solving			Social Literacy and Cross/ Multicultural Literacy		
	Communication (oral and written)			Productivity and Accountability		
	ICT Literacy			Leadership and Responsibility		
	Collaboration			Financial, Economic and Entrepreneurial Literacy		
	Information Literacy			Civic Literacy		
	Flexibility and Adaptability			Health Literacy		
	Initiative and Self-Direction					

(Continued)

(Continued)

			Presentation Audience
Student Work	Major group product(s):	Business plan, multimedia presentation	Class
			School
			Community experts
	Major individual product(s):	Persuasive Essay	Web
			Other

Assessment and Reflection	**Rubric**(s) I'll use (check all that apply)	Collaboration		Content Knowledge	
		Critical Thinking		CTE Competencies	
		Oral Communication		Physical Education skills	
		Written Communication		Physical Education skills	
		Visual and Performing Arts (multimedia presentation)			
	Other **assessments, benchmarks,** and **checkpoints** (check all that apply)	Quizzes/tests		Practice presentations	
		Self-evaluations		Notes	
		Peer evaluations		Checklists	
		Online tests/exams		Concept maps	
	Reflections	Survey		Focus group	
		Discussion		Learning plan	
		Journal write/learning log			

Resources	On-site personnel	Principal, counselors, teachers
	Technical (equipment)	Flip cameras, computers with Internet access, printer
	Community resources	Rockwall Business Education Council (RBEC)
	Material resources	Economic magazines
	Online resources	BLS.gov, Businessweek.com CIA World Factbook (theodora.com), BEA.gov

What instructional strategies does Tracey use throughout the project? What culturally responsive, standards-based strategies did you find?

_____

_____

_____

❖   ❖   ❖

Heather, a colleague of Tracey's and Jason's at Maurine Cain Middle School, engages her students in middle school science class by giving them a real task to complete. This lesson involves collaboration and higher level thinking skills.

Roller Coaster Project

Heather Ross

Part 1: Design and Build a Model Roller Coaster

Objectives

- Create and build a model roller coaster that can be used in student experiments.
- Differentiate between speed, velocity, and acceleration by determining the speed, velocity, and acceleration of different points on a model roller coaster created by a student.

Follow These Guidelines

1. The roller coaster must be reasonable and successful.

2. Passenger safety in the "cars" (simulated by marbles of varying sizes) is most important. It cannot come off the track!

3. The roller coaster should be attached to a neatly cut piece of cardboard or foam board (not poster board).

4. Record the exact length of track used to construct the roller coaster. Make a sign that displays the total length of the track. *This is very important!*

5. The roller coaster is constructed using only approved materials. The track should be made of cardstock and the support beams should be made of cardstock or Popsicle sticks.

6. Make up a unique name for your roller coaster and create a marquee sign and attach it to the board or coaster.

7. Give a name to two important or interesting features, like curves, hills, and loops. Put a small sign at these locations on your coaster. (Partners must complete four signs.)

8. Have an attached starting gate at the beginning of the coaster.

9. Have an attached ending gate at the end of your coaster to safely catch the car.

10. The roller coaster must have at least two 90° turns. (Partners must have four.)

11. The roller coaster must have at least two 180° turns. (Partners must have four.)

12. The roller coaster must have at least one full loop. (Partners must have two.)

13. The roller-coaster ride must last for at least fifteen seconds from starting gate to ending gate. (Partners' ride must last for at least twenty-five seconds.)

14. Identify and *label* on the roller coaster the following physics concepts:

    a. Calculate the average speed of your roller coaster:

$$\text{Speed} = \frac{\text{The total length of the track in centimeters}}{\text{The time it takes a marble to complete the coaster in seconds}}$$

    b. Choose five different sections of track and calculate the speed of the marble as it travels through these sections (cm/s). (Partners are responsible for ten speeds.)

        i. You will always start the marble at the very beginning, but you will only time the section that you are measuring. (This is kind of tricky. You will need to do it a few times to get it right—please see me if you do not understand.)

    c. Choose five different sections of the track and determine the velocity of the marble as it travels through these sections (cm/s + the direction). (Partners are responsible for ten velocities.)

    d. Label five sections of the track that demonstrate acceleration. Label the points with the specific type of acceleration (speeding up, slowing down, starting, stopping, turning). (Partners are responsible for ten accelerations.)

Extra Credit

You can receive ten bonus points for creating a project that makes me say WOW (in a good way). Think creative themes, extreme numbers of special features (such as loops), extra large or long, unique uses of roller-coaster pieces, and so on.

Note: Remember your coaster is made out of paper; it will not respond well to moisture. Please think about this when you are bringing your project to school.

Part 2: Conducting the Experiment and Collecting Data

Objective

Determine if mass affects the average speed of a roller-coaster ride by completing an experimental investigation using the model roller coasters.

Question

How does the number of passengers affect the speed of a roller coaster?

After your roller coaster is built, you will be given three marbles of different masses. These marbles will represent the increased number of passengers in the roller-coaster cars.

Read all of the following directions carefully. Ask yourself these questions:

- What am I trying to find out?
- How will I measure what I find out?
- How will I record what I measure?

Your experiment will be titled "The Effect of Mass on Average Roller Coaster Speed."

Create an ExD *before* you begin the experiment. Look back in your IAN to remind yourself about the parts of an ExD. Make sure to include

- Your hypothesis in the "If . . . then:" format. (How the independent variable (IV) affects the dependent variable (IV))
- Identify the IV, DV, control, number of trials, and constants.
- Your data table should include the following measurements or calculations for each of the marbles: mass, distance, time, average time, average distance, and average speed. Your data table should have space for three trials for time.
- Sketch of what the experiment will look like.

Materials

- Three different marbles
- Triple beam balance
- Roller coaster
- Timer

Procedure for Testing Your Hypothesis

1. Measure the mass of each of the marbles. Record the data on your data table.

2. Begin with the marble with the lowest mass.

3. Place the marble at the starting point on your roller coaster.

4. At the moment that the marble is released from the starting point, start the timer. Stop the timer when the marble reaches the end point.

5. Record the data in your data table.

6. Repeat Steps 4 through 6 for a total of three trials.

7. Repeat Steps 4 through 7 with each marble.

8. Use the average time and average distance traveled for each marble to calculate the average speed.

Note: Do not count trials that are incomplete because the marble falls off or does not move down the entire track.

What instructional strategies does Heather use throughout this project? What culturally responsive, standards-based strategies does she use?

_____

_____

_____

❖   ❖   ❖

Kim James is math department head at Maurine Cain Middle School and a colleague to Tracey and Heather. She really knows how to connect student interests to her curriculum. Kim shares why she designed "The Car Project" and how she implements it in her middle school math classes.

How Much Does a Car Really Cost?

Kim James

Let's face it, students today must feel some sort of reasoning behind everything that they do when it comes to education. One of the projects that I use in my classroom every year takes a "rite of passage" for many soon-to-be-high school students and puts it into a realistic format—buying a car. "The Car Project," as my students have come to call it, allows middle school students to get the real-world perspective of all of the expenses involved in buying a car and allows them to take ownership of the main aspect in the project, choosing their car. Students are completely engaged throughout this project because, once they have chosen the car they want to purchase, they are invested in the outcome. They truly want to see the final outcome and actually care about the accuracy more than the teacher. Parents become involved as well in discussing savings plans with their students. Students are working within the three upper levels of Bloom's taxonomy throughout the project as they apply the standards of percentages and proportions, analyze the data they gather, and then synthesize their findings into a proposal for the purchase of their new car. Each year that I assign this project, I have so many students walk away with not only the understanding of the materials that will be tested, but with a new understanding of life concepts.

Project Planning Form		
Name of Project	*How much does a car really cost?*	*Duration: 1 Week*
Class(es)	*Eight Grade Math—Regular and Pre-AP*	*Semester: 1*
Content/Curriculum areas to partner with	Math and BIM	
Project Idea (investigation, scenario, problem, challenge, issue, and so on)	Students will choose a car that piques their interest, yet is reasonable to purchase. They will research the actual cost of the simple interest loan needed including taxes, title, license, and interest. They will determine their monthly payments on the loan and additional expenses that it will take to maintain the car, such as insurance and gas. Students also will calculate the commission earned by the salesperson.	
Entry Event (grabber) to launch inquiry and spark curiosity	Teacher presents a slide show of different cars and then polls students to get their thoughts on what it would cost to own and drive a car.	

(Continued)

(Continued)

The driving question, problem or challenge statement or issue	How much does it really cost to own a car?
Content and Skills Standards addressed	8.1(B)—select and use appropriate forms of rational numbers to solve real-life problems including those involving proportional relationships. 8.2(B)—use appropriate operations to solve problems involving rational numbers in problem situations. 8.3(B)—estimate and find solutions to application problems involving percentages and other proportional relationships such as similarity and rates. 8.14(A)—identify and apply mathematics to everyday experiences, to activities in and outside the school, with other disciplines and with other mathematical topics. 8.14(B)—use problem-solving model that incorporates understanding the problem, carrying out the plan and evaluating the plan for reasonableness. 8.14(D)—select tools such as real objects, manipulatives, paper and pencil, and technology or techniques such as mental math, estimation, and number sense to solve problems.

		T	P		T	P
Partnership for P21 skills to be taught (T) and practiced (P): Check all that apply.	Critical Thinking/ Problem Solving		•	Social Literacy and Cross/ Multicultural Literacy		
	Communication (oral and written)		•	Productivity and Accountability		•
	ICT Literacy			Leadership and Responsibility	☐	
	Collaboration	☐		Financial, Economic and Entrepreneurial Literacy	•☐	
	Information Literacy	☐		Civic Literacy		
	Flexibility and Adaptability	•☐		Health Literacy		
	Initiative and Self-Direction		•			

			Presentation Audience	
Student Work	Major individual product(s):	Written proposal and multimedia presentation	Class	X
			School	X
	Major group product(s):		Community Experts	X
			Other	X

Assessment and Reflection	Rubric(s) I'll use (check all that apply)	Collaboration	•	Content Knowledge	•
		Critical Thinking	•	CTE Competencies	•
		Oral Communication	•	Physical Education skills	
		Written Communication	•	Physical Education skills	
		Visual and Performing Arts (multimedia presentation)	•		
	Other assessments, benchmarks, and checkpoints (check all that apply)	Quizzes/tests	•	Practice presentations	•
		Self-evaluations	•	Notes	
		Peer evaluations		Checklists	•
		Online tests/exams		Concept maps	
	Reflections	Survey		Focus group	
		Discussion	•	Learning plan	
		Journal write/ learning log	•		
Resources	On-site personnel	Principal, counselors, teachers			
	Technical (equipment)	Computers with Internet access and printers			
	Community resources	Local car dealerships, with explanation on calculating title, taxes, and license, examples			
	Material resources	Pen and papers, calculators			
	Online resources	Tax guides			

What instructional strategies does Kim use during the car project? What culturally responsive, standards-based strategies does she use?

_____

_____

_____

❖   ❖   ❖

HIGH SCHOOL LESSONS

The following lessons are from high school teachers in the West Contra Costa Unified School District in Richmond, California. The administrators in these high schools are committed to equity. They work tirelessly to support their teachers with professional development that offers them culturally responsive instructional strategies. A cadre of teachers at the schools have been engaged for the past three years learning culturally responsive instruction and doing peer observations in an effort to learn from their colleagues and share best practices. Teachers also have the opportunity to participate in Saturday workshops focusing on culturally responsive, standards-based instruction. Although all the administrators are committed to this work, I have to give a shout-out to the ones I worked especially closely with over the past few years: Terri Ishmael, Sue Kahn, Reggie Marsh, and Jessica Smith-Kennan. In addition, I must acknowledge the other administrators, department heads, instructional coaches, teachers, and other educators who continue the challenging work in this district to improve instruction for all students.

Tiffany Holliday is a young, dedicated educator who teaches English at Pinole Valley High School and is also Lead Teacher of the Health Careers Academy at her school. This lesson, taught in her English class, prepares students for career readiness and college preparation.

Work Ready—College Ready—Life Ready

Tiffany Holliday

Subject: English 3, Day 2B: Work Readiness Skills—Time Management Skills	Essential Question for This Unit: What is fitness?
Time: 42 minutes (Advocacy Class)	Goals/Objectives (from Stage 1 of UbD): Students will be able to . . . • Identify which work readiness skills they need to develop and practice more by reading attributes of ten skills • Explain how they will improve on a particular work readiness skill this week by writing goals for themselves
Materials • Equipment • Laptop • Projector • Remote control	Lesson Activities • Lesson Springboard • Each student will get a copy of the work readiness skills survey and they will rate themselves on each of the ten skills.
Resources • Forty copies of work readiness skills survey and worksheet • Student reflection journals • Access to work readiness poll	Lesson Development Direct Instruction: Work Readiness Skills As a class we will review each of the ten skills and take an informal survey of the class about how they rated themselves on each of the skills. We will discuss examples and non-examples of each skill to gain a better understanding of what these skills look like at school or in the workplace.
Prior Student Learning: (Stage 2 of UbD Template)	Interactive Survey Using Poll Everywhere, students will text their vote to the number given to determine which of the ten work readiness skills they need to work on the most (wherever they rated themselves the lowest). Before students take the poll, I will ask the class what their predictions are for which skill they think the class needs to work on the most. The poll can be accessed at http://www.poleverywhere.com. We will then discuss the results and reactions that students have—were their predictions correct?

(Continued)

(Continued)

Homework: Work on achieving time management goals this week	**Goal Setting** During this first week of our project, students will focus on improving their time management skills. They will work on the second page of their work readiness skills handout, where they will describe where they currently rate with this skill and what about their behavior demonstrates that level of skill, and write a goal for themselves around time management for this week. I will provide them with an example.
	Lesson Closure Students will share with me and with each other what their goals are for the week.
	Possible Prior Student Misconceptions (if applicable) Regardless of which skill comes up as the one to work on most as a class, this week we will work on time management skills. UPDATE: It just so happened that the skill they rated themselves as needing to work on the most was time management!
	Student Assessment Artifacts (from Stage 2 of UbD Template) Student artifact: work readiness skills worksheet
	Variations and Extensions "Hired/Fired" Cards—Students will receive a "hired" or "fired" card based on their work throughout the day. Whoever has a "hired" card at the end of the day will earn extra points. Watch clips of TV shows (fiction or reality) where the setting is a workplace. They can look for positive and negative examples of the skill we are currently focusing on.

Monday: The work readiness skill I am working on this week is _____.

For this skill, I rated myself as _____.

By Friday I hope to rate myself as: _____.

1. Why do you think this skill is considered a "work readiness skill"?

2. What does it look like when someone is very good at this skill? What would a person who is very good at this skill do at school or work?

3. What does it look like when someone is very bad at this skill?

4. In order to improve on this work readiness skill this week, I will:

    A. _____

    _____

    B. _____

    _____

    C. _____

    _____

Friday: I now rate myself as _____ for this week's work readiness skill.

1. Did you meet this week's goal for work readiness skills? Why or why not?

2. What can you do to continue being good at or improving on this goal in the future?

Work-Ready/Essential Skills

Keith Archuleta

In today's knowledge and innovation-based economy, the skills necessary for success in the workplace have converged with those needed for success in college. These are the work-ready/essential skills most identified by employers that students must develop to be ready after high school graduation to enter the workforce *and* to successfully transition to college. *They are skills for life.*

1. Communication

I pay attention to instructions; listen and observe; articulate thoughts and ideas clearly and effectively in written form; speak clearly, assertively, and decisively with appropriate speed, inflection, and volume; and use technology appropriately to communicate.

| I Need Some Help | I'm Working on It | I'm OK | I'm Pretty Good! | I'm AWESOME at This! |

2. Information Management

I seek out, locate, and organize information; read to understand and evaluate information for quality of content, validity, credibility, and relevance; reference sources of information appropriately; and ask probing and clarifying questions if I don't understand.

| I Need Some Help | I'm Working on It | I'm OK | I'm Pretty Good! | I'm AWESOME at This! |

3. Quantitative Reasoning

I use quantitative reasoning to describe, analyze, and solve problems; perform basic mathematical computations quickly and accurately; and use applied math and/or data to develop possible strategies and solutions.

| I Need Some Help | I'm Working on It | I'm OK | I'm Pretty Good! | I'm AWESOME at This! |

4. Technology

I select and use appropriate technology to accomplish tasks; apply technology skills to problem solving; use computer programs such as Word, Excel, and PowerPoint easily; and can quickly access information from reliable sources online.

| I Need Some Help | I'm Working on It | I'm OK | I'm Pretty Good! | I'm AWESOME at This! |

5. Initiative/Self-Direction/Resourcefulness

I listen actively and seek out necessary information and the means to solve problems and get things done; take initiative and can work independently as needed; am open to learning; actively seek out new knowledge and skills; and monitor my learning needs.

| I Need Some Help | I'm Working on It | I'm OK | I'm Pretty Good! | I'm AWESOME at This! |

(Continued)

(Continued)

6. Critical Thinking and Problem Solving

I think about how to describe and analyze both the symptoms and the causes of problems; use cost/benefit analysis to determine the advisability of a course of action and make effective decisions; make judgments and evaluate alternatives based on evidence and previous findings; and use knowledge, facts, and data to generate workable solutions.

| I Need Some Help | I'm Working on It | I'm OK | I'm Pretty Good! | I'm AWESOME at This! |

7. Professionalism and Ethics

I am punctual and manage time effectively; set goals and prioritize tasks; bring tasks and projects to completion; demonstrate integrity and ethical behavior; act reliably with others in mind; learn from my mistakes and take responsibility for my actions.

| I Need Some Help | I'm Working on It | I'm OK | I'm Pretty Good! | I'm AWESOME at This! |

8. Workplace Context and Culture

I understand workplace culture, etiquette, and practices and know how to navigate in organizations; understand how to build, use, and maintain a professional network of relationships and the role such a network plays in personal and professional success; pay attention to detail, dress appropriately on the job, and understand the value of rules that protect the health and safety of others.

| I Need Some Help | I'm Working on It | I'm OK | I'm Pretty Good! | I'm AWESOME at This! |

9. Creativity and Innovation

I demonstrate originality and inventiveness; communicate new ideas to others; and integrate knowledge across different disciplines.

| I Need Some Help | I'm Working on It | I'm OK | I'm Pretty Good! | I'm AWESOME at This! |

10. Collaboration

I build collaborative relationships with colleagues and customers; consider others' time and ideas to be valuable and can work within a team, contributing appropriately to the team effort; motivate and support others; resolve conflicts and negotiate reasonable solutions; foster mutual respect, understanding, and cooperation; learn from and work collaboratively with individuals representing diverse cultures and ethnicities, ages, gender, religions, lifestyles, and viewpoints; and use technology to support collaboration.

| I Need Some Help | I'm Working on It | I'm OK | I'm Pretty Good! | I'm AWESOME at This! |

SUGGESTIONS FOR STUDENTS

- ✓ Take classes that emphasize these skills.
- ✓ Document the acquisition of these skills in a portfolio throughout high school.
- ✓ As you gain these skills, include them on your resume.
- ✓ Describe the skills you have gained on your college and job applications.

From Archuleta (n.d.). Used with permission from Keith Archuleta, President, Emerald HPC International, LLC.

While doing this, we focused on one skill for just one week at a time. Ideally, I think the skill should be focused on for maybe a month at a time to give students a real opportunity to improve on the skill. If you have questions or wish to contact me, you may do so at hollidayteacher@gmail.com.

What instructional strategies does Tiffany use during this project? What culturally responsive, standards-based strategies does she use?

_____

_____

_____

Cecilia Distefano is a Spanish teacher at Kennedy High School. She tried something new this year that worked well, and she wanted to share it with us. Even though this is high school Spanish, this web idea would work in most grade levels and across most content disciplines.

Five-Paragraph Essay

Cecilia Distefano

Teacher Name : Distefano	Date: 3/14 to 3/22
Course Name: Spanish 1	
Lesson Topic/Function: Present information, conceptual ideas to the audience of (readers) on a variety of topics.	Goal: SWBAT: write extended sentences by using a web to brainstorm adjectives or other descriptive words and phrases. SWBAT: write a five-paragraph essay by brainstorming extended topic sentence, four detail sentences, and a concluding sentence. SWBAT: write a title and a reflection for their five-paragraph essay by analyzing (Bloom's Taxonomy) and synthesizing.
Standard Addressed: Stage I: Standard 1.1: Students address discrete elements of daily life.	ESLR Addressed: G: Set goals, develop and utilize a plan to achieve these goals (with guided practice). E: Use concise, logical language coherently.

Assessment

Students are assessed according to the rubric provided and the quality of their work. They also will be assessed when I get back in the classroom by writing a paragraph on their own in class. Students may use their reference vocabulary portfolio.

Research-Based Strategies Used: Marzano's essential 9: Explicit instruction; Bloom's taxonomy

Lesson Plan Note and Reflection

Planning

I had to prepare a lesson plan for my substitute to be able to carry out while I was away from class in a two-week period (for coordination of WASC visit).

I decided to do a project: My students would write a five-paragraph essay from one's personal point of view or about another person regarding things that one does in everyday life. And they had to be able to do it almost independently so the sub would not go crazy.

Student Assessment: Informal

Before my leave, students had practiced answering personal questions. Most students know to answer in complete sentences by now. But the sentences tend to rely on easy ideas (I like X, I do X) and be very repetitive with vocabulary.

Thinking about Marzano's teaching strategy of explicit instruction, I showed students how to write more interesting sentences with a web graphic organizer.

I showed students how to brainstorm ideas by answering questions (what, how, who, when, etc.). We listed and used prepositions in order to form adverbial clauses (in the room, under the table, on the chair, with my friend). We practiced with a graphic organizer. We also went at the problem backward by having students label ready-made sentence parts (subject and verb) and clauses responding to the question-labels who, what, where, when, how, etc.

We also have been working all quarter on being cognizant of the difference between two types of basic Spanish sentences. (Indirect sentences like "Me gusta + infinitive verb + subject" and "Soy + adjective.")

The Project

I left two big chart papers detailing the first phase of the project, with a clear rubric. Students were told what would be considered A, B, or C work.

Scaffolding for Paragraphs

After working on extending sentences, students had to make a paragraph. A rubric with instructions showed students how to first brainstorm a topic sentence and then the detail sentences. And finally how to write a concluding sentence (a question or a comment on the subject of the paragraph) (see Appendix E).

Afterward, students received the actual project guidelines, a five-paragraph essay, complete with a title and a reflection. Finally, students are required to write a reflection on the process of writing the five paragraphs.

Student Assessment: Formal

As part of their end of the quarter assessment, students will have to write a paragraph. They may use their reference folders, but they have to write a paragraph on their own in class, using the same procedures.

Reflection

The care I had to take in detailing instructions and writing rubrics (and explaining it to the substitute, who is an effective teacher in her own right) produced some of the best individual work I have seen all year. I arrived at the final product after reviewing each night the work students were doing and handing in. I returned the work to the classroom each day with feedback either to the substitute or recognizing the great work the students were doing.

What instructional strategies does Cecilia use? What culturally responsive, standards-based strategies does she use?

_____

_____

_____

Maricris Cruzat is one of the most exciting math teachers I have observed. Her classroom is always filled with students (often more than forty) working together in groups and collaborating on projects. Her freshman algebra class, consisting of many students who have failed the class in the past, is taught in a format where students must depend on each other for problem solving. Students are expected to present to the entire class from the front of the room, showing their work on a document reader as groups check their answers. Students stay on and are kept on task due to the group makeup of the class and the expectations for their success. Notice how Ms. Cruzat has a *community component* in her project as well as collaboration and problem solving.

Math Multimedia Project

Maricris Cruzat

Common Core Math Standards

F.IF.7; S.MD.1; S.MD.2; S.MD.5; F.IF.9; F.BF.1; F.BF.3; AS.SE.1; AS.SE.3; S.CP.4; S.MD.6; S.MD.7; N.Q.1; N.Q.2; N.Q.3

Objective

The purpose of this project is to create a multimedia presentation that will highlight or showcase various math concepts or issues related to math *and relevant to the community.* The project must be *informative, relevant, and engaging.*

Examples

- Tracking Urban Lions (http://science.kqed.org/quest/video/tracking-urban-lions/)
- Restoration of the San Joaquin River Slideshow (http://science.kqed.org/quest/video/web-extra-restoration-of-the-san-joaquin-river-slideshow/)

Media Format

The project can be presented in the following formats:

- Audio
- Slideshow
- Video

Mechanics for the Project

1. Collaboration and teamwork will be the driving force behind this project. Each team consists of three or four students. You will be allowed to choose your own members (choice) for this project since it will involve meetings outside classroom time.

2. This project aim is to inspire your group to explore, experiment, and create an effective media presentation communicating your ideas to your audience. This is a two or three minute media presentation. In order to be successful, there will be four phases for this project that will follow a given timeline.

  A. **Planning Time:** Determining what resources are accessible to your group, how much time is available, and what you want to illustrate. Find time to read the tools in pdf format for your guide.

    Output: Story Board

  B. **Media Planning Tool Kit**
    - Tools: Writing a script
    - Media-making resources slideshow
    - Media-making video resources
    - Choosing your media content, equipment, and format
    - Interview techniques

  C. **Producing:** Taking photos, shooting video, recording sound, editing clips, and working with materials

    Output: Proof of photos, preliminary video, and interview saved on a flash drive to show that you have begun the project

  D. **Presentation/Publishing:** Showing the finished product, uploading content to the Web, exporting media files, and demonstrating learning.

    Output: Actual project on a flash drive presentation will be on _____.

3. The tools for the project are anything that is available to your group. There are many sophisticated, powerful, and expensive tools on the market, but perhaps surprisingly, there are also many less sophisticated yet still powerful hardware and software options, and many are free. Interestingly, the final media projects tend to be of similar quality whether they are created by the free or the expensive tools. Most people end up using a combination of both.

4. You will be given one day of access to the library computers during class time. If you need more time, you are expected to make the necessary arrangements outside class time.

5. You will be graded based on the following components:

  A. Introduction—10 points

  B. Delivery—15 points

  C. Technical Production—20 points

  D. Images and Graphics—20 points

  E. Content—20 points

  F. Group Collaboration and Individual Contribution—15 points

A more detailed rubric will be provided for each group in order to have a clear set of expectations for each component. This is worth 100 points, and the final project is due on _____.

What instructional strategies does Maricris use in this lesson? What culturally responsive, standards-based strategies does she use?

_____

_____

_____

Michele Lamons-Raiford teaches English and American Sign Language (ASL) at Pinole Valley High School, in addition to presenting workshops in the area of professional development. Michele is forceful, passionate, engaging, and smart. Students flock to her classes. The following lessons demonstrate her use of collaborative, interactive instruction to engage high school students and support academic achievement.

Beginning American Sign Language Bull Game/Numbers Exercise

Michele Lamons-Raiford

Date: 2011–2012
Class/Subject: ASL 1 (Grades 9–12)
Title of Lesson: Beginning American Sign Language Bull Game/Numbers Exercise

Length of Lesson

One class period, or about 55 minutes

Content Area Objectives/Standards

Student will be able to

- Acquire a basic functional vocabulary in American Sign Language. (WCCUSD—Course of Study—Course Outline—Performance Objectives 2.1.15)
- Demonstrate the content components of the numbers 1 to 100. (3.1.4)
- Increase speed in signing numbers.

Computer Functions

Student should be able to use the American Sign Language Browser Web site (http://commtechlab.msu.edu/sites/aslweb/browser.htm) to look up the correct ASL numbers as necessary.

Materials Needed

Class set of hardcopy photos of ASL numbers 1 to 100. (Use handouts from textbook.)

Problem Specification

- Students need to apply their knowledge of the Internet.
- Students go to a Web site and search for the video examples of ASL numbers as necessary.

Hook (Approx. Five Minutes)

Activities Before Using the Computer

Students become engaged with the lesson through the use of *collaboration*. Students gather into groups of three or four and practice with each other on the signing of ASL numbers 1 to 100. (The teacher may choose to pair struggling signers with more advanced ones.)

Discussion (Debrief) (Approx. Five Minutes)

Supporting Activity

Students switch groups. Students practice as well as test each other.

Activity 1 (Approx. Five Minutes)

Activities While Using Computer
Allow students to use the computer to look up video demonstrations of the numbers at their leisure. (Some students may feel more comfortable looking up things themselves rather than asking for help.)

Mini Lecture/Model (Approx. Ten Minutes)

1. Have everyone gather into a large circle along the walls of the room.

2. Explain the bull game: You must sign the numbers 1 to 100 but leave out anything that has a seven in it. If you come to that number, you must sign "bull" or else you are "out" and must sit down.

3. The teacher starts going around the room and speaking the numbers, helping those who are struggling or who forget and sign 7, 17, 27, and so on.

4. Caution that anyone who falls in the seventies (numbers 70 to 79) must be very careful to pay attention. (The teacher may choose to put a struggling signer next to an advanced signer who can silently help.)

5. After at least one practice round, the teacher advises that this is a *silent* game and that if you get lost, you must sign "again" or "slower" to the person next to you to make sure you do not get "out." Talking and laughing also constitutes an "out."

6. A bag of healthy snacks (e.g., fruit gummy bears, granola) can act as rewards (incentives) for whoever is left standing.

Activity 2 (Approx. Fifteen to Twenty Minutes)

1. The teacher begins the game, reiterating that it is a silent game.

2. The teacher may provide limited help to students but encourage help to silently come from their peers.

3. The ultimate authority in determining who is "out" is the teacher.

4. The teacher times this first game to keep a record of how the class speed improves. (Later, there will be competitions where classes compete against each other for faster times.)

Discussion (Debrief) (Approx. Five Minutes)

Supporting Activity

The teacher asks for volunteers to communicate their frustrations with trying to remember numbers, paying attention to where they were in the game, or trying to improve their speed.

Data Manipulation and Presentation of Results

Students are encouraged to find other signing Web sites or online ASL dictionaries that will help in the memorization or practice of ASL numbers.

Evaluation Methods

Students will be individually and privately tested on their numbers after the fifth week of school. They must be able to sign the numbers 1 to 25 in twenty seconds. The time may be adjusted and modified as necessary, but *all* students must show an improvement in sign speed two weeks later.

Review/Summary (Approx. Five Minutes)

Supporting Activity

The teacher explains the importance of studying ASL numbers and the difference between ASL numbers, other sign systems, and English.

Homework Assignment

Activities After Using the Computer

Each student will be encouraged to study at home or with partners outside of class and be reminded of the impending individual ASL numbers test.

Assessment of Student Learning During and After Class

- Did students acquire a basic functional vocabulary in ASL?
- Could the students demonstrate the content components of the numbers 1 to 100?
- Were the students able to increase their speed of signing numbers?
- Could the students apply their knowledge of the Internet and go to a Web site and search for the video examples of ASL numbers as necessary?

English-Language Arts Content Standards for California Public Schools

Grades 11–12, Reading

2.0 Reading Comprehension (Focus on Informational Materials): Students read and understand grade-level-appropriate material. They analyze the organizational patterns, arguments, and positions advanced.

National Education Technology Standards

2. Communication and Collaboration: Students use digital media and environments to communicate and work collaboratively, including at a distance, to support individual learning and contribute to the learning of others. (a, b, and c)

3. Research and Information Fluency: Students apply digital tools to gather, evaluate, and use information. (a, b, c, and d)

What instructional strategies does Michele use? What culturally responsive, standards based-strategies does she use?

_____

_____

_____

❖   ❖   ❖

Music as Poetry

Michele Lamons-Raiford

Date: 2011–2012
Class/Subject: AP LIT (Grades 11–12)
Title of Lesson: Music as Poetry

Length of Lesson

One class period, or about fifty-five minutes

Content Area Objectives/Standards

Student will be able to

- Apply prior knowledge and experience to a variety of music.
- Recognize themes and motifs in music lyrics.
- Define and practice the application of literary or poetic devices.

Materials Needed

- Class set of music lyric handouts from a variety of musical genres
- Class set of poetic devices handouts
- CDs or burned compilations of a variety of music from different genres

Hook

Students will become engaged with the activity through the use of a quick-write, a short burst of writing based on the following questions.

Topic

Do you think of music as poetry? How and why? Does your answer only pertain to a certain type of music? What is your favorite genre (type) of music? Do you consider yourself to be eclectic (varied or diverse) in your musical preferences?

Discussion (Debrief)

Have students get into groups of three or four and share their answers. Or implement an "idea wave," randomly selecting students or asking for volunteers to share their quickwrites. Teachers also may wish to further engage students by asking them to think about which artists they find to be the *most* poetic and why. Teachers may wish to enter into the hook as well and share their own personal musical preferences. This would work the best if the teacher's musical preferences were eclectic, if the teacher was open-minded, and if he or she were "up" on some of the latest and current music.

Mini Lecture

1. Explain the concept of music as poetry.

2. Create an eclectic, open-minded, and safe learning environment so that the discussion of hip-hop/rap, R&B, rock, alternative, reggae, pop, jazz, and top forty can be readily accepted as another tool to explore literary themes, poetic devices, and ways in which to understand and practice the application of literary and poetic devices. Mandate a climate of respect of differing opinions and ideas.

3. Review literary and poetic devices.

Activity 1

1. Pick a song from hip-hop/rap, R&B, rock, alternative, reggae, pop, jazz, or top forty (or another genre) with no profanity, no blatant sexuality, an array of literary and poetic devices, and possibly different interpretations that can be drawn from the content.

2. Model this first activity by playing the song, reviewing the lyrics with the students afterwards, pointing out literary and poetic devices, and discussing possible themes.

Discussion (Debrief)

Have the students introduce a theme they see in the song and support it with lyrical references. Or have them gather into groups of three or four and share how they might be able to analyze a contemporary song that they like the same way.

Activity 2

1. The students should receive lyrics from another song (of a different genre).

2. The students should have the literary and poetic devices handout next to the lyrics so that as they listen to the song they can reference which lyrics may exemplify which literary or poetic devices.

3. The students also should look for a theme that may readily lend itself to the song.

Discussion (Debrief)

Have students gather into groups of three or four and share their ideas about the song, compare literary and poetic devices and themes, and eventually come back together as a larger group to share, discuss, agree, and sometimes disagree as a class.

Assessment of Student Learning During and After Class

- Could students effectively apply prior knowledge and experience to reading music lyrics?

- Did the students recognize themes and motifs in music lyrics?
- Did the students successfully define and practice the application of literary or poetic devices?

English-Language Arts Content Standards for California Public Schools

Reading, Grades 11–12

3.0. Literary Response and Analysis

3.2. Analyze the way in which the theme or meaning of a selection represents a view or comment on life, using textual evidence to support the claim.

3.3. Analyze the ways in which irony, tone, mood, the author's style, and the "sound" of language achieve specific rhetorical or aesthetic purposes or both.

3.4. Analyze ways in which poets use imagery, personification, figures of speech, and sounds to evoke readers' emotions.

❖ ❖ ❖

CULTURALLY RESPONSIVE STRATEGIES

These lessons from a variety of teachers share commonalities that support culturally responsive and standards-based instruction. For the most part, the lessons shared have the following characteristics:

- Student centered and inquiry based or project oriented
- Aligned with standards
- Prepare students for career readiness and college
- Use higher level thinking
- Students work in groups
- Incorporate Differentiated Instruction (DI)
- Keep students in the general classroom, working at Tier I of RTI
- Make all students visible through teacher-student interaction and peer interaction
- Respectful of learning time and space

What instructional strategies does Michele use? What culturally responsive, standards based-strategies does she use?

_____

_____

_____

❖ ❖ ❖

This chapter illustrates how teachers can incorporate culturally responsive strategies into the lessons already designed for their classroom use. After you design your lessons, either by yourself or ideally with your professional learning group, examine them to see how many culturally responsive practices are embedded and what others you can add. All of these women are diligent, passionate teachers who have devoted their lives to children. What can you take away from this chapter?

_____

_____

_____

_____

_____

The final chapters focus on a call to action and ask you to step outside your comfort zone and work for personal and social change. The next chapter offers several models for student groups at all levels. Consider a model that might work at your school.

Which lessons offer possibilities for you to use in the classroom?

_____

_____

_____

PART IV

A Call to Action

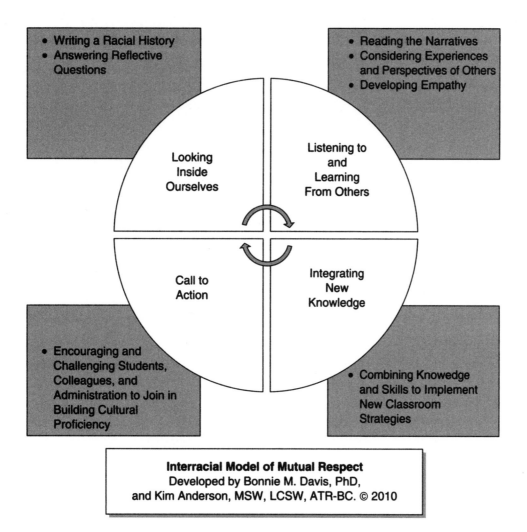

- Writing a Racial History
- Answering Reflective Questions

- Reading the Narratives
- Considering Experiences and Perspectives of Others
- Developing Empathy

Looking Inside Ourselves

Listening to and Learning From Others

Call to Action

Integrating New Knowledge

- Encouraging and Challenging Students, Colleagues, and Administration to Join in Building Cultural Proficiency

- Combining Knowedge and Skills to Implement New Classroom Strategies

Interracial Model of Mutual Respect
Developed by Bonnie M. Davis, PhD,
and Kim Anderson, MSW, LCSW, ATR-BC. © 2010

17

A Call to Action

Sponsoring Academic Student Support Groups

Students need to interact with other students who look like them and face similar challenges. Student support groups based on ethnicity or racial identity offer that. In this chapter, several educators share the models they use to provide this for their culturally diverse students. In addition to these individuals who have started student support groups, many schools, universities, public agencies, and churches are supporting students' academic achievement through tutoring and leadership programs. You can find out about these by calling local agencies, school districts, and churches. For example, a school in St. Louis County uses Washington University students as tutors for their after-school program. The university students volunteer, and the middle school students have both a mentor and a tutor. It is a win-win situation.

A high school in a neighboring district implemented a mentoring program where the African American high school students travel weekly to two elementary schools in the district to mentor the fifth-grade African American students. The students volunteer their time, and the feedback is tremendous. An unexpected positive effect has been the *improvement in the academic achievement of the high school students.* They said they had to do better in order to be good examples for their mentees.

The following are several models created by educators for the students in their schools.

HIGH SCHOOL

The African American Academic Achievement Club: The 4 As

Researching the work of Banks (1994), Kunjufu (1988), and others, my colleagues and I organized an academic club at a high school that met weekly to support student achievement. We proposed a model for a school club that would give external rewards to high school girls for their improved academic achievement. We received a district grant to fund the club following a study of the academic achievement gap between African American students and other students at this high school. The sponsors' goal was for the girls to make As, so we created a name that included As: the African American Academic Achievement Club (AAAA), or the 4 As.

After receiving the grant, we invited all the African American high school girls to join. During the previous year, I had developed a relationship with five girls with whom I met weekly. Each Tuesday morning they met for twenty minutes before the first class of the day. Mainly, they knew they could count on me to be there, and if they ran into trouble at school, they knew they could come to me for support. These girls were the first to join, so they helped put up flyers throughout the school, announcing the new academic achievement club. Just seeing the flyers with "African American" and "Academic Achievement" on the same poster prompted some educators to make positive comments to the sponsors about the idea of the group.

The girls met weekly after school for approximately thirty minutes, and those who could not make the afterschool meetings met for twenty minutes before school in one sponsor's room. The focus was solely on improving their grades. At the end of the first quarter of the school year, there was dramatic improvement in the girls' grades. No girl's grade had fallen, and most had significant improvement in their overall grade point average. The improvement continued throughout the year, and more and more girls joined the club. By the end of the year, nearly every African American girl in the school was a member.

A club for the boys also existed, and its model was based on a coaching model where the boys met in the sponsor's room each morning and huddled and set goals, much like players on a team. This group was called the American Black Achievers (ABA). Because of the expertise of the male sponsor, he used a model that was a better fit for the boys.

Each sponsor has different strengths, and each club has different strengths. The sponsors stressed academics, because we believed that if the girls achieved B and A averages, they would begin to see themselves differently and the staff would view them differently. School behaviors would change—if they had been previously negative—when the girls began to experience academic success.

We explicitly taught and modeled what the girls had to do if they wanted to make Bs and As in the highly competitive, college prep school in which they found themselves. Most of these girls were taking part in the St. Louis Voluntary Desegregation Program, and they lived in the city of St. Louis. They traveled daily to this affluent district where resident students had years of sibling models; parents and older siblings often had attended Ivy League schools. Resources were available to support most of their educational needs, including such things as weekly tutors to organize them, Kumon math, ACT/SAT prep classes, and so on.

On the other hand, these girls needed to learn the hidden rules of this district, choose the best course of study, learn how to study most effectively, develop relationships with staff and students who could support their efforts, and withstand negative peer pressure. They were told that they needed to do approximately three hours of homework a night, as well as eliminating most, if not all, phone use and television during the week. The club brought in speakers, role models, other teachers, and anyone else who would encourage the girls to succeed. The girls ran the meetings and had individual responsibilities within the club; they did the attendance and much of the paperwork—it was their club.

At the end of the first semester, a popular television personality came to the awards ceremony to speak to the club and to distribute the rewards to the girls. She posed for a picture with each girl. The superintendent, the assistant superintendent, the principal, and the assistant principal attended, showing the girls and the staff that this club was important. A poignant moment occurred when a Black parent said that this was the first time she had come to the school for something positive rather than punitive regarding her child. The parents were so proud and turned out in large numbers. Teachers who had complained that Black parents didn't come to school functions now saw them proudly attending a celebratory function for their children. Eventually the club dropped its use of external rewards, and the girls continued because they wanted the support and camaraderie that the club offered them.

After the first semester, teachers began commenting about the "improved attitudes" of the "Black girls." These comments, along with proof of the improved grade point averages and the girls' attitudes toward schoolwork, made this club a success.

The 4 As club model can improve student achievement and change beliefs about student abilities. The model can function also as a staff development tool, because it forces staff to confront their attitudes about minority achievement, and, hopefully, to examine teaching practices. The club can and does work for the following reasons:

- It has a single focus—academic achievement.
- It offers concrete rewards in its first year for academic achievement.
- It meets weekly or more often.
- It teaches students how to study.
- It teaches students the hidden rules of the school culture.
- It teaches students the expectations that staff has for honor roll students.
- It reinforces academic achievement with ceremony and recognition.
- It continually reinforces participants' perceptions of themselves as academic achievers.
- It stresses to its participants that they will attend college and offers college visits.
- It offers tutorial assistance and other necessary support for participants to achieve academic excellence.
- It evolves differently in each setting, depending on its sponsors and members.
- It receives support for its sponsors through staff support and networking.
- It has sponsors who are willing to take risks while risking the criticism of their colleagues.
- It has sponsors who are willing to make mistakes, learn from the students, and grow professionally.

An academic achievement group, such as the 4 As club, is but one strategy to improve the academic achievement of diverse learners, but it is a powerful strategy because it can change belief systems. It says to diverse learners that, yes, they are capable and they can achieve academically. And it says to the staff that, yes, these students are capable and they can achieve academically.

How might an academic achievement group work in your school setting?

_____

_____

_____

I met Graig Meyer at a national conference more than ten years ago, and we have become close colleagues, collaborating around issues of social justice, especially pertaining to racial identity. Below Graig describes the Blue Ribbon Mentor-Advocate program.

Blue Ribbon Mentor-Advocate Program

Graig Meyer

What does it take to make sure every single student is successful? What do they need as individuals? What do their families need? What does the system need to do?

My goal is to answer those questions for every student in the Blue Ribbon Mentor-Advocate (BRMA) program. As the program's coordinator for fourteen years, I've seen 95 percent of our students graduate from high school and 100 percent of those graduates go on to college. We've learned a lot of answers to those questions, but the only real answer is that every student needs something different.

We have learned that the most powerful transformation you can make in most students' lives is to help develop their individual strengths and interests. We take on some challenges with intervention strategies as necessary, but our real goal is to help every student figure out his or her singular gifts and foster those so that they become a pedestal for future success.

We know you have to start early and stick with it. Students enter our program in the fourth grade and we keep working with them all the way through college. Volunteer mentors provide our primary support for the students, and we've learned that the duration of a mentoring relationship is the strongest predictor of its impact. Some kids might have a couple of mentors during their time in our program, but more than 60 percent have had the same mentor the whole way through. It's not just the students who benefit from these relationships either. Mentors report just as high a level of benefit as our students, and I truly believe that the whole community is better because of these bonds across lines of age, class, and race difference.

Many efforts at various tutoring programs have taught us that no amount of academic help outside of school is as good as having a good learning experience inside school. That's why we train all of our mentors and parents to work together on school advocacy tasks like going to parent-teacher conferences. While they're doing that, we're taking on systemic advocacy initiatives to create better support for our students and all of those who are like our students.

We have seen time and again that our students thrive when they have access to cultural enrichment, summer learning experiences, college exposure, and leadership development. They have so much untapped potential and I'm reenergized every time one of our activities with a group of students lights a few sparks amongst them.

There is one thing that I have learned which almost all of our program participants already know. When working with People of Color, you've got to deal with the issue of race. As a White man, I have spent years in a listening and learning position to understand how our families want their race and culture to be strengths for their children. I've learned to follow the lead of our students when they talk about the impediments they face because of institutionalized racism. Perhaps most importantly, I've learned not to be scared. They're not. And they can't afford for me to be. For every student to be successful, I have to be courageous enough to fight for racial equity.

More Information on the Program

Blue Ribbon Mentor-Advocate Provides Local Students Quality Comprehensive Support

The Blue Ribbon Mentor-Advocate program is the flagship mentoring program of the Chapel Hill–Carrboro City Schools, working to increase student achievement and reduce the achievement gap. The program relies on the relationship between mentor-advocates and students as the foundation for providing a variety of individualized student supports. BRMA students benefit from mentoring, advocacy, tutoring, enrichment opportunities, leadership development, and college scholarships. Mentor-advocates help determine a student's strengths and interests, and the program tries to provide support that will help develop those to their full potential. Over the program's fourteen-year history, 95 percent of student participants have graduated from high school, with 100 percent of those students enrolling in institutions of higher education.

History

The Chapel Hill-Carrboro City Schools have a strategic focus on improving the achievement of African-American and Latino students. These students have not performed to the same level as their White and Asian peers in our schools. In 1994, the Blue Ribbon Task Force on the Achievement of African-American Students made a recommendation that the school district sponsor a mentoring program to provide assistance to some of these students. In 1995, Blue Ribbon Mentor-Advocate was launched in response to that recommendation. BRMA continues to be one of the district's many efforts to support these students as they progress through our schools.

(Continued)

(Continued)

Program Logistics

The role of the BRMA program is to provide students with the adult support they need to attain their personal and academic potential. The mentor-advocate plays a dual role, establishing a meaningful relationship with a young person as well as promoting the child's success in school by working as an advocate in conjunction with the child's family and school personnel.

Children are carefully selected for the program because of their ability to benefit from the increased support it offers. The neediest students are not necessarily chosen to participate.

Rather, students who are chosen have shown particular promise, perhaps in the form of motivation, citizenship, academic ability, or determination. Students must also show a desire for additional interaction with adults, and their families must be willing to support the program through involvement with the mentor. Students enter the program in fourth grade, and we continue to support them through graduation from high school and enrollment in postsecondary education.

Likewise, adult volunteers are carefully selected to serve as mentors. Volunteers make a two-year, two hour minimum per week commitment to a child. All volunteers must attend preservice training and make regular reports to the program on the progress of their match. In exchange, the program offers volunteers multiple forms of support to enhance their effectiveness as a mentor.

Student Services Provided

Mentoring—The one-on-one relationship is the fundamental component of the program. The mentor exposes the child to new experiences while also helping the student pursue his or her interests and talents.

Advocacy—Mentors and parents collaborate to support their student by working within the school and community to develop and utilize resources that support the student's success.

Tutoring—Students have the opportunity to receive tutoring in community-based, evening tutorials. Tutorial sessions include peer support, college exposure, and creative learning activities.

Social and Cultural Enrichment—The program sponsors social and cultural events for mentors and mentees. Scholarship funds are also used to provide opportunities for student engagement in activities such as summer camps, arts lessons, and athletic leagues.

College and Career Exposure—Students are provided with regular opportunities to explore options for attending college and pursuing the career of their choice. BRMA sponsors college tours, workshops, and assistance through the college application and enrollment process. Mentors provide students with individualized guidance throughout a student's time in the program.

Parental Involvement—BRMA provides direct support to parents through individualized assistance intended to support their child's success in school.

Youth Leadership Institute—The Blue Ribbon Youth Leadership Institute operates a leadership summer camp and year-round service club that encourages students to develop their leadership skills through service-learning activities. This program serves more students than just those who are officially part of BRMA.

Scholarships—BRMA provides scholarship funds for students who wish to pursue postsecondary education.

The Haidt Scholars fund is an endowed scholarship that aids in paying the tuition of a student attending a four-year college or university. The Sponsor a Scholar fund uses community donations to assist students who wish to attend any type of postsecondary educational institution.

Donations/Gift Giving

Another way BRMA provides to students is through monetary investment in secondary education. These funds are raised though the Sponsor a Scholar initiative. The goal of Sponsor a Scholar is to raise $500 for each of the eight years a child is enrolled in the Blue Ribbon Mentor-Advocate program. Of that amount, half is invested for postsecondary study and the other half for enrichment experiences.

BRMA maintains support from the community because of the local social-justice centered ethos. Chapel Hill has built a reputation as being a leader in North Carolina on social, economic, and environmental issues. The Town Council has introduced programs to holistically address issues of sustainability through social equity, economic vitality, and environmental protection. Programs like BRMA, seeking to give back to members of the community, gain community buy-in as a result.

For more information on the program, visit www.blueribbonmentors.org.

❖ ❖ ❖

MIDDLE SCHOOL

Dorothy Kelly puts students first. When she became the only Administrator of Color in a middle school, she knew she needed to do something to support the Students of Color who were the racial minority in the school. Here she describes the student support groups she started at the school.

Dorothy Kelly, whose racial history and "A Day in the Life" are found in Chapters 3 and 5, shares the school support groups she founded for middle school students.

The Kids in Cooperation and Future Focus Programs

Dorothy Kelly

I believe students should have opportunities to connect with one another and learn how to be leaders in a safe environment. This belief became a source of strength to me when I served as an assistant principal at Washington Junior High School in a suburban school district south of St. Louis City. The district participated in a desegregation program called the Voluntary Student Transfer (VST) program. This program allowed African American students from St. Louis City to attend the suburban St. Louis County schools. The results of desegregation and/or integration did not always leave the St. Louis City children with a sense of security in knowing that they belonged in the schools they attended. Over the years while I was a teacher and later an administrator, many African American students expressed their feelings of discontent to me. They believed they were not liked by people at the schools they volunteered to attend. Some students wanted to go back to their home schools.

The principal, Mike McGough, and I were concerned that our African American students did not have "real" connections to the school or to their peers. While African American students rode the same buses to school every day, they usually did not live in the same neighborhoods, and this resulted in neighborhood clashes because they either belonged to rival gangs or did not associate with one another outside of the school day. The phenomenon of not associating with their peers was pervasive among the high to mid-level achievers. Although they did their schoolwork, they were not distinguished as individuals or as a group of achievers. Further adding to that group's isolation was tracking in math and literacy classes. When the high-achieving African American students were placed in advanced classes, they were usually the only African American student in that class. They did not go home with White students after school, participate in sleepovers, or get invited to parties on the weekends, although they spent most of their days with these students. As an administrator, I knew the results of tracking could be isolation, but observing and experiencing a whole population of children being ignored or not seen as worthy peers was disheartening. The principal and I sensed that the African American students were not as tolerant of each other as we knew they should be and they were not perceived as significant peers by their White classmates. This was perhaps the most agonizing part of our school culture and had to be eradicated.

To me the answer was simple: let's create a fun program for them to participate in! To reach our goals I decided that I needed a hook and an interesting activity for them to do. Previously, Dr. Bonnie Davis had sponsored an academic club for the African American girls at a neighboring high school, and it was very successful. She generated positive feedback and the girls expressed that they felt more connected to their school as a result of being in the club. However, the idea of academics being the focus was not the direction I initially wanted to take. I was leaning more toward a "team" type activity or event with a culminating experience for them to accomplish. Once I gained a following, I would drop the academics on them! So Kids in Control (KIC) was launched as a drill/dance team.

Kids in Control Program

We started with the name, Kids in Control, and it morphed into Kids in Cooperation, because the culture among the African American students seemed to change over the years—less conflict, more cooperation. Activities for the Kids in Cooperation (KIC) club were centered around practicing dance/drill routines and participating in career field trips.

The structure of the club for the first year was a combination of seventh and eighth girls and boys. The following year the club was only open to eighth graders. This was part of building the image of "something special" to the seventh graders: "When I get to eighth grade I can join KIC." This marketing strategy worked, because the second year more students were on board. In order to pull off what we planned, cooperation was paramount, and the truly dedicated leaders knew this. I considered all students leaders; however, as I observed and interacted with them over time, I identified the co-captains of the drill team. I supported them with consensus-building skills and how to develop a capacity for tolerance. My idea was to encourage them to become models of cooperation and tolerance, teaching students how to get along when you do not agree without resorting to name calling, degrading others, or fighting. Eligibility requirements for the KIC program: eighth-grade student, 2.5 or above GPA, and no out-of-school suspensions for violence or illegal acts. Activities include: weekly meetings and practices; fund raising for snacks, team T-shirts, supplies, and bus costs; design dance/drill team T-shirts; be a dancer or part of the technical crew for the annual performance; and participate in two career-oriented field trips per year.

The KIC program became an established program at our school and became culturally diverse. Membership included African American, Latina, and White girls. Students, parents, and teachers looked forward to our performances at school spirit assemblies.

Future Focus Program

A second club was launched three years later—it was called Future Focus—which incorporated an academic component and introduced a peer-tutoring model to the students. Both programs offered leadership development activities such as goal setting, decision making, social and study skills, career-oriented field trips, fund raising, and hosting guest speakers.

The main goals of the Future Focus program were to connect with high-achieving African American students and move the average achievers to higher levels in their daily work by establishing academic goals and achieving those goals through peer tutoring. The membership of this club included African American students who were achieving a 2.5 and/or basic level to advance level on their state tests. The club was named Future Focus because I wanted students to understand that they had control over their futures. Activities included peer tutoring and career field trips. Again, we were attempting to develop a culture of leadership and self-advocacy among the students. Once eighth graders were functioning under the established norms and demonstrated full commitment, then at the beginning of second semester the seventh-grade students were brought on board. Students set academic goals at the first meeting and again at the beginning of each quarter. Their goals were to increase and/or maintain

(Continued)

(Continued)

a particular grade in a class. The choice was C or above; C− or lower goals were not allowed. Occasionally the school counselors and Volunteer Student Transfer counselors would visit our meetings and speak about the achievement gap, high school life, or social skills. However, the "meat and potatoes" of our meetings was peer tutoring. Everyone would bring their text books, assignments, and supplies. They would group together by expertise; then participants would tutor their peers that needed help. Perhaps the most rewarding aspect of the Future Focus club was observing them peer teach. They were talking like their teachers, demonstrating how to solve equations or write grammatically correct paragraphs. Students would scold or praise to motivate their tutee.

Eligibility requirements for the Future Focus program: eighth-grade students (all year), seventh-grade students (second semester), 2.5 or above GPA, basic or above results on state achievement assessment, and no out-of-school suspension for violence or illegal acts. Activities included two weekly meetings, goal setting, volunteering as a peer tutor, and participation in two field trips.

The main goals with the KIC and Future Focus programs were to develop leadership skills within and among the students. Second, but just as powerful, was for the students to develop connections to Washington Junior High School beyond the classroom. We wanted the African American students to remember something fun and important about their junior high years. We wanted them to learn to view themselves in a positive light. For all participants, leadership would mean learning to build consensus, tolerance of peers, practicing self-control, and strengthening the capacity to persevere. My role was more of a facilitator than a director, and the principal's role was one of a motivator. I believe the students accepted our guidance for two reasons: they knew we cared about them and that we were on a mission for them.

Overall, I believe the KIC and Future Focus programs were successful because they fulfilled a need among an isolated group of students. Once these two clubs were established, our school culture changed. Other staff members got on board: the librarian filmed our performances; the FACS teacher provided use of the lab to design T-shirts (no one was ever allowed to use FACS room after school); the school counselors attended our meetings; the secretaries helped with paperwork; and some teachers volunteered to supervise field trips. Of course we met challenges, mainly funds. Programs could not receive funds if they were racially exclusive. Our club was not billed as racially exclusive, but it appeared to be, even after other ethnicities joined us, so no funding came our way. So we had to raise funds to pay for T-shirts, supplies, snacks, and buses for our field trips. Lack of school funding actually benefited us, because the students sold candy—they loved doing it and it taught them budgeting skills, too. The principal and I simply saw this as yet another function of leadership—figure out how to overcome setbacks.

The KIC and Future Focus students became noticed and distinguished for being leaders. The results of the end-of-the-year program evaluations were always positive, especially when students were asked if they thought belonging to KIC and Future Focus was beneficial to them. Past members would come to meetings and performances. Overwhelmingly, students reported that they liked the clubs and felt more connected to Washington Junior High School, and they also said KIC and Future Focus clubs made them feel important.

❖   ❖   ❖

Tracey Black was inspired by learning about the 4 As during a summer professional development held in her district in Rockwall, Texas. She decided, with the support of her principal, to start an academic achievement club for the girls in her school based on the 4 As. Tracey's group includes African American and Hispanic students.

Sisters of Class

Tracey Black

My interest in starting Sisters of Class began with a spark from Jason Johnston, my principal. After attending a diversity workshop with Dr. Bonnie Davis, he and I had a conversation that centered on whether we were doing enough to reach all students. After careful thought, I shared the idea of Sisters of Class with him, and he supported the idea from day one. I wanted to form an academic group that was founded on the values of excellence, integrity, and service. The group is comprised of girls of various ethnic groups and open to all girls, even though the mission of Sisters of Class seeks to empower African-American girls through increased academic achievement while creating opportunities to serve school and community. The vision of Sisters of Class is to inspire African American girls to excel in academic achievement and social responsibility through school and community service and interactive workshops that focus on college and career readiness, twenty-first century leadership skills, interpersonal skills, and character building.

I looked at grades and test scores of the student population and wanted to aid in helping all students, especially African American females. Since I am African American, I felt that I could positively impact their academic performance as well as social. When I was a student in elementary, middle, and high school, there was a majority Caucasian student population. It was easy for me and my other African American friends to just camouflage ourselves and just try to blend in with everyone else and not draw too much attention. Therefore, I felt that Sisters of Class could be a place where all girls could feel welcome and be a part of paving the way for the continued success of all girls.

We have weekly meetings in the mornings on Thursdays for thirty minutes and rap sessions after school. The morning meetings are designed to have workshops on various topics, such as study skills, math skills, writing skills, leadership skills, healthy living, etc.

In a reflective paragraph written by one of the Sisters of Class members, who is also African American, she shares that she is very shy but feels that she has found a group where she can really find herself. She has learned how to study and gain better skills in math. I was touched when I read her reflection, and other girls who share similar stories. I continue to feel the positive results with this group as so many colleagues and other Rockwall School District staff members show support.

Sisters of Class

Front row left to right: Domanique King, Devynn King, Kayli Lusk. Back row left to right: Tracey Black (sponsor), Cecil Ene, Kajol Maheshwari, Michelle Perez, Nayeli Rodriguez, Kim Lusk (parent), Hilina Tesfaye (cosponsor).

Photo by Kimberly Henderson.

December 19, 2011
Dear Parent or Guardian:

It is my pleasure to inform you of a new group, Sisters of Class, forming at Cain Middle School that promotes the success of our students. Sisters of Class (SOC) seeks to empower African American girls through increased academic achievement while creating opportunities to serve school and community and is open to all girls.

Ms. Hilina Tesfaye and I, with the support of our principal, Mr. Johnston, would like to invite you and your daughter to be a part of SOC. The founding values of SOC are integrity, excellence, and service. We will hold weekly meetings to encourage these young ladies to continue to excel in the classroom, create service opportunities, as well as providing mentoring. The group will work with high school students as well as adult mentors to gain a full understanding of the skills necessary to build a foundation of success.

The vision of Sisters of Class is to inspire African American females to excel in academic achievement and social responsibility through school and community service and interactive workshops that focus on college and career readiness, twenty-first century leadership skills, interpersonal skills, and character building. If you would like your child to be part of Sisters of Class, please send me an e-mail with the following information:

- Student Name
- Parent/Guardian Name

- Telephone and E-mail
- One Interest Your Student Has

The launch of Sisters of Class will be held on Thursday, January 19, at 8:00 a.m. Afterwards, we will collaborate with the students and decide which day for weekly meeting works best. If you have any questions, please do not hesitate to contact me. We look forward to working with your daughter. Happy Holidays!

Sincerely,
Tracey Black
CTE Department Chair
Maurine Cain Middle School

Tracey includes her officer descriptions below.

Sisters of Class Officers

Position Descriptions

All members are expected to demonstrate good leadership traits on campus and maintain good academic and behavioral standards.

President

The president's responsibilities include:

- Supervise and coordinate Sisters of Class activities.
- Call and preside over regular and special meetings.
- Serve as a key liaison with the school administration, faculty, staff, and other organizations.
- Oversee the responsibilities of all officers.
- Collaborate with school sponsor to plan meeting agenda and field trips.

Vice President

The vice president's responsibilities include:

- Preside over the Sisters of Class meetings in the absence of the president.
- Serve as a resource for the campus organizations.
- Assume the duties of the president on an interim basis if the president is unable to complete her term.

Secretary

The secretary's responsibilities include:

- Give notice of the Sisters of Class meetings (journalism class).
- Take meeting minutes.
- Maintain a permanent attendance record of all Sisters of Class meetings.

(Continued)

(Continued)

Historian

The *historian's* responsibilities include:

- Take photographs at group events.
- Maintain a photo album for the group.
- Create a history log of the group activities (idea: create a monthly newsletter).

Write an essay that describes why you will be a great candidate for the position of your choice. Turn in your essay to Ms. Black by Friday, February 17.

Upcoming Event: Step Into Black History Program

Featuring Our Cain Middle School Step Team

Date: February 28, 2012
Time: 6:30 to 7:30 p.m.
Where: Cain Cafeteria

Tracey recently launched her Sisters of Class. The group picture is from a college visit, and Sisters of Class has many more events planned for the future.

❖   ❖   ❖

ELEMENTARY SCHOOL

At the elementary level, Roberta McWoods and Damian Pritchard, two teachers at North Glendale Elementary School in the Kirkwood School District, started student support groups at a school that is predominately White and in which most of the Students of Color come to the school from a different part of town.

Sista Club

Roberta McWoods

Literacy Specialist Roberta McWoods established the Sista Girl club in 2003. The goal of the club is to support girls who need additional support in developing their social skills, self-esteem, and social/emotional concerns (i.e., respect, responsibility, cooperation, diversity, and literacy). A group of girls from Grades 1 through 5 meet weekly during their lunch recess, working on a variety of activities from literacy, hands-on projects, field trips, and conflict resolution. Guest speakers have been brought in as role models to help support the goals that were being taught. The Brotherman Group was established in 2005 to assist with the boys needing the same reinforcement. Both groups (SGBM) were involved in similar activities that helped support them as students. The clubs take field trips to a Cardinals baseball game, a television station, Katherine Dunham Exhibits, Chase Park Plaza Hotel, Cheesecake Factory, Kirkwood Park, and the Girl-Talk/Girl-Power (fifth grade girls only) Conference at the University of Missouri/St. Louis. Basketball, cheerleading, and beauty clinics were also held at the school. Guest speakers over the years have included Chief Justice of the Missouri Supreme Court Ronnie White, former Rams player Mike Jones, and a host of other speakers.

The success of the group at North Glendale has prompted other elementary schools in Kirkwood to form a Sista Girl group. This year we created the first annual Girl Power Conference, and fifty Girls, ten from each of the five elementary schools, participated in a half day of sessions that included an African American Kirkwood police officer who addressed bullying, a skin-care class by an African American Mary Kay consultant, and dance instruction. The emphasis of the Conference was to Celebrate the Beauty Within. *The success of this conference makes this an annual event in the Kirkwood School District.*

The Brotherman Group

Damian Pritchard

The Brotherman Group's intent was to match up boys with male teachers in the building. The group started out with mostly (but not all) African American and Latino boys who did not have a strong positive male role model in their lives. These boys were also having trouble at school—some academically and some with behavior issues. Within a short time, the group was expanded to include any boy who was having trouble at school, including students who struggled socially. This year the group is about 50 percent African American boys and 49 percent White boys and 1 percent Latino (however, 100 percent of the African American boys in fifth grade are in the group, and only a small percentage of the white boys).

The success of the group for me is being able to build a positive relationship with the boys by meeting once a week. I really try to really listen to the students and address the topics that are on their minds. We also address issues that are brought up by other teachers in the school. However, the bases for our weekly meetings are driven by the boys. Issues that almost always come up are homework, friendship, sportsmanship, and issues with teachers.

Recently I met with just the African American boys and we discussed race. I have addressed race with the Brotherman Group every year. It is an honor to be a part of these conversations. Listening to ten- and eleven-year-old boys talk

(Continued)

(Continued)

so insightfully about race, and explain so many things to me, are some of the most powerful experiences I have had as an educator. I know how much I have learned, but I also feel that these conversations have a powerful effect on the boys. It seems to me that after we have one of our great conversations, the boys seem to be walking a little more proudly down the hall and sitting a little taller in class. The power of having a White teacher (me) listen without judgment, without dominating the conversation, and really wanting to learn and understand, gives the boys something that is so valuable.

Three fifth-grade Males of Color from the group expressed what they liked about the group:

Shelby   *"It helps you with concentrating and focusing on your work. Mr. Pritchard talks to us about learning."*

Arvell   *"It teaches us how to act in school and outside of school."*

Jerry   *"It is making me a better student and teaching me to pay more attention and not talk while the teacher is teaching."*

The girls and boys look forward to their weekly lessons in the club.

❖   ❖   ❖

Barb Swalina, first grade teacher at North Glendale Elementary School, continues academic student support services with the Believing is Seeing Tutoring Program.

Believing Is Seeing Tutoring Program

Barb Swalina

In 2008, North Glendale Elementary in the Kirkwood School District began participating in the Believing Is Seeing Tutoring Program, a program begun by Robinson Elementary, to connect primarily to Students of Color who live across town in Meacham Park, a historically Black area. Our goals are to provide one-on-one academic and social support while nurturing relationships between our elementary students and local high school students, senior volunteers, teacher assistants, and teachers in a safe and supportive environment. Each year we have been able to secure more tutors and therefore, invite more students to participate. Initially, we began with twelve students, and this past year we had twenty students in the program.

Our principal and teachers identify children who would most benefit by being included in the program. Once a week, tutors work with students on homework (math, reading, spelling, or anything else) the child's classroom teacher assigned.

After completion of homework, students work out of carefully selected and designed reading and math activity books based on their individual Tungsten test results and other concepts in which students need additional support.

At 5 p.m. students are given choices. They may play math, word, or strategy board and card games.

At the end of the academic school year, we hold a picnic for both schools in Meacham Park and invite all students and their families who have participated in the program. We truly feel that our program has helped our students become more successful academically and socially. Furthermore, the Believing Is Seeing Tutoring Program has allowed us, White educators, to become visible members within the community in which our students live.

❖   ❖   ❖

In this chapter, you learned several models created by educators (nearly all full-time classroom teachers) in their districts for their students. These educators truly heed the call to action and realize it in their lives. You may contact any of these educators for more information. Please send your e-mail requests to a4achievement@earthlink.net, and I will make sure you receive a reply. These student groups, elementary through high school, focus on academic achievement and leadership.

How do these groups support student success?

_____

_____

_____

What steps can you take to create a student support group in your school?

_____

_____

_____

❖   ❖   ❖

The final chapter is just for you: how do you take care of yourself? Learn strategies to keep yourself at the peak of wellness in your body and your mind.

SUGGESTED READINGS

Peters, Stephen G. *Inspired to Learn: Why We Must Give Children Hope* (Marietta, GA: Rising Sun, 2001).

Wynn, Mychal. *Empowering African-American Males to Succeed: A Ten-Step Approach for Parents and Teachers* (Marietta, GA: Rising Sun, 1992).

18

A Call to Action

Taking Care of Yourself

Teaching is hard. I don't care what color, ethnicity, racial identity, gender, or age your students are. It is exhausting. What follows are some of the things I learned from others and figured out myself to stay in sound physical, mental, and emotional health. This doesn't mean I was always successful, but that speaks to the need for the suggestions listed in this chapter. These are for teachers of any color who teach students of any color. They are shared to make your life easier. Enjoy!

As one reader shared, "I wish I'd read this chapter twenty years ago." I hope you feel the same.

Since you made it this far in the book, you are confronting your own fears as you take the journey to learn what you *don't know you don't know* about yourself and cultural others. Parker Palmer (1998), in his great book, *The Courage to Teach: Exploring the Inner Landscape of a Teacher's Life*, says:

> If we embrace diversity, we find ourselves on the doorstep of our next fear: fear of the conflict that will ensue when divergent truths meet. . . . If we peel back our fear of conflict, we find . . . the fear of losing identity. Many of us are so deeply identified with our ideas that when we have a competitive encounter, we risk losing more than the debate: we risk losing our sense of self. (p. 38)

In order not to lose your sense of self, you must care for your *self*. It may seem peculiar to name taking care of yourself as a *call to action*, yet unless you take care of yourself, you cannot retain your sense of self and you cannot take care of others. Self-care is not a "New Age, touchy-feely" concept; it is a necessity. Therefore, self-care is critical to your well-being and to the well-being of your students.

How do you take care of yourself?

_____

_____

_____

In this chapter, clinical social worker and expressive arts psychotherapist Kim L. Anderson shares suggestions for self-care.

The Importance of Self-Care to Teacher Well-Being and Student Success

Kim L. Anderson, MSW, LCSW, ATR-BC

Educators have always made up a sizable portion of my clientele. School-age children have made up another large portion. From this vantage point, I am privy to the internal struggles of each. Teachers tell me they are overwhelmed with tasks that have nothing to do with teaching. They have little leeway in their work. Assigned curriculum and test scores take up much of their time. Common core standards are beginning to pose further challenges.

Children tell me they don't like going to school. They feel their teachers are mean or don't pay attention to them. They often say things like, "Ms. Johnson looks mad all the time," or "Mr. Beason frowns a lot and sometimes raises his voice." In their own way, students are often aware these are signs of stress. As children will do, they are fearful they have caused their teachers to be frustrated, angry, or tired. In some instances students do contribute to teacher stress, but more often both teachers and students are verbalizing a recognition that things are out of balance and teachers need to "get a break," as my young client Walton puts it. "Mrs. Renner should do yoga like my mom," he says. Pointing to his brow, he tells me, "She's getting that same line on her forehead as Mom has—you know—the worry line."

I am a big believer in the adage Physician heal thyself, or in my profession, Helper help herself. Many years ago, I discovered that our own self-care is imperative to the quality of our personal life and the satisfaction of our professional work. I began to share this with other clinicians, and in the past few years, I have begun to share it with other helping professionals, educators among them. In Culturally Considerate School Counseling: Helping Without Bias _(2010), I wrote:_

> _Individual circumstances such as illness, family matters, or a death are profound and spillage into our work is inevitable. Occupational circumstances such as changes in job or school policies, conflicts within the work environment, or the challenge of dual relationships naturally affect our work performance. Global circumstances (significant historic or political events, natural disasters, war) may intrude upon our professional space without time to prepare._

Health is a personal issue but when illness causes visible symptoms, absenteeism, or affects work performance, we must recognize our limitations and adjust for them. Family matters are equally personal. Problems with personal relationships, children, aging parents, or issues such as a spouse's job loss or military deployment ride with us to work each day. Certainly supervisors, administrators, and some co-workers need to be apprised of situations which may require attention during ordinary work days or a temporary leave of absence, but finding a truthful, yet boundaried and balanced way of sharing personal information is important to privacy and comfort levels. Global circumstances seem to reach into our lives and into our schools at unprecedented rates these days. Some inspire hope and change; others arouse fear and anguish. (pp. 142–143)

Norma Day-Vines writes, "We have no recourse but to mine our reservoirs of wellness, even in the midst of tragedy. The seemingly impossible juxtaposition of two diametrically opposed states (wellness midst tragedy and adversity), will likely lead to the journey toward healing and wholeness" (Day-Vines & Holcomb-McCoy, 2007).

Self-care is fundamental to caring for others. Those of us in the position of influencing the lives of others—especially the delicate lives of children—are obligated to pursue our own wellness (Anderson, 2010). I originally created Inward Bound for clients as a "road map to wellness" which inserts simple wholistic practices for mind, body, psyche, and spirit into daily life. It has become a TripTix for anyone who needs to get away from habits and hindrances which may be interfering with personal balance or professional effectiveness. These new behaviors and routines might feel awkward, irritating, or time-consuming at first, but in time, they can become second nature. Practices such as writing sunrise pages; setting a daily intention; establishing a food plan; incorporating movement into each day; including affirmations; writing twilight pages; identifying gifts of gratitude; centering before bedtime; connecting with family and friends; expanding education, vocation, or avocation; creating something; nurturing something; recreation; helping others and giving back; defining a spiritual practice; and connecting with nature contribute to overall health, well-being, and balance.

In taking care of ourselves, we not only model good practices for our students, but we benefit from the clarity of thought and attitude self-care provides. Basic principles of personal growth can be the best way to begin our transition from cultural carelessness to cultural consciousness and integrate new knowledge and practices. By changing how we feel inwardly, we also change how we think and feel outwardly. Diminishing biases about our own abilities gives way to alleviating bias toward others (Anderson & Davis, 2012).

Kim offers us a pathway for wholistic self-care. Below I bring it back to the classroom. While in the classroom, teaching five or six classes a day, I needed concrete strategies to help me make it through the day and be the best I could be for all students.

Consider the strategies that speak to you; you know yourself better than anyone else. Perhaps students never "drive you crazy" and you don't get stressed in the classroom. But I did, so I offer what worked for me in the suggestions below.

HOW-TO STRATEGIES FOR WELLNESS ON THE DAYS YOU TEACH

- Begin the day with a form of meditation and setting intention. This can be meditation, prayer, walking, running, sitting still, and thinking. At the end of your sitting or walking meditation, set your intention for the day, such as "Today I get to teach poetry, and it is for you, my students. Please let me do the best I can do to support student learners in engaging with these poems and growing from them."
- Use an inspirational book to begin your day: a religious book, a book of poetry, an inspirational book. Consider *Teaching With Fire: Poetry That Sustains the Courage to Teach* (Intrator & Scribner, 2003). Just reading a couple of minutes of inspiration can gird us for the day.
- Keep stimulants to a minimum. Have a cup of coffee or tea if you choose, but don't drink coffee all day. I used to and was so wired I drove my students crazy. Ultimately, I realized the caffeine had to go, and I switched to decaf and lived happily ever after.
- Wear comfortable clothing. I love style and fashion, so this doesn't mean you have to be frumpy; however, clothing should caress you, not bind you (this includes shoes!).
- Eat every two hours. Consider a healthy snack every couple of hours. This can be organic carrots you keep in a bag on your desk or (since we're teachers) an apple or a slice of cheese. If you keep your blood sugar stable through frequent eating, you won't get that light-headed, "I think I'm going to faint because you're driving me crazy" feeling.
- Take a break during your break! Come on, put your stuff down, go outside and take ten deep breaths, scream (silently) if you want, wave your arms, jump a little, and walk a little more; take a break during your break!
- During lunch, sit with friends and decompress. But don't ignore others. Take a few moments and stop and say hi to Mr. Grump and Ms. Isolation. And by the way, say hi to the substitute that everyone ignores and the consultant and literacy coach who work in the school that few acknowledge. You might even consider inviting these folks to join your special group.
- Smile.
- Drink water (but, of course, not too much since you don't get bathroom breaks when you want them).
- Laugh. Consider asking for a student volunteer to be the "laughter person" for the week. This person is ready with a joke (appropriate) when you call on them.
- At the beginning of each class, set your intention—a positive one. Look for positive behaviors from your most challenging students—you might be surprised, they might reciprocate with some.
- Walk around during class. Proximity is one of the most powerful learning strategies you can use, and it does a body good, too!

- Use music in your classroom, play it in your car, and listen to it at home. Music elevates moods and calms us, depending on which music you choose.
- Between class, deep breaths, then to your door to welcome students. Of course, you have to find a restroom sometime. Take care of your body first so you can take care of all the bodies that will be coming through the door.
- Keep a journal. When stress really got to me when I was teaching in middle school, I kept a journal and had the students stop for journal breaks while I did the same. Stopping and writing for five minutes was a great "cool down."
- Plan rewards for yourself. Bring a one-ounce piece of dark chocolate each day and gift it to yourself at your lowest point of the day. I always needed it about 2:00 p.m. Yum.
- Think through your homework policy. Are you giving homework that truly supports practice, learning, and growth? If not, throw it out—that way you won't be spending time grading it. (You don't have to throw out all homework, but assess whether what you're assigning is really worth doing—I found assigning thirty pages a night to read in a self-selected novel worked well.)
- Think through all your instructional processes. What can go? What needs to stay? Reflect on and really get to know what and why you are doing things. This knowledge can lower stress.
- Ask for help. If, due to a personal problem, you need to see a professional, do so.
- Ask for help. Use your professional learning group as a resource. Ask your colleagues for help. Don't try to do everything yourself.
- Celebrate yourself and others. Celebrate successes, birthdays, awards, and so on. Celebrate as often as you can—you deserve it.
- Create crazy rituals with your team or favorite colleagues. Wear the same colors, become characters in your discipline, create a special handshake or cheer—anything to liven it up and make it fun!
- When you leave school, leave school! Try to do something completely different for a few hours: go to a gym, take a walk, read a book, knit, cook, clean—anything but school. Try your hardest to get as much work done on site so at the end of the school day, you have a life.
- Always have a long-term goal. Consider working on an advanced degree, running a marathon, or planning a major trip. Keep your mind focused outside the classroom as well as inside it.
- End your day with a healthy meal, stretching, relaxation, and a good night's sleep. Before you drift off, assess your day, citing what you are grateful for, and go to sleep thinking positive thoughts. Consider doing "yoga" in your mind as you drift off to sleep. Imagine you are in the poses as you do them. Or if you are not into that, count sheep, pray, or think happy, calming thoughts.

My personal secret is walking. Throughout my life, walking has provided me with a daily meditation and time for solitude in which to think and create.

My best lesson ideas stem from thoughts I have while walking. Stress leaves my body with each step I take. Nature bestows sun, humidity, heat, cold, rain, and snow. I notice and enjoy and am grateful for the seasons. There is no need for diets; walking miles a day keeps the metabolism moving and burns extra calories while offering a special private "spa" period each day.

How do you stay well? Fortunately, there are so many good books, periodicals, and Web sites that address wellness that you can find what you're looking for with the touch of your fingers. One of these resources is Allen N. Mendler, one of my favorite authors on discipline, who writes about wellness in his 2012 book, *When Teaching Gets Tough: Smart Ways to Reclaim Your Game*. He gives a myriad of exercises to practice (pp. 150–178) to destress and "reclaim our game"—teaching. So put yourself first, and remember what my mother always said: "Your health comes first." She is so right—unless you are healthy and feel good both inside and outside, you can't reach and teach the smiling (or not smiling) children who walk through your door.

What strategies from the list above will you consider integrating into your teaching life?

_____

_____

_____

❖ ❖ ❖

SUGGESTED READINGS

Intrator, Sam M., and Megan Scribner, editors. *Teaching With Fire: Poetry That Sustains the Courage to Teach* (Bainbridge Island, WA: Center for Teacher Formation, 2003).
Palmer, Parker. *The Courage to Teach* (San Francisco: Jossey-Bass, 1998).
Mendler, Allen N. *When Teaching Gets Tough: Smart Ways to Reclaim Your Game* (Alexandria, VA: ASCD, 2012).

FINAL THOUGHTS

Mark Nepo, a cancer survivor and author of *The Book of Awakening: Having the Life You Want by Being Present to the Life You Have*, writes, "So many times we suppose ourselves out of existence, imagining that if we speak our heart we will be rejected or ignored" (2011, p. 121). His words seem poignant and particularly relevant to thousands of White women teachers who inhabit today's classrooms. Even though today's women are told to speak out and share their truths, there are often still repercussions for doing so, resulting in too many teachers staying silent. Our Children of Color, too, encounter challenges and are often silenced when they speak their heart (and our Colleagues of Color might be ignored or ostracized when they do). This silencing undergirds a continuance of oppression. So the question must be, how do we create a culture where every voice is respected and given the opportunity to be heard without fear of reprisals? How do we create a culture where each of us is allowed to speak our heart and receive the respect we deserve? Hopefully, this book gives you some tools to do that.

In the beginning of the book, we read that the journey to creating this culture begins with the self, knowing and understanding your own cultural lens and understanding what respect "looks like" to persons of other cultures. Throughout the next chapters, you listened to and learned about others from cultures both familiar and unfamiliar. Then we examined school culture and strategies for creating positive cultures and building relationships with colleagues, students, and their families. You found numerous lessons aligned to the CCSS and to the cornerstones of culturally responsive instruction to connect with culturally diverse learners. Finally, the "Call to Action" section of the book gives you ways to act. Sometimes, it is our own practice we need to question; if so, ask your students and colleagues what you need to change or do and listen to their responses. In this section, there are descriptions of several student groups and tutoring you might consider for your call to action. And finally, this section ends with actions you can take for your own well-being, underscoring the idea that if you do not take care of yourself, you cannot be there to support and teach others.

The next time you think you see injustice and you just want to question a practice at your school site or in your community, remember Mark Nepo's words and do not "suppose yourself out of existence." Instead, speak from your heart. In *Teaching With Fire: Poetry That Sustains the Courage to Teach*, Sam Intrator (2003) writes that "meaningful and enduring change cannot happen without individuals convening in community to speak to those potent hopes and concerns that live in the center of our hearts and minds" (p. 207). When we speak from our hearts, telling our truths, others respond. They sense our authenticity; they share responses to assuage our ignorance; and they support us as we continue our journey to learn "what we don't know we don't know." We have learned that convening in community with our colleagues to examine what is important for all students is the catalyst for whole school change. Hopefully, this book gave you one of many tools for doing that. Thank you for sharing this book journey with me.

Please consider the final reflection questions below.

You've finished the book. What are your thoughts? What worked for you? What did not work? What will you take with you into your classroom and implement?

_____

_____

_____

_____

_____

_____

_____

_____

_____

_____

_____

_____

_____

_____

_____

_____

_____

_____

_____

_____

_____

Final thought: Do something nice for yourself tonight!

References and Resources

Abel-Fattah, R. (2010). *Where the streets had a name.* New York: Scholastic.

Adams, J. Q., & Strother-Adams, P. (2001). *Dealing with diversity.* Dubuque, IA: Kendall/Hunt.

Al Abdullah, R., & DiPucchio, K. (2010). *The sandwich swap.* New York: Hyperion Books.

Alexander, F. (1997). *Mother Goose on the Rio Grande.* Chicago: Passport Books.

Allen, D. W., & LeBlanc, A. C. (2005). *Collaborative peer coaching that improves instruction: The 2+2 performance appraisal model.* Thousand Oaks, CA: Corwin.

Allen, J. (1999). *Words, words words: Teaching vocabulary in grades 4–12.* York, ME: Stenhouse.

Allen, R. (2002). *Impact teaching.* New York: Allyn & Bacon.

Allington, R. L., & McGill-Franzen, A. (1990). Children with reading problems: How we wrongfully classify them and fail to teach many to read. In *Early reading difficulties: Their misclassification and treatment as learning disabilities* (ERS Research Digest, pp. 4–10). Arlington, VA: Educational Research Service.

American Anthropological Association. (1998). *American Anthropological Association statement on "race."* Arlington, VA: American Anthropological Association. Retrieved from http://www.aaanet.org/stmts/racepp.htm

Anderson, K. L. (2010). *Culturally considerate school counseling: Helping without bias.* Thousand Oaks, CA: Corwin.

Anderson, K. L., & Davis, B. M. (2012). *Creating culturally considerate schools: Educating without bias.* Thousand Oaks, CA: Corwin.

Applebee, A., & Langer, J. A. (1987). *How writing shapes thinking: A study of teaching and learning.* Urbana, IL: National Council of Teachers of English.

Archuleta, K. (n.d.). *Work ready/essential skills.* Unpublished worksheet used in professional trainings. Antioch, CA: Emerald HPC International, LLC (emeraldconsulting.com).

Arthur, J. (2000). *Invisible sojourners: African immigrant diaspora in the United States.* Westport, CT: Praeger.

Artiles, A. J., & Ortiz, A. A. (Eds.). (2002). *English language learners with special education needs: Identification, assessment, and instruction.* Washington, DC: Center for Applied Linguistics.

Atwell, N. (1987). *In the middle: Writing, reading, and learning with adolescents.* Portsmouth, NH: Boynton/Cook.

Atwell, N. (1998). *In the middle: New understandings about writing, reading, and learning* (2nd ed.). Portsmouth, NH: Boynton/Cook.

Avioli, J., & Davis, B. M. (1994). *Literature of migration and immigration: An anthology of curriculum guides for novels, short stories, poetry, biography and drama.* St. Louis, MO: International Education Consortium.

Bailey, B. (2000). *Conscious discipline: 7 basic skills for brain smart classroom management.* Oviedo, FL: Loving Guidance.

Banks, J. (1994). *Multiethnic education: Theory and practice* (3rd ed.). Needham, MA: Allyn & Bacon.

Barr, R., & Parrett, W. (2003). *Saving our students, saving our schools.* Glenview, IL: Pearson Professional Development.

Barringer, H. R., Takeuchi, D. T., & Xenos, P. (1990). Education, occupational prestige, and income of Asian Americans. *Sociology of Education, 63*(1), 27–34.

Beam, C. (2011). *I am J.* Boston: Little, Brown Books for Young Readers.

Beers, K. (2003). *When kids can't read: What teachers can do.* Portsmouth, NH: Heinemann.

Bernal, G., Sáez, E., & Galloza-Carrero, A. (2009). Evidence-based approaches to working with Latino youth and families. In F. A. Villarruel, G. Carlo, J. M. Grau, M. Azmitia, N. J. Cabrera, & T. J. Chahin (Eds.), *Handbook of U.S. Latino psychology: Developmental and community-based perspectives* (pp. 309–328). Thousand Oaks, CA: Sage.

Bishop, J. (2003). *Goal setting for students.* St. Louis, MO: Accent on Success.

Blankstein, A. M. (2004). *Failure is not an option: Six principles that guide student achievement in high-performing schools.* Thousand Oaks, CA: Corwin.

Blankstein, A. M. (2011). *The answer is in the room: How effective schools scale up student success.* Thousand Oaks, CA: Corwin.

Bomer, R. (1995). *Time for meaning: Crafting literate lives in middle and high school.* Portsmouth, NH: Heinemann.

Booth, C. (2011). *Bronxwood.* New York: Scholastic/Push.

Boykin, A. W., & Bailey, C. T. (2000). *The role of cultural factors in school relevant cognitive functioning* (Report No. 43). Baltimore: Center for Research on the Education of Students Placed at Risk.

Brough, J., Bergman, S., & Holt, L. (2006). *Teach me, I dare you!* Larchmont, NY: Eye On Education.

Brown, D. F. (2002). *Becoming a successful urban teacher.* Portsmouth, NH: Heinemann.

Brown, D. S. (1994). *Books for a small planet: A multicultural-intercultural bibliography for young English language learners.* Alexandria, VA: Teachers of English to Speakers of Other Languages.

Brown v. Board of Education. 347 U.S. 483 (1954) (USSC+).

Burke, J. (1999a). *The English teacher's companion: A complete guide to classroom, curriculum, and the profession.* Portsmouth, NH: Boynton/Cook.

Burke, J. (1999b). *I hear America reading: Why we read, what we read.* Portsmouth, NH: Heinemann.

Burke, J. (2000). *Reading reminders: Tools, tips, and techniques.* Portsmouth, NH: Boynton/Cook.

Burke, J. (2001). *Illuminating texts: How to teach students to read the world.* Portsmouth, NH: Heinemann.

Burke, J. (2003). *Writing reminders: Tools, tips, and techniques.* Portsmouth, NH: Heinemann.

Burke, K. (2010). *Balanced assessment: From formative to summative.* Bloomington, IN: Solution Tree.

Caine, R. N., & Caine, G. (1997). *Unleashing the power of perceptual change: The potential of brain-based teaching.* Alexandria, VA: ASCD.

Calderón, M. E., & Minaya-Rowe, L. (2011). *Preventing long-term ELs: Transforming schools to meet core standards.* Thousand Oaks, CA: Corwin.

Calkins, L. (1986). *The art of teaching writing.* Portsmouth, NH: Heinemann.

Calkins, L., Montgomery, K., & Santman, D. (1998). *A teacher's guide to standardized reading tests: Knowledge is power.* Portsmouth, NH: Heinemann.

Cameron, J. (1992). *The artist's way: A spiritual path to higher creativity.* New York: Putnam.

Carbo, M. (1994). Sharply increasing the reading ability of potential dropouts. In R. C. Morris (Ed.), *Using what we know about at-risk youth: Lessons from the field* (pp. 129–138). Lancaster, PA: Technomic.

Card, O. S. (1985). *Ender's game.* New York: Tom Doherty.

Carlson, G. R., & Sherrill, A. (1988). *Voices of readers: How we come to love books.* Urbana, IL: National Council of Teachers of English.

Carlson, L. (Ed.). (1994). *Cool salsa: Bilingual poems on growing up Latino in the United States.* New York: Henry Holt.

Carnegie Corporation of New York. (1998). *Turning points: Preparing American youth for the 21st century.* Retrieved from http://carnegie.org/publications/search-publicati ons/?word=Globalizing+American+Studies=project

Carnegie Council on Advancing Adolescent Literacy. (2010). *Time to act: An agenda for advancing adolescent literacy for college and career success.* New York: Carnegie Corporation of New York.

Chall, J. S., & Curtis, M. E. (1992). Teaching the disabled or below-average reader. In S. J. Samuels & A. E. Farstrup (Eds.), *What research has to say about reading instruction* (2nd ed., pp. 253–276). Newark, DE: International Reading Association.

Chambers, A. (1985). *Booktalk.* London: Bodley Head.

Chayil, E. (2010). *Hush.* New York: Walker.

Christenbury, L. (1994). *Making the journey: Being and becoming a teacher of English language arts.* Portsmouth, NH: Boynton/Cook.

Cisneros, S. (1984). *The house on Mango Street.* New York: Random House.

Cisneros, S. (1991). *Woman Hollering Creek and other stories.* New York: Random House.

Cisneros, S. (1994). *La casa en Mango Street. Traducido por Elena Poniatowska.* New York: Random House.

Cofer, J. O. (1995). *An island like you.* New York: Penguin.

Cohen, D., & Francisco, D. (2004). *Si, se puede!/Yes, we can!* El Paso, TX: Cinco Puntos Press.

Cole, R. (Ed.). (1995). *Educating everybody's children: Diverse teaching strategies for diverse learners.* Alexandria, VA: ASCD.

Cole, R. (2001). *More strategies for educating everybody's children.* Alexandria, VA: ASCD.

College Board's National Task Force on Minority Achievement. (1999). *Reaching the top: A report of the national task force on minority high achievement.* New York: Author.

Collins, K. (2004). *Growing readers: Units of study in the primary classroom.* Portland, ME: Stenhouse.

Compton-Lilly, C. (2004). *Confronting racism, poverty, and power: Classroom strategies to change the world.* Portsmouth, NH: Heinemann.

Covey, S. R. (1989). *The seven habits of highly effective people.* New York: Simon & Schuster.

Crawford, J. (2012). *Aligning your curriculum to the common core state standards.* Thousand Oaks, CA: Corwin.

Cross, G. (2011). *Where I belong.* New York: Holiday House.

Crow Dog, M. (1990). *Lakota woman.* New York: Grove Weidenfeld.

Csikszentmihalyi, M. (1991). *Flow: The psychology of optimal experience.* New York: HarperPerennial.

Culham, R. (2003). *6+1 traits of writing.* Portland, OR: Northwest Regional Educational Laboratory.

Cunningham, P. M. (2000). *Phonics they use: Words for reading and writing.* New York: Longman.

Cunningham, P., & Allington, R. (1999). *Classrooms that work: They can all read and write.* New York: Longman.

Daniels, H., & Bizar, M. (2005). *Teaching the best practices way: Methods that matter, K–12.* Portland, ME: Stenhouse.

Darling-Hammond, L. (1997). *The right to learn: A blueprint for creating schools that work.* San Francisco: Jossey-Bass.

Davidson, J., & Koppenhaver, D. (1993). *Adolescent literacy: What works and why.* New York: Garland.

Davis, B. M. (1988). *A rationale for the reconstruction of the American literary canon* (Unpublished dissertation). St. Louis University, St. Louis, MO.

Davis, B. M. (1989). Feminizing the English curriculum: An international perspective. *English Journal, 78*(6), 45–49.

Davis, B. M. (Ed.). (1990). *Freedom rising: Viewer guide to video production.* St. Louis, MO: Voluntary Interdistrict Council.

Davis, B. M. (1994). A cultural safari: Dispelling myths and creating connections through multicultural and international education. *English Journal, 83*(2), 24–26.

Davis, B. M. (1996). Writing across the ages: A working writer's workshop. *English Journal, 85*(1), 37–39.

Davis, B. M. (1999). Women in Faulkner's novels. In Robert W. Hamblin & Charles Peek (Eds.), *A William Faulkner encyclopedia* (pp. 439–442). Westport, CT: Greenwood Press.

Davis, B. M. (2006). *How to teach students who don't look like you: Culturally relevant teaching strategies.* Thousand Oaks, CA: Corwin.

Davis, B. M. (2007). *How to coach teachers who don't think like you: Coaching literacy across the content areas.* Thousand Oaks, CA: Corwin.

Davis, B. M. (2009). *The biracial and multiracial student experience: A journey to racial literacy.* Thousand Oaks, CA: Corwin.

Day-Vines, N. L., & Holcomb-McCoy, C. (2007). Wellness among African American counselors. *Journal of Humanistic Counseling, Education and Development, 46*(1), 82–97.

Delgado, R., & Stefancic, J. (Eds.). (1997). *Critical white studies: Looking behind the mirror.* Philadelphia: Temple University Press.

Delpit, L. (1995). *Other people's children: Cultural conflict in the classroom.* New York: New Press.

Delpit, L. (1997). Ebonics and cultural responsive instruction. *Rethinking Schools: An Urban Educational Journal, 12*(1), 6–7.

Delpit, L. (2012). *"Multiplication is for white people": Raising expectations for other people's children.* New York, NY: The New Press.

Dickens, H., & Churches, A. (2012). *Apps for learning: 40 best iPad/iPod Touch/iPhone apps for high school classrooms.* Thousand Oaks, CA: Corwin.

Dodge, L., & Whaley, L. (1993). *Weaving in the women: Transforming the high school English curriculum.* Portsmouth, NH: Boynton/Cook.

Dornan, R., Rosen, L. M., & Wilson, M. (1997). *Multiple voices, multiple texts: Reading in the secondary content areas.* Portsmouth, NH: Boynton/Cook.

Dotson-Blake, K. R., Foster, V. A., & Gressard, C. F. (2009). Ending the silence of the Mexican immigrant voice in public education: Creating culturally inclusive family-school-community partnerships. *Professional School Counseling, 12*(3), 230–240.

Draper, S. (1994). *Tears of a tiger.* New York: Simon & Schuster.

Draper, S. (1997). *Forged by fire.* New York: Simon & Schuster.

Dreschler, F. (2011). *Being Wendy.* New York: Grosset & Dunlap.

Dweck, C. S. (2006). *Mindset: The new psychology of success.* New York: Ballantine Books.

Ecroyd, C. A. (1991). Motivating students through reading aloud. *English Journal, 80*(6), 76–78.

Educational Research Service. (1999). *Reading at the middle and high school levels: Building active readers across the curriculum.* Arlington, VA: Educational Research Service.

Edwardson, D. D. (2011). *My name is not easy.* Tarrytown, NY: Marshall Cavendish.

Ehrenreich, B. (2001). *Nickel and dimed: On (not) getting by in America.* New York: Henry Holt.

Ellison, R. (1952). *Invisible man.* New York: Random House.

Estrella, A. (2012). Seeing a bright future. *Educational Leadership, 69*(7), 94.

Fielding, L. C., & Pearson, P. D. (1994). Reading comprehension: What works. *Educational Leadership, 52*(5), 62–68.

Fisher, D., Frey, N., & Rothenberg, C. (2011). *Implementing RTI with English learners.* Bloomington, IN: Solution Tree.

Fleischman, P. (1997). *Seedfolks.* New York: HarperTrophy.

Fleischman, P. (1998). *Whirligig.* New York: Henry Holt.

Fletcher, R. (1996). *Breathing in, breathing out: Keeping a writer's notebook.* Portsmouth, NH: Heinemann.

Fletcher, R., & Portalupi, J. (1998). *Craft lessons: Teaching writing K–8.* York, ME: Stenhouse.

Fountas, I. C., & Pinnell, G. S. (2001). *Guiding readers and writers, Grades 3–6: Teaching comprehension, genre, and content literacy.* Portsmouth, NH: Heinemann.

Fountas, I. C., & Pinnell, G. S. (2006). *Teaching for comprehending and fluency: Thinking, talking, and writing about reading, K–8.* Portsmouth, NH: Heinemann.

Fox, M. (2001). *Reading magic: Why reading aloud to our children will change their lives forever.* New York: Harcourt.

Fox, M. (2006). *Whoever you are.* San Anselmo, CA: Sandpiper.

Freedman, S. W., Simons, E. R., Kalnin, J. S., Casareno, A., & M-Class Teams. (1999). *Inside city schools: Investigating literacy in multicultural classrooms.* Urbana, IL: National Council of Teachers of English.

Freire, P. (2000). *Pedagogy of the oppressed* (30th anniv. ed.). New York: Continuum.

Freire, P. (2003). *From risk to opportunity: Fulfilling the educational needs of Hispanic Americans in the 21st century* (Final report of the president's advisory commission on educational excellence for Hispanic Americans). Retrieved from http://www.YesICan.gov/paceea/finalreport.pdf

Gallagher, K. (2004). *Deeper reading: Comprehending challenging texts, 4–12.* Portland, ME: Stenhouse.

Gardner, H. (1983). *Frames of mind: The theory of multiple intelligences.* New York: Basic Books.

Gates, H. L., Jr. (1992). *Loose canons: Notes on the culture wars.* New York: Oxford University Press.

Gay, G. (2000). *Culturally responsive teaching: Theory, research, & practice.* New York: Teachers College Press.

Gilligan, C. (1982). *In a different voice: Psychological theory and women's development.* Cambridge, MA: Harvard University Press.

Ginsberg, M. B., & Wlodkowski, R. J. (2000). *Creating highly motivating classrooms for all students: A schoolwide approach to powerful teaching with diverse learners.* San Francisco: Jossey-Bass.

Giroux, H. A. (1997). *Pedagogy and the politics of hope: Theory, culture, and schooling.* Boulder, CO: Westview.

Glasser, W. A. (1990). *Quality school: Managing students without coercion.* New York: HarperCollins.

Goldenberg, C., & Coleman, R. (2010). *Promoting academic achievement among English learners: A guide to the research.* Thousand Oaks, CA: Corwin.

Golding, W. (1959). *Lord of the flies.* New York: Perigee Books.

Goleman, D. (1995). *Emotional intelligence.* New York: Bantam.

Gollnick, D. M., & Chinn, P. C. (2012). *Multicultural education in a pluralistic society: (9th ed.).* Upper Saddle River, NJ: Pearson.

Gonzalez, M. L., Huerta-Macias, A., & Tinajero, J. V. (1998). *Educating Latino students: A guide to successful practice.* Lancaster, PA: Technomic.

Graves, D. H. (1989). *Experiment with fiction.* Portsmouth, NH: Heinemann.

Graves, D. H. (2002). *Testing is not teaching: What should count in education.* Portsmouth, NH: Heinemann.

Gregory, G., & Chapman, C. (2002). *Differentiated instructional strategies: One size doesn't fit all.* Thousand Oaks, CA: Corwin.

Gruwell, E. (1999). *The freedom writers diary: How a teacher and 150 teens used writing to change themselves and the world around them.* New York: Doubleday.

Haberman, M. (1995). *STAR teachers of children in poverty.* West Lafayette, IN: Kappa Delta Pi Biennial.

Haddix, M. P. (1998). *Among the hidden.* New York: Simon & Schuster.

Hale, J. (2001). *Learning while black: Creating educational excellence for African-American children.* Baltimore: Johns Hopkins University Press.

Hale-Benson, J. E. (1986). *Black children: Their roots, culture, and learning styles* (Rev. ed.). Baltimore: Johns Hopkins University Press.

Hamanaka, S. (1999). *All the colors of the earth.* New York: HarperCollins.

Hanley, M. S., & Noblit, G. (2009). *Cultural responsiveness, racial identity and academic success: A review of literature.* A paper prepared for the Heinz Endowments. Retrieved May 15, 2012, http://www.heinz.org/programs_cms.aspx?SectionID=233

Harvey, S. (1998). *Nonfiction matters: Reading, writing, and research in Grades 3–8.* Portland, ME: Stenhouse.

Haycock, K. (2001). Closing the achievement gap. *Educational Leadership, 58*(6), 6–11.

Haycock, K., & Hanushek, E. A. (2010). An effective teacher in every classroom. *Education Next, 10*(3). Retrieved from http://educationnext.org/an-effective-teacher-in-every-classroom/

Hayes Jacobs, H. (2006). *Active literacy across the curriculum: Strategies for reading, writing, speaking, and listening.* Larchmont, NY: Eye On Education.

Hede, M. (2009). *Hispanic vs. Latino.* Retrieved from http://www.hispanic-culture-online.com/hispanic-vs-latino.html

Henze, R., Katz, A., Norte, E., Sather, S., & Walker, E. (2002). *Leading for diversity: How school leaders promote positive interethnic relations.* Thousand Oaks, CA: Corwin.

Hicks, T. (2009). *The digital writing workshop.* Portsmouth, NH: Heinemann.

Hill, J. D., & Flynn, K. M. (2006). *Classroom instruction that works with English language learners.* Alexandria, VA: ASCD.

Hiller, A. (Director). (1984). *Teachers* [Motion picture]. United States: MGM/United Artists.

Hinojosa, R. (1987). *This migrant earth.* Houston, TX: Arte Publico Press.

Hoffman, M. (1991). *Amazing Grace.* New York: Dial.

Hofstede, G. (1991). *Culture's consequences: Comparing values, behaviors, institutions, and organizations across nations* (2nd ed.). Thousand Oaks, CA: Sage Publications.

Holly, M. L. (1989). *Writing to grow: Keeping a personal-professional journal.* Portsmouth, NH: Heinemann.

Honigsfeld, A., & Dove, M. G. (2010). *Collaboration and co-teaching: Strategies for English learners.* Thousand Oaks, CA: Corwin.

Hooks, B. (2004). *Skin again.* New York: Jump at the Sun.

Howard, G. R. (1999). *We can't teach what we don't know: White teachers, multiracial schools.* New York: Teachers College Press.

Hoyt, L. (1999). *Revisit, reflect, retell: Strategies for improving reading comprehension.* Portsmouth, NH: Heinemann.

Hoyt, L. (2000). *Snapshots: Literacy minilessons up close.* Portsmouth, NH: Heinemann.

Humes, K. R., Jones, N. A., & Ramirez, R. R. (2011). *Overview of race and Hispanic origin: 2010.* Washington, DC: U.S. Census Bureau. Retrieved from http://www.census .gov/prod/cen2010/briefs/c2010br-02.pdf

Hunt, I., & Pucci, A. J. (1964). *Across five Aprils.* Chicago: Follett.

Hutchins, D. J., Greenfeld, M. D., Epstein, J. L., Sanders, M. G., & Galindo, C. L. (2012). *Multicultural partnerships: Involve all families.* Larchmont, NY: Eye On Education.

Intrator, S. M., & Scribner, M. (Eds.). (2003). *Teaching with fire: Poetry that sustains the courage to teach.* Thousand Oaks, CA: Corwin.

Jago, C. (2002). *Cohesive writing: Why concept is not enough.* Portsmouth, NH: Heinemann.

Jensen, E. (1998). *Teaching with the brain in mind.* Alexandria, VA: ASCD.

Jensen, E. (2009). *Teaching with poverty in mind: What being poor does to kids' brains and what schools can do about it.* Alexandria, VA: ASCD.

Jimenez, F. (1998). *The circuit.* Albuquerque: University of New Mexico Press.

Johnson, R. S. (2002). *Using data to close the achievement gap: How to measure equity in our schools.* Thousand Oaks, CA: Corwin.

Johnson, R. S., & La Salle, R. A. (2010). *Data strategies to uncover and eliminate hidden inequities: The wallpaper effect.* Thousand Oaks, CA: Corwin.

Jones, N. A., & Smith, A. S. (2001). *U.S. Census Bureau: The two or more races population: 2000.* (Census 2000 Brief Series C2KBR/0I-6, 2001). Washington, DC: U.S. Census Bureau. Retrieved from http://www.census.gov/prod/2001pubs/c2kbroi-6.pdf

Katz, K. (2002). *The colors of us.* New York: Henry Holt.

Keene, E. O., & Zimmermann, S. (1997). *Mosaic of thought: Teaching comprehension in a reader's workshop.* Portsmouth, NH: Heinemann.

Kiang, P. N., & Kaplan, J. (1994). Where do we stand? Views of racial conflict by Vietnamese American high-school students in a black and white context. *Urban Review, 26*(20), 95–119.

Killens, J. O., & Ward, J. W., Jr. (Eds.). (1992). *Black southern voices: An anthology of fiction, poetry, drama, nonfiction, and critical essays.* New York: Penguin.

Kindler, A. (2002). *Survey of the states' limited English proficient students and available educational programs and services, 2000–01 summary report.* Washington, DC: U.S. Department of Education.

Kingsolver, B. (1988). *The bean trees.* New York: Harper Perennial.

Koppelman, S. (1996). *Women in the trees: U.S. women's short stories about battering & resistance, 1839–1994.* Boston: Beacon Press.

Kozol, J. (1991). *Savage inequalities.* New York: Crown.

Krogness, M. M. (1995). *Just teach me, Mrs. K: Talking, reading, and writing with resistant adolescent learners.* Portsmouth, NH: Heinemann.

Kunjufu, J. (1988). *To be popular or smart: The black peer group.* Chicago: African-American Images.

Kuperminc, G. P., Wilkins, N. J., Roche, C., & Alvarez-Jimenez, A. (2009). Risk, resilience, and positive development among Latino youth. In F. A. Villarruel, G. Carlo, J. M. Grau, M. Azmitia, N. Cabrera, & T. J. Chahin (Eds.), *Handbook of U.S. Latino psychology: Developmental and community-based perspectives* (pp. 213–234). Thousand Oaks, CA: Sage.

Ladson-Billings, G. (1994). *The dreamkeepers: Successful teachers of African American children.* San Francisco: Jossey-Bass.

Landsman, J. (2001). *A white teacher talks about race.* Lanham, MD: Scarecrow Press.

Lane, B. (1993). *After the end: Teaching and learning creative revision.* Portsmouth, NH: Heinemann.

Langer, J. (1995). *Envisioning literature: Literary understanding and literature instruction.* New York: Teachers College Press.

Lee, S. J. (1996). *Unraveling the "model minority" stereotype: Listening to Asian American youth.* New York: Teachers College Press.

Levine, M. (2002). *A mind at a time: America's top learning expert shows how every child can succeed.* New York: Simon & Schuster.

Levy, J. (2005). *Alley oops.* Brooklyn, NY: Flashlight Press.

Lindsey, R. B., Nuri Robins, K., & Terrell, R. D. (2003). *Cultural proficiency: A manual for school leaders.* Thousand Oaks, CA: Corwin.

Lindsey, R. B., Roberts, L. M., & CampbellJones, F. (2005). *The culturally proficient school: An implementation guide for school leaders.* Thousand Oaks, CA: Corwin.

Linton, C. (2011). *Equity 101: The equity framework.* Thousand Oaks, CA: Corwin.

Linton, C., & Davis, B. (2012). *Equity 101: Culture.* Thousand Oaks, CA: Corwin.

Lombard, J. (2006). *Drita, my homegirl.* New York: Putnam Juvenile.

Long, E. (2011). *Chamelia.* New York: Little, Brown Books for Young Readers.

Long, M., & Richards, J. (Eds.). (1987). *Methodology in TESOL: A book of readings.* Boston: Heinle & Heinle.

Macrorie, K. (1984). *Writing to be read.* Upper Montclair, NJ: Boynton/Cook.

Malcolm X & Haley, A. (1973). *The autobiography of Malcolm X.* New York: Ballantine Books.

Martinez, V. (1998). *Parrot in the oven: Mi vida.* New York: HarperTrophy.

Marzano, R. (2003). *Classroom management that works.* Alexandria, VA: ASCD.

Marzano, R. (2004). *Building background knowledge for academic achievement.* Alexandria, VA: ASCD.

Marzano, R., & Kendall, J. S. (1997). *Content knowledge: A compendium of standards and benchmarks for K–12 education* (2nd ed.). Alexandria, VA: ASCD.

Marzano, R., & Pickering, D. J. (2011). *The highly engaged classroom.* Bloomington, IN: Marzano Research Laboratory.

Marzano, R., Pickering, D. J., & Pollock, J. E. (2001). *Classroom instruction that works: Research-based strategies for increasing student achievement.* Alexandria, VA: ASCD.

Mathis, S. B. (1986). *The hundred penny box.* New York: Viking.

McCall, G. G. (2011). *Under the mesquite.* New York: Lee & Low Books.

McEwan, E. K. (2002). *Ten traits of highly effective teachers: How to hire, coach, and mentor successful teachers.* Thousand Oaks, CA: Corwin.

McEwan-Adkins, E. K. (2010). *40 reading strategies for K–6 students: Research-based support for RTI.* Bloomington, IN: Solution Tree.

McIntosh, P. (1998). White privilege and male privilege: A personal account of coming to see correspondences through work in women's studies. In M. L. Andersen & P. Hill-Collins (Eds.), *Race, class, and gender: An anthology* (pp. 70–81). Wellesley, MA: Wellesley College Center for Research for Women.

McIntyre, A. (1997). *Making meaning of whiteness: Exploring racial identity with white teachers.* New York: State University of New York Press.

McIntyre, E., Hulan, N., & Layne, V. (2011). *Reading instruction for diverse classrooms.* New York: Guilford Press.

McKinley, J. (2010). *Raising black students' achievement through culturally responsive teaching.* Alexandria, VA: ASCD.

McKissack, P., & McKissack, F. (1999). *Black hands, white sails: The story of African-American whalers.* New York: Scholastic.

Medina, J. (1999). *My name is Jorge on both sides of the river.* Honesdale, PA: Boyds Mills Press.

Mehrabian, A. (1990). *Silent messages: Implicit communication of emotions and attitudes.* New York: Wadsworth.

Mendler, A. N. (2012). *When teaching gets tough: Smart ways to reclaim your game.* Alexandria, VA: ASCD.

Morrison, T. (1987). *The song of Solomon.* New York: Penguin.

Morrow, L. M., Rueda, R., & Lapp, D. (2010). *Handbook on literacy and diversity.* New York: Guildford Press.

Moss, P. (2010). *One of us.* Gardner, ME: Tilbury House.

Mowry, J. (1992). *Way past cool.* New York: Farrar, Straus & Giroux.

Muhammad, A. (2009). *Transforming school culture: How to overcome staff division.* Bloomington, IN: Solution Tree.

Murray, D. (1985). *A writer teaches writing.* Boston: Houghton Mifflin.

Murray, D. (1990). *Shoptalk: Learning to write with writers.* Portsmouth, NH: Boynton/Cook.

Myers, J. (2000). *Afraid of the dark: What whites and blacks need to know about each other.* Chicago: Lawrence Hill.

Myers, W. D. (1988). *Fast Sam, cool Clyde & stuff.* New York: Viking Press.

Myers, W. D. (1990). *Scorpions.* New York: HarperTrophy.

Myers, W. D. (1991). *Fallen angels.* New York: Scholastic.

Myers, W. D. (1996). *The glory field.* New York: Scholastic.

Myers, W. D. (1998). *Slam.* New York: Scholastic.

Myers, W. D. (1999). *Monster.* New York: HarperCollins.

National Center for Education Statistics. (2000). *NAEP trends in academic achievement.* Washington, DC: U.S. Department of Education.

National Council of Teachers of English/International Reading Association. (1994). *Standards for the assessment of reading and writing.* Urbana, IL: National Council of Teachers of English.

Nepo, M. (2011). *The book of awakening: Having the life you want by being present to the life you have.* San Francisco: Conari Press.

Nieto, S. (1996). *Affirming diversity: The sociopolitical context of multicultural education* (2nd ed.). White Plains, NY: Longman.

Nieto, S. (2000). *Affirming diversity: The sociopolitical context of multicultural education* (3rd ed.). Reading, MA: Addison Wesley.

Noguera, P. A., & Akom, A. (2000). The opportunity gap. *The Wilson Quarterly, 24*(3), 86–87.

Nuri Robins, K., Lindsey, R. B., Lindsey, D. B., & Terrell, R. D. (2002). *Culturally proficient instruction: A guide for people who teach.* Thousand Oaks, CA: Corwin.

Nuri Robins, K., Lindsey, R. B., Lindsey, D. B., & Terrell, R. D. (2012) *Culturally proficient instruction: A guide for people who teach* (3rd ed.). Thousand Oaks, CA: Corwin.

O'Brien, T. (1990). *The things they carried.* Boston: Houghton Mifflin.

Odean, K. (2002). *Great books for girls: More than 600 books to inspire today's girls and tomorrow's women.* New York: Random House.

Ogbu, John. (1991). Immigrant and involuntary minorities in comparative perspective. In J. Ogbu & M. Gibson (Eds.), *Minority status and schooling* (pp. 184–204). New York: Garland.

Ogle, D. (1986). K-W-L: A teaching model that develops active reading of expository text. *Reading Teacher, 39*(6), 564–570.

Okorafor, N. (2011). *Akata witch.* New York: Penguin Group/Viking.

Paley, G. (1979). *White teacher.* Cambridge, MA: Harvard University Press.

Palmer, P. J. (1998). *The courage to teach: Exploring the inner landscape of a teacher's life.* San Francisco: Jossey-Bass.

Papalewis, R., & Fortune, R. (2002). *Leadership on purpose: Promising practices for African American and Hispanic students.* Thousand Oaks, CA: Corwin.

Parr, T. (2009). *It's okay to be different.* New York: Little, Brown Books for Young Readers.

Paulsen, G. (1995). *Nightjohn.* New York: Laurel Leaf.

Paulsen, G. (1999). *Sarny.* New York: Laurel Leaf.

Pearson, D. P., Rohler, L. R., Dole, J. S., & Duffy, G. G. (1992). Developing expertise in reading comprehension. In S. J. Samuels & A. E. Farstrup (Eds.), *What research has to say about reading instruction* (2nd ed., pp. 145–199). Newark, DE: International Reading Association.

Perera, A. (2011). *Guantanamo boy.* Park Ridge, IL: Albert Whitman.

Peters, S. G. (2001). *Inspired to learn: Why we must give children hope.* Marietta, GA: Rising Sun.

Pollock, J. E. (2012). *Feedback: The hinge that joins teaching and learning.* Thousand Oaks, CA: Corwin.

Pollock, M. (2008). *Everyday antiracism: Getting real about race in school.* New York: New Press.

Portalupi, J., & Fletcher, R. (2001). *Nonfiction craft lessons: Teaching information writing K–8.* Portland, ME: Stenhouse.

Raschka, C. (1998). *Yo! Yes?* New York: Scholastic.

Ratekin, N., Simpson, M., Alvermann, D. E., & Dishner, E. K. (1985). Why teachers resist content reading instruction. *Journal of Reading, 28*(5), 432–437.

Reeves, D. B. (2006). *The learning leader: How to focus school improvement for better results.* Alexandria, VA: ASCD.

Reglin, G. (1995). *Achievement for African-American students: Strategies for the diverse classroom.* Bloomington, IN: National Education Service.

Rico, G. L. (1983). *Writing the natural way: Using right-brain techniques to release your expressive powers.* Los Angeles: J. P. Tarcher.

Rief, L. (1992). *Seeking diversity: Language arts with adolescents.* Portsmouth, NH: Heinemann.

Rief, L. (1998). *Vision and voice: Extending the literacy spectrum.* Portsmouth, NH: Heinemann.

Robb, L., Nauman, A., & Ogle, D. (2002). *Reader's handbook: A student guide for reading and learning.* Wilmington, MA: Great Source.

Rockquemore, K., & Laszloffy, T. (2005). *Raising biracial children.* Lanham, MD: Rowman & Littlefield.

Rodriguez, E. R., & Bellanca, J. A. (2007). *What is it about me you can't teach: An instructional guide for the urban educator* (2nd Ed.). Thousand Oaks, CA: Corwin.

Rodriguez, L. (1993). *Always running.* Willimantic, CT: Curbstone Press.

Romano, T. (1987). *Clearing the way: Working with teenage writers.* Portsmouth, NH: Heinemann.

Rong, X. L., & Preissle, J. (2009). *Educating immigrant students in the 21st century: What educators need to know* (2nd ed.). Thousand Oaks, CA: Corwin.

Rosenblatt, L. (1995). *Literature as exploration* (5th ed.). New York: Modern Language Association of America.

Rosenbloom, S. R., & Way, N. (2004). Experiences of discrimination among African American, Asian American, and Latino adolescents in an urban school. *Youth and Society, 35*(4), 420–451.

Rotner, S., & Kelly, S. (2009). *Shades of people.* New York: Holiday House.

Routman, R. (2000). *Conversation: Strategies for teaching, learning, and evaluating.* Portsmouth, NH: Heinemann.

Sachar, L. (1998). *Holes.* New York: Farrar, Straus & Giroux.

Saifer, S., Edwards, K., Ellis, D., Ko, L., & Stuczynski, A. (2011). *Culturally responsive standards-based teaching: Classroom to community and back* (2nd ed.). Thousand Oaks, CA: Corwin.

Santa, C. M. (1988). Changing teacher behavior in content reading through collaborative research. In S. J. Samuels & P. D. Pearson (Eds.), *Changing school reading programs: Principles and case studies* (pp. 185–206). Newark, DE: International Reading Association.

Schreck, M. K. (2009). *Transformers: Creative teachers for the 21st century.* Thousand Oaks, CA: Corwin.

Schreck, M. K. (2011). *You've got to reach them to teach them: Hard facts about the soft skills of student engagement.* Bloomington, IN: Solution Tree.

Senge, P. (2000). *Schools that learn: A fifth discipline fieldbook for educators, parents, and everyone who cares about education.* New York: Doubleday-Currency.

Shange, N. (1985). *Betsey Brown.* New York: Picador.

Sherman, C. W. (1994). *Sisterfire: Black womanist fiction and poetry.* New York: HarperPerennial.

Short, D. J., & Fitzsimmons, S. (2007). *Double the work: Challenges and solutions to acquiring language and academic literacy for adolescent English language learners.* Washington, DC: Alliance for Excellent Education.

Silven, M., & Vauras, M. (1992). Improving reading through thinking aloud. *Learning and Instruction, 2*(2), 69–88.

Silver, H. F., Strong, R. W., & Perini, M. J. (2000). *So each may learn: Integrating learning styles and multiple intelligences.* Alexandria, VA: ASCD.

Singham, M. (1998). The canary in the mine: The achievement gap between black and white students. *Kappan, 80*(1), 9–15.

Singleton, G. (2003, August). *De-institutionalizing racism.* Workshop for Cooperating School Districts, University of Missouri, St. Louis.

Singleton, G. E., & Linton, C. (2006). *Courageous conversations about race: A field guide for creating equity in schools.* Thousand Oaks, CA: Corwin.

Sleeter, C. (1996). *Multicultural education as social activism.* Albany: State University of New York Press.

Soto, G. (1991). *A summer life.* New York: Laurel Leaf.

Soto, G. (1992a). *Living up the street.* New York: Laurel Leaf.

Soto, G. (1992b). *Taking sides.* New York: Harcourt.

Soto, G. (1993). *Pieces of the heart: New Chicano fiction.* New York: Chronicle.

Soto, G. (1995). *New and selected poems.* New York: Chronicle.

Soto, G. (1997). *Junior college.* New York: Chronicle.

Soto, G. (1999). *Buried onions.* New York: HarperTrophy.

Soto-Hinman, I., & Hetzel, J. (2009). *The literacy gaps: Bridge-building strategies for English language learners and standard English learners.* Thousand Oaks, CA: Corwin.

Sousa, D. (2001). *How the brain learns.* Thousand Oaks, CA: Corwin.

Spinelli, J. (2000). *Stargirl.* New York: Random House.

Steele, C. (1999). Thin ice: "Stereotype threat" and black college students. *Atlantic Monthly, 284*(2), 44–47, 50–54.

Stone, R. (2002). *Best practices for high school classrooms: What award-winning secondary teachers do.* Thousand Oaks, CA: Corwin.

Sylwester, R. (2000). *A biological brain in a cultural classroom: Applying biological research to classroom management.* Thousand Oaks, CA: Corwin.

Tannen, D. (1990). *You just don't understand: Men and women in conversation.* New York: Ballantine.

Tate, M. L. (2003). *Worksheets don't grow dendrites: Instructional strategies that engage the brain.* Thousand Oaks, CA: Corwin.

Tate, M. L. (2004). *"Sit and get" won't grow dendrites: 20 professional learning strategies that engage the adult brain.* Thousand Oaks, CA: Corwin.

Tatum, B. D. (1997). *Why are all the black kids sitting together in the cafeteria?* New York: Basic Books.

Taylor, K., & Walton, S. (1998). *Children at the center: A workshop approach to standardized test preparation, K–8.* Portsmouth, NH: Heinemann.

Terrell, R., & Lindsey, R. (2009). *Culturally proficient leadership: The personal journey begins within.* Thousand Oaks, CA: Corwin.

Thompson, G. L. (2010). *The power of one: How you can help or harm African American students.* Thousand Oaks, CA: Corwin.

Thornton, Y. S. (1995). *The ditchdigger's daughters: A black family's astonishing success story.* New York: Penguin.

Tileston, D. W. (2004). *What every teacher should know about diverse learners.* Thousand Oaks, CA: Corwin.

Tileston, D. W. (2011). *Closing the RTI gap: Why poverty and culture count.* Alexandria, VA: Solution Tree.

Tileston, D. W., & Darling, S. K. (2008). *Why culture counts: Teaching children of poverty.* Bloomington, IN: Solution Tree.

Tomlinson, C. A. (1999). *The differentiated classroom: Responding to the needs of all learners.* Alexandria, VA: ASCD.

Tomlinson, C. A. (2003). *Fulfilling the promise of the differentiated classroom: Strategies and tools for responsive teaching.* Alexandria, VA: ASCD.

Tovani, C. (2000). *I read it, but I don't get it: Comprehension strategies for adolescent readers.* Portland, ME: Stenhouse.

Tovani, C. (2004). *Do I really have to teach reading? Content comprehension, Grades 6–12.* Portland, ME: Stenhouse.

Trueman, T. (2000). *Stuck in neutral.* New York: HarperCollins.

Trumbull, E., & Rothstein-Fisch, C. (2008). *Managing diverse classrooms: How to build on students' cultural strengths.* Alexandria, VA: ASCD.

Tsujimoto, J. (2001). *Lighting fires: How the passionate teacher engages adolescent writers.* Portsmouth, NH: Heinemann.

Tyler, M. (2005). *The skin you live in.* Chicago: Chicago Children's Museum.

U.S. Census Bureau. (2010). *Poverty tables—families.* Washington, DC: U.S. Census Bureau. Retrieved from http://www.census.gov/hhes/www/poverty/data/historical/families.html

U.S. Census Bureau, Ethnicity and Ancestry Branch Population Division. (2006). *Hispanics in the United States.* Washington, DC: U.S. Census Bureau. Retrieved from www.census.gov/population/www/socdemo/hispanic/reports.html

Veljkovic, P., & Schwartz, A. J. (Eds.). (2001). *Writing from the heart: Young people share their wisdom.* Philadelphia: Templeton Foundation Press.

Viadero, D. (2000, May 1). Bridging the gap. *Education Week Teacher, 2*(8), 30. Retrieved from http://www.edweek.org/tm/articles/2000/05/01/08blacks1.h11.html

Villarruel, F. A., Carlo, G., Grau, J. M., Azmitia, M., Cabrera, N. J., & Chahin, T. J. (Eds.). (2009). *Handbook of U.S. Latino psychology: Developmental and community-based perspectives.* Thousand Oaks, CA: Sage.

Vygotsky, L. (1994). *Thought and language* (A. Kosulin, Trans. & Ed.). Cambridge: MIT Press.

Walker, A. (1983). *In search of our mother's gardens.* New York: Harcourt Brace Jovanovich.

Ward, J. (Ed.). (1997). *Trouble the water: 250 years of African-American poetry.* New York: Putnam.

Wiggins, G., & McTighe, J. (1998). *Understanding by design.* Alexandria, VA: ASCD.

Wilhelm, J. D. (1995). *"You gotta be the book": Teaching engaged and reflective reading with adolescents.* New York: Teachers College Press.

Williams, B. (Ed.). (1996). *Closing the achievement gap: A vision for changing beliefs and practices.* Alexandria, VA: ASCD.

Williams, L. (2002). *It's the little things: The everyday interactions that anger, annoy, and divide the races.* New York: Harcourt.

Wong, H. K., & Wong, R. T. (1998). *The first day of school: How to be an effective teacher* (Rev. ed.). Mountain View, CA: Harry K. Wong.

Woodbury, J. (1997). No more rules! Simplify your discipline plan with these five statements. *Learning, 26*(3), 25–27.

Wynn, M. (1992). *Empowering African-American males to succeed: A ten-step approach for parents and teachers.* Marietta, GA: Rising Sun.

Zack, N. (2002). *Philosophy of science and race.* New York: Routledge.

Zeni, J., Krater, J., & Cason, N. D. (1994). *Mirror images: Teaching writing in black and white.* (Action research from the Webster Groves Writing Project). Portsmouth, NH: Heinemann.

Index

AAA. *See* American Anthropological Association (AAA)

Academic achievement
expectations, questions on, 21
hidden rules of, 67
peer pressure and, 66–67

Academic course work, 102–103

Acculturation, 8–9

Across Five Aprils (Hunt, Pucci), 187

Active Literacy Across the Curriculum (Jacobs), 182

Administrators, 129
insults by, 50, 54
strategies for, 129
teachers and, 108, 126–128
walk throughs by, 130

African American Academic Achievement Club, 242–243

African American Academic Achievement: Building a Classroom of Excellence (Davis), x

African Americans
academic achievement of, 66–67
call-and-response pattern and, 62
collectivism among, 85
colorblindness of, 68–69
cultural homogenates of, 14–15
learning gaps of, 96
learning styles of, 64–65
literature about, 189
multimodel learning by, 64
poverty of, 98–99
school connections and, 248
skin color prejudice and, 67–68
stereotyping by, 71

African Americas
insults, 50

Akata Witch (Okorafor), 158

Aligning Your Curriculum to the Common Core State Standards (Crawford), 169

All the Colors of the Earth (Hamanaka), 157

Alvarez, Brenda, 84

Amazing Grace (Hoffman), 158

American Anthropological Association (AAA), 38–39, 42, 45

American Sign Language, 231–234

Anderson, Kim, 75–76, *x*

Anderson, Kim L., 260

Andrade, Christina Amelia, 85–86

The Answer Is in the Room: How Effective Schools Scale Up (Blankstein), xv

Apps for Learning: 40 Best iPad, iPod Touch or IPhone Apps for High School Classrooms (Dickens, Churches), 143

Asian Americans
literature about, 189
poverty of, 99
stereotype of, 71–72

Asian immigrants, 90–91

Assessments. *See also* Standardized tests
emotional, 117
feedback, 150–151
questions, 152–154
types of, 151

Atwell, Nancie, 184

The Autobiography of Malcolm X, 186

Bailey, Becky, 197

Balanced Assessment (Burke), 151

Banks, James, 28

Barajas-Alexander, Mani, 85

Beard, Donna, 39–40

The Bean Trees (Kingsolver), 175

Behavior
classroom, 63–64
cultural, 41–42
expectations of, 4–6
modeling of, 20–21
poverty and, 99
welcoming rituals, 113–114

Being Wendy (Dreschler), 157

Believing Is Seeing Tutoring Program, 256–257

Benben, Todd, 196–197

Bias, test, 104–195

The Biracial and Multiracial Student Experience (Davis), 29, 41
The Biracial and Multiracial Student Experience: A Journey to Racial Literacy (Davis), 41
Biracial children, 40
Black immigrants (African, Caribbean), 91–92
Black, Tracey M., 210, 251
Blacks. *See* African Americans
Blankstein, Alan, *xv*
Blue Ribbon Mentor-Advocate Program (BRMA)
    district history, 245
    goal of, 244
    role of, 246
    student services provided, 246–247
    training for, 244–245
Bluford Series, 156
Body language
    impact of, 115–116
    monitoring of, 116
    questions on, 20
    reflective questions on, 117
The Book of Awakening: Having the Life You Want by Being Present to the Life You Have (Nepo), 264
Bronxwood (Coe), 158
Brotherman Group, 255–256
Brown v. Board of Education, 30
Building Culturally Considerate Schools (Davis, Anderson), 75
Burke, Kay, 151

Calderón, M. E., 148
Call-and-response pattern, 62
"The Canary in the Mine: The Achievement Gap Between Black and White Students" (Singham), 66
Car project, 217–219
CCSS. *See* Common core state standards (CCSS)
Chamelia (Long), 157
Chapel Hill-Carrboro City Schools, 245–246
Chapman, Carolyn, 184
Chavez, Ray, 132
Check-in questions, 118–119
Chinese students, 66
Churches, Andrew, 143
Cisneros, Sandra, 60, 86
Classroom Instruction That Works (Pollock, et. al.), 150
Classroom Instruction That Works with English Language Learners (Hill, Flynn), 147

Classrooms
    behaviors in, 63–64
    emotional climate in, 117–118
    environment of, 20–21, 112–114
    management of, 144–146
Cliffs Notes project, 170, 174–176
Closing the Achievement Gap (Williams), 105
Code-switch, 9
Coleman, Rhoda, 146–147
College Academy for Parents, 132
College and career readiness (CCR), 185
The Colors of Us (Katz), 157
Color blindness, 68–69
The Color Purple (Walker), 189
Common core state standards (CCSS), 3
    Cliffs Notes project, 174–176
    curriculum criteria, 162–170
    guidebook project, 171–172
    high school reading class, 188
    informational material, 234
    literary analysis, 237
    oral history project, 172
    poetry assignment project, 177
    reading, 156
    reading implications, 183, 185–187
    seventh-grade reading class, 187
    teaching strategies, 172
    use of, 22
    writing, 162, 189, 205
    you can be a book project, 178
Communication
    body language, 115–116
    misreading, 62–63
    style differences in, 61–62
    tone of, 115
Conversations About Race (Singleton, Linton), 25–26
The Courage to Teach: Exploring the Inner Landscape of a Teacher's Life (Palmer), 19, 259
Crawford, Joe, 169
Crow Dog, Mary, 189
Cultural behaviors, 41–42
Cultural capital, 8
Cultural considerations
    definition of, *x*
    equity skill building and, *xii–xiii*
    function of, 10
    web sites, 18
Cultural expectations. *See* Hidden rules
Cultural homogenates, 14–15
Cultural proficiency, 9–10
Cultural Proficiency: A Manual for School Leaders (Lindsey et. al), 7

Culturally Considerate School Counseling: Helping Without Bias (Anderson), 75–76, 260
Culturally diverse learners. *See also* English language learners
  characterization of, *xiii–xiv*
  classroom behaviors of, 63–64
  code-switching by, 9
  communication styles of, 61–63
  engagement assessment, 150–154
  how-to strategies for, 60
  instructional strategies for, 141–143
  language issues of, 6
  learning styles of, 64–65
  overview of, 59–60
  peer pressure on, 66–67
  professional development for, 7
  reaching, 73–74
  technology for, 143–144
  vignette, 139–140
  web sites, 74
Culturally responsive teaching, 8
Culturally Responsive Teaching: Theory, Research, & Practice (Gay), 8
Culture. *See also* School culture
  building bridges to, 13–14
  collectivist, 85
  definition of, 7–8
  factors of, 12
  hot beverage, 10
  organizational, 10
  purpose of, 6
  race *vs.*, 42
  respeto for, 115
  world view and, 3–4
Culture and Instruction (Curtis, Davis), xi

Data Strategies to Uncover and Eliminate Hidden Inequities: The Wallpaper Effect (Johnson, La Salle), 96
Davis, Eva Salomé Alvarez, 33
Day-Vines, Norma, 261
Delpit, Lisa, 165
Dickens, Harry, 143
Distefano, Cecilia, 226
Dotson-Blake, K. R., 76
Drita, My Homegirl (Lombard), 157
Dweck, Carol, 152

"Educationalese," 10
Educating Everybody's Children: Diverse Teaching Strategies for Diverse Learners (Cole), 170
Educating Immigrant Students in the 21st Century: What Educators Need to Know (Rong, Preissle), 89

Ehrenreich, Barbara, 188
Elementary school projects
  math lesson, 198–200
  overview of, 196–197
  poetry books, 205–209
  science inquiry, 201–204
Ellison, Ralph, 28
Engagement
  assessment questions, 152–154
  feedback on, 150–151
  reading, strategies for, 155–162
  reflective questions for, 153–154
  suggested books, 154
  writing, strategies for, 162–166
English language learners. *See also* Culturally diverse learners
  backgrounds of, 146
  building relationships with, 149–150
  research strategies for, 147–148
  suggested books, 154
  web sites for, 154
English language learners (ELLs), 3
Equity
  basics of, *xi–xii*
  data on, 96
  framework, 115
  professional development and, 13
  skill building, *xii–xiii*
  teachers' views on, 195–196
Equity 101 (Curtis), *xi*
Estrella, Angela, 106
Ethnicity
  definition of, 11
  poverty and, 98

Family centers, 131–132
Feedback, 150–151
Feedback: The Hinge That Joins Teaching and Learning (Pollock), 150–151
Fisher, D., 148–149
Five-paragraph essay, 226–227
Foster, V. A., 76
Fountas, Irene C., 184
Frey, N., 148–149
Frontloading, 146
Future Focus Programs, 249–250

Gay, Geneva, 8
Gilligan, Carol, 197
Goal setting, *xiv–xv*
Goldenberg, Claude, 146–147
Golding, William, 179
The Grapes of Wrath (Steinbeck), 186
Graves, Donald, 184, 185
The Great Gatsby (Fitzgerald), 187
Gregory, Gayle, 184

Gressard, C. F., 76
Gribbins, Marti, 157
Guantanamo Boy (Perera), 158
Guidebook project, 171–172
Guiding Readers and Writers, Grades 2-6: Teaching Comprehension, Genre, and Content Literacy (Fountas, Pinnell), 184

Haycock, Kay, 108
Hidden rules
    academic achievement, 67
    behavior, 4–5
    code-switch and, 9
    definition of, 7
    learning gaps and, 96–98
    white women's, 197
High fives, 119
High school projects
    American Sign Language, 231–234
    five-paragraph essay, 226–227
    math multimedia, 228–230
    music as poetry, 235–238
    overview of, 220
    work ready-college ready-life ready, 221–225
The Highly Engaged Classroom (Marzano, Pickering), 152
Hispanic learners. *See* Latino/a/Hispanic learners
Holliday, Tiffany, 221
Homogenates, 14–15
"Hot beverage" culture, 10
The House on Mango Street (Cisneros), 60
How-to strategies
    academic course work, 102–103
    administrators, 129
    Asian immigrants, 91
    Black immigrants, 92
    classroom, 16–17
    collaborative relationships, 130–131
    communication, 63
    culturally diverse learners, 60
    family relationships, 132–133
    Latino/a/Hispanic learners, 86–87
    learning styles, 65–66
    Middle Eastern immigrants, 93
    music uses, 62
    overview of, 15–16
    poverty, 101
    racial identity, 34–35
    reaching diverse learners, 73–74
    relationship building, 119–122
    respeto, 115
    school culture, 127

self-care, 262–264
skin color prejudice, 69–70
staff attitudes, 128–129
stereotype threat, 72–73
teacher expectations, 107
test bias, 104–195
Huerta-Macias, ?, 65
Hush (Chayll), 158

I am Big! (Silkwood), 208
I am J (Beam), 158
Idea wave, 235
Immigrants
    Asian, 90–91
    Black, 91–92
    Middle Eastern, 93
Implementing RTI with English Learners (Fisher et. al.), 148
In the Middle: Writing, Reading and Learning With Adolescents (Atwell), 184
Instructional strategies
    Cliffs Notes project, 174
    oral history project, 172
    poetry assignment project, 177
    you can be a book project, 179
International business project, 210–212
International Society for Technology in Education (ISTE), 144
Interracial Model of Mutual Respect, 1, *xi figure*
Intrator, Sam, 265
Invisible Man (Ellison), 28
It's Okay to Be Different (Parr), 158

James, Kim, 217
Johnson, Jason, 251
Johnson, Ruth S., 96, 98
Johnston, Jason L., 209
Jones, Jessica, 144–146
Jones, Mike, 255
Journal writing, 22–23, 189

Kanjufu, J., 66
Kelly, Dorothy, 29, 247
Kids in Control, 249–250
Kids in Cooperation, 249
Kindergarten, 77
Kingsolver, Barbara, 175

La Salle, Robin Avelar, 96
Lakota Woman (Crow Dog), 189
Lamons-Raiford, Michele, 231–235
Latino/a/Hispanic learners
    Brenda's story, 78–84

common legacies of, 77–78
geographical distribution of, 84
how-to strategies for, 86–87
in kindergarten, 77
learning gaps of, 96
learning styles of, 65
literature about, 189
NAEP scores, 79
native born, percentage of, 77
population growth of, 76–77
poverty of, 99
risks of, 77
suggested books, 94
term use, discussion of, 75–76
web sites, 94
League of United Latin American Citizens,
Latinos, 84
Learning gaps
academic course work and, 102–103
cognitive development rates and, 97
cultural expectations and, 96–98
definition of, 95
persistence of, 96
poverty and, 98–100
school environment and, 98
suggested books, 110
teacher expectations, 105–107
teacher quality, 108–109
test bias, 104–105
Learning styles, 64–66
Lee, Stacey J., 72
Librarians, 157
Linton, Curtis, 42, *viii, xi*
Literacy lessons. *See also* Reading;
Writing
Cliffs Notes project, 174–176
criteria for, 170
guidebook project, 171–172
oral history project, 172–174
poetry assignment project, 177–178
teacher's role, 190–192
theme book project, 180
writing contests, 180–182
you can be a book project, 178–180
The Lord of the Flies (Golding), 179
Louis, Karen, 105

Making the Meaning of Whiteness
(McIntyre), 29
Managing Diverse Classrooms: How to
Build on Students' Cultural
Strengths (Trumbull), 84
Marzano, Robert J., 98–99, 150–152,
187
Math lesson, 198–200

Math multimedia project, 228–230
McCormac, Nancy, 157
McIntosh, Peggy, 47
McIntyre, Alice, 29
McWoods, Roberta, 157, 254–255
Mehrabian, Albert, 115
Mendler, Allen N., 264
Meyer, Graig, 43, 45, 244
Middle Eastern immigrants, 93
Middle school projects
car costs, 217–219
international business, 210–212
overview of, 209
roller coaster, 213–216
Minaya-Rowe, L., 148
Mindset: The New Psychology of Success
(Dweck), 152
Model minority, 71–72
Morning announcements, 126
Multimodel learning, 64
Multiracial children, 40
Murray, Donald, 192
Music as poetry, 235–238
Music in classroom, 62, 119
Mutual respect models, 1
My Name Is Not Easy (Edwardson), 158

NAEP. *See* National Assessment of
Education Progress (NAEP)
National Assessment of Education
Progress (NAEP), 79
National Education Association (NEA),
75
National Education Technology
Standards, 234
National Education Technology
Standards (NETS), 144
Nationality, 11
Native Americans, 61–62, 96
Nepo, Mark, 264–265
Nickel and Dimed (Ehrenreich), 188
Nieto, Sonia, 59
North Glendale Elementary School,
196–197

Obama, Michelle, 68
Of Mice and Men (Steinbeck), 186
Ogbu, John, 66
One of Us (Moss), 157
Online tools, *xi–xii*
Oral history project, 172–174
Organization for the Appreciation of
Black Culture, 28
Other People's Children (Delpit), 165
Otherness, 19

Palmer, Parker, 19, 259
"Paper-bag test, 67
PD 360, *xi*
Peer pressure
   achievement and, 66–67
   skin color and, 67–68
   types of, 66
Pendulums, 201–204
Personal or professional journals,
   22–23
Personal racial histories
   author's, 27–29
   benefits of, 46
   Bonnie's, 48–49
   Brenda's, 33–34
   Dorothy's, 29–32, 49–51
   Keith's experience with, 51–53
Phenotypes, 38–39
Philosophy of Science and Race
   (Zack), 39
Pickering, Debra J., 150–152
Pinnell, Gay Su, 184
Poetry
   assignment project, 177–178
   book publication, 205–209
   exploring words through, 206–207
   first-grade pattern, sample, 208–209
   music as, 235–238
   rubrics scoring, 206
Poets and Writers, 180
Pollock, Jane E., 150–151
Possessing the Secret of Joy (Walker), 189
Poverty
   behavioral effects of, 99
   educators' assumptions of, 101
   generational impact of, 101
   how-to strategies, 101
   mediation strategies, 100–101
   myths of, 98–99
   rates of, 98–99
   schools of, 100
   standardized test scores and, 100
The Power of One: How You Can Help or
   Harm African American Students
   (Thompson), 64–65
Preissle, Judith, 89–90
Prejudice, skin color, 67–68
Preuss, Deb, 200
Preventing Long-term ELs (Calderón,
   Minaya-Rowe), 148
Prison class, 186–187
Pritchard, Damian, 255–256
Privilege, 54
Professional development, 7, 13

Promoting Academic Achievement Among
   English Learners (Goldenberg,
   Coleman), 146–147

Questions. *See* Reflective questions

Race
   AAA definition of, 38–40
   biological, 38–39
   concept, evolution of, 40
   concept, lessons on, 45–46
   cultural behaviors and, 41–42
   culture *vs.*, 42
   existence of, 43
   learning about, 54
   multiracial aspects of, 40–41
   understanding of, 37
Racial identity
   author's story, 27–29
   Brenda's story of, 33–34
   concept, lessons on, 45–46
   definition of, 11
   development of, 43–45
   Dorothy's story of, 29–32
   history of, 26–27
   how-to strategies of, 34–35
   omnipresence of, 25–26
   reflecting on, 35–36
Racial profiling, 39
Racism, 43–45
Readers and writers workshops
   CCSS and, 183–184
   college class, 188–189
   high school class, 188
   list for, 186
   prison class, 186–187
   seventh-grade class, 187
   suggested books, 193
   web sites, 193
   web sites for, 184
   writing guidelines, 189
Reading. *See also* Writing
   CCSS implications, 156, 185–187
   creating passion for, 155–156
   culturally reflective texts for, 156–158
   curricular strategies, 160–162
   life history survey, 158–159
   resistance to, reasons, 155
   suggested books, 166–167
Reading history survey, 159–160
Reflective questions
   academic course work, 103
   acculturation, 9
   body language, 117

classroom experiences, 19–23
cultural expectations, 97–98
cultural factors, 13
culturally responsive teaching, 8
engagement, 153–154
ethnic/racial identity, 11–12
final thoughts, 265–266
good teaching, 138
Latino/a/Hispanic learners, 84
peer cultures, 70
poverty, 100
privilege, 53–55
reading history, 159–160
relationship building, 122
school culture examples, 126
skin color prejudice, 67
student welcoming, 112–113
teacher expectations, 106–107
teacher quality, 108–109
writing, 163, 166
Relationship building
    body language and, 115–116
    classroom environment and, 112–114
    collaborative, 130–131
    community, 132
    emotions and, 117–118
    English language learners, 149–150
    families, 131–133
    grade-level based, 118–122
    how-to strategies for, 119–122
    overview of, 111
    readiness factor, 119
    reflective questions for, 122
    respeto and, 114–115
    staff, 127–131
    student greeting and, 116–117
    students, 119–122
    suggested books, 112
Respeto, 114–115, 130
Response to Intervention (RTI)
    cliffnotes project, 175
    definition of, 170
    English language learners and,
        148–149
    oral history project, 173
    poetry assignment project, 177
    you can be a book project, 179–180
Revisions, 192–193
Rituals
    classroom management, 144–146
    teachers', 118
    welcoming, 113–114
Roller coaster project, 213–216
Rong, Xue Lan, 89–90

Rosenblatt, L., 187
Ross, Heather, 213
Rothenberg, C., 148–149
Rothestein-Fisch, C., 85
Rubrics, 182, 206

Sammon, Laura, 197
The Sandwich Swap (Al Abdullah,
    DiPucchio), 157
School culture
    administrators, 129
    collaborative relationships in,
        130–131
    district A example, 124–125
    district B example, 125
    district C example, 125–126
    how-to strategies, 127–129
    importance of, 123–124
    overview of, 123
    professional attitudes in, 127–128
    reflective questions for, 126
    staff, 128–129
    staff and, 127–131
    suggested books, 133
School Improvement Network, *viii, xi*
School/Digger.com, 196
Schreck, Mary Kim, 117, 144
Science inquiry, 201–204
Self-care
    importance of, 260–261
    overview of, 259
    strategies for, 262–264
    suggested books, 264
Self-edit ideas, 191–192
Shades of People (Rotner, Kelly), 157
Shared lesson plans
    American Sign Language, 231–234
    car project, 217–219
    fifth grade math, 198–200
    five-paragraph essay, 226–227
    international business project,
        210–212
    math multimedia project, 228–230
    music as poetry, 235–238
    publishing student poetry, 205–209
    roller coaster project, 213–216
    science inquiry, 201–204
    work ready-college ready-life ready,
        221–225
Silkwood, Zoe, 280
Singham, Mano, 66
Singleton, Glenn E., 42, 47
Sista Club, 254–255
Sisters of Class, 251–254

Skin Again (Hooks), 157
Skin color prejudice, 67–70
The Skin Your Live In (Tyler), 157
Smith, BetsAnn, 105
Speaking rubrics, 182
St. Louis schools, 248
St. Louis Voluntary Desegregation
    Program, 28
Staff
    collaborative relationships among,
      130–131
    collegial culture among, 127–128
    culture of, 10, 14
    development system, 152
    family connections and, 123, 131
    learning about, 13
    niceness of, 66
    problem solving by, 73
    technology for, 143
Standardized tests
    bias in, 104–105
    poverty and, 100
    scores, 96
    stereotypes and, 71
Steele, Claude, 71, 73
Steinbeck, John, 186
Stereotype threat
    definition of, 71
    experience of, 70–71
    hot-to strategies for, 72–73
    model minority, 71–72
Strategies. *See* How-to strategies;
    Instructional strategies
Student support groups
    books on, 257
    high school, examples, 241–247
    middle school, examples, 247–254
    overview of, 241
Students
    assessment by, 150–151
    cognitive development rates, 97
    greeting, 116–117
    interactions with, 20
    tardy, 112
    technology for
    transition time for, 117–118
    welcoming, 112–114
Subject content, 21–22
Swalina, Barb, 256

Tannen, Deborah, 197
Tardiness, 112
Teacher Expectations: Student
    Achievement (TESA), 121
Teachers
    color blindness among, 68–69

interactions of, 20
learning gap role of, 105–107
literacy role, 190–192
poverty assumptions by, 101
quality of, 108
rituals of, 118
self-care for, 259–265
student deficit assistance by, 83–84
unconventional experiences, learning
    from, *xiii*
Teaching. *See also* Culturally responsive
    teaching
    culturally responsive, 8
    good, characteristics of, 152–153
    standards of practice, 148
*Teaching With Fire: Poetry That Sustains
    the Courage To Teach* (Intrator), 265
Technology
    cliffnotes project, 175
    guidebook project, 171–172
    national standards for, 234
    oral history project, 173–174
    poetry assignment project, 177–178
    21st century learning and, 143–144
TESA. *See* Teacher Expectations: Student
    Achievement (TESA)
Theme book project, 180
Thompson, Gail L., 64–65
Tinajero, ?, 65
Tomlinson, C. A., 96
Tortilla Flat (Steinbeck), 186
*Transformers: Creative Teachers for 21st
    Century* (Schreck), 144
Transition time, 117–118
Trumbull, Elise, 84–85
Twenty-first century learning, 143–144

Under the Mesquite (McCall), 158
Using Data to Close the Achievement
    Gap (Johnson), 98

Velazuez, Rosalinda, 87
Voice, tone of, 115–116
Voluntary Student Transfer, 248

Walker, Alice, 189
*When Teaching Gets Tough: Smart Ways to
    Reclaim Your Game* (Mendler), 264
Where I Belong (Cross), 158
Where the Streets had a Name (Abel-
    Fattah), 158
"White talk," 29
White privilege
    awareness of, 47
    Bonnie's experience with, 48–49
    characterization of, 47–48

Dorothy's experience with, 49–51
examination of, 197
Keith's experience with, 51–53
White Women's Hidden Rules, 7
White, Ronnie, 255
"White Privilege and Male Privilege,"
    47–48
Whites
    academic achievement of, 66–67
    colorblindness of, 68–69
    cultural homogenates of, 14–15
    peer pressure on, 66
    skin color prejudice ad, 67–68
    stereotyping by, 71
Whoever You Are (Fox), 157
Work ready-college ready-life ready,
    221–225
Writing
    CCSS for, 162, 205

contests, 180–182
groups, 164
guidelines for, 189
journal, 189
life history survey, 163–164
love of, survey, 162–163
reflective questions for, 163
revisions, 192–193
self-edit ideas, 191–192
strategies for, 164–166
suggested books, 166–167

Yo! Yes? (Raschka), 157
You can be a book project,
    178–180
You've Got To Reach Them to Teach Them
    (Schreck), 117

Zack, Naomi, 39

CORWIN

A SAGE Company

The Corwin logo—a raven striding across an open book—represents the union of courage and learning. Corwin is committed to improving education for all learners by publishing books and other professional development resources for those serving the field of PreK–12 education. By providing practical, hands-on materials, Corwin continues to carry out the promise of its motto: **"Helping Educators Do Their Work Better."**